Envisioning America

ASIAN AMERICA
A series edited by Gordon H. Chang

The increasing size and diversity of the Asian American population, its growing significance in American society and culture, and the expanded appreciation, both popular and scholarly, of the importance of Asian Americans in the country's present and past—all these developments have converged to stimulate wide interest in scholarly work on topics related to the Asian American experience. The general recognition of the pivotal role that race and ethnicity have played in American life, and in relations between the United States and other countries, has also fostered the heightened attention.

Although Asian Americans were a subject of serious inquiry during the late nineteenth and early twentieth centuries, they were subsequently ignored by the mainstream scholarly community for several decades. In recent years, however, this neglect has ended, with an increasing number of writers examining many aspects of Asian American life and culture. Moreover, many students of American society are recognizing that the study of issues related to Asian America speak to, and may be essential for, many current discussions on the part of the informed public and various scholarly communities.

The Stanford series on Asian America seeks to address these interests, including works from the humanities and social sciences—history, anthropology, political science, American studies, law, literary criticism, sociology, and interdisciplinary and policy studies.

A full list of titles in the Asian America series can be found online at www.sup.org/asianamerica.

Envisioning America

NEW CHINESE AMERICANS
AND THE POLITICS OF BELONGING

Tritia Toyota

STANFORD UNIVERSITY PRESS
STANFORD, CALIFORNIA

Stanford University Press
Stanford, California

Printed in the United States of America on acid-free,
archival-quality paper

Library of Congress Cataloging-in-Publication Data

Toyota, Tritia.
  Envisioning America : new Chinese Americans and the politics of
belonging / Tritia Toyota.
    p. cm. — (Asian America)
  Includes bibliographical references and index.
  ISBN 978-0-8047-6241-0 (cloth : alk. paper) — ISBN 978-0-8047-6242-7
(pbk. : alk. paper)
  1. Chinese Americans—California, Southern—Political activity—History—20th century. 2. Asian Americans—California, Southern—Political
activity—History—20th century. 3. Identity politics—California,
Southern—History—20th century. 4. Chinese Americans—Ethnic
identity. 5. Asian Americans—Ethnic identity. 6. United States—Race
relations—Political aspects. I. Title. II. Series: Asian America.
  E184.C5T75 2010
  305.895'107949—dc22

                               2009023019

Typeset by Bruce Lundquist in 11/14 Adobe Garamond

Contents

Acknowledgments

Were it not for Don Nakanishi (director of the Asian American Studies Center at UCLA), I would never have produced this book. Over a period of 20 years, during which I worked full time in television news, he remained steadfast as a sounding board for my developing theoretical frameworks and a constant support in my academic endeavors. His knowledge of racialized political history and his vision and commitment to enlarge the discussion and create social change continue to inform my own positions. In addition, it was extremely providential that I had the opportunity to work with Karen Brodkin (professor of anthropology at UCLA). I am grateful for her never-ending patience, her spot-on critiques regarding the co-constitutive nature of race and global capital projects, and now her friendship. Her repeated entreaties to just "Tell the story!" kept me focused on what ethnography is all about and its continuing value to the discipline of anthropology. It has guided my own teaching. Most of all, to the new Chinese activists who didn't run when they saw me, my deepest thanks for permitting me, not just to *repeat* your stories, but to *share* them here, in a way that privileges what it means to be a twenty-first-century American.

In addition, I thank the following community organizations and elected officials for their permission to quote from public speeches, statements, letters, and press releases: the Asian American Journalists Association, the Asian Pacific American Legal Center, the Center for Asian Americans

United for Self Empowerment, Chinese Elected Officials, the Committee of 100, California State Board of Equalization member Judy Chu, former California governor Gray Davis, California state assemblyman Mike Eng, and former Los Angeles city council member Mike Woo.

Envisioning America

Introduction

For more than three decades, I have been privileged to have front-row seats at what is one of the most—for me anyway—exciting games in town. The game is about politics and, more specifically, about the construction of a community's political identity. The ground rules are changeable; the players, the outline and location of the playing field, and the rewards of the game are in constant flux. It is a continually unpredictable process occurring within the Asian American community in Southern California, and since the late 1960s, the variability of alterations and modifications characterizes a community undergoing major transformation. I witnessed most of this dynamic struggle as a journalist of color in the Los Angeles area, working for the local news stations of two major U.S. television networks.

Being a journalist requires one to be a perpetual student and observer, something of which I always took advantage. There never was a time when I wasn't keen to insinuate myself into social processes in which people were actively fashioning membership in the Asian American community. My position as a news reporter and anchor gave me entrée (though not always welcome) and allowed me to penetrate community structures, become acquainted with acknowledged leadership, and understand contextually how and why issues translated into collective agendas and actions. I came to know countless individuals, most of them, like myself, American-born and politically progressive. We were products of the contested discourses that expanded racial and social paradigms during the 1960s.

For my part, I was not permitted, either by news management or by viewers, to forget my own role in the grand experiment of diversity undertaken by major news corporations. In the aftermath of the transformative 1960s, a few enlightened members of television news media looked around the newsroom and saw a staff of mostly white men. I was a "three-fer" and a first: young, female, and Asian American. I felt an overwhelming responsibility to ensure that newsworthy stories in the Asian American community were covered fairly and accurately. During the early 1970s, most of my bosses, co-workers, and the viewing public did not share this enthusiasm. Other than the occasional story about Chinese New Year or the Nisei Week Parade, most other coverage of Asian America was insignificant. In part, this reflected the numerically small and largely politically insignificant Asian American community in Southern California at the time. That, of course, was about to change.

In the space of just one decade, I became aware of a large, new cohort of different Asian actors whose rapid appearance after 1965 was facilitated by dramatic changes in U.S. immigration law. They quickly enlarged everyday notions of a more traditional Asian American political identity. These putative new leaders, and therefore newsmakers, in Southern California were speaking English with accents. They were Chinese from Taiwan, Hong Kong, and even Mainland China. They were Asian Americans, but immigrant and naturalized. I did not know them, nor was I familiar with their leadership, methods of organizing, associations, important issues, or even where they lived. A television documentary I wrote and produced during the early 1980s was my attempt at making sense of the sweeping changes and increasing heterogeneity in the community.

Journalism gave me an elementary understanding, but it was not until my doctoral research in anthropology that I began to have a more thorough theoretical grasp of the relationship between a group's politicized identity and the instantiation of structures of power in historical context. Within this matrix and grounded in the realities of continuing immigration from Asia, a major reordering in the meanings and construction of politicized group membership among new Chinese activists and within the larger Asian American community has occurred. As a social researcher, I could not ignore this change.

I was, in fact, quite literally forced to pay attention by some of the more active naturalized Chinese members of a political advocacy organization based in

Southern California called Chinese Americans United for Self Empowerment (CAUSE) who began to push for a larger pan–Asian American identity—a project of integration with other, more traditional, and largely native-born Asian Americans. This came after a decade of numerous ethnic-specific strategies in the organization and culminated in 2003 when the topic of changing the group's name came up at a board retreat. The new version replaced *Chinese American* with *Asian American.* Nobody was saying ethnic-specific strategies were inconsequential. Yet the realization was growing among the most active members that their new citizenship reflected not just their ethnic Chineseness but their racialization as Asians. Some felt that a wider, more instrumentally useful rubric had become necessary. Although only a spectator at the meeting, I was asked what I thought about the group's plan to pursue a pan–Asian American political outlook and identity. Not much.

In the years I had spent observing all manner of pan–Asian Pacific American politics locally and nationally, I was dismayed to realize that not much had come of it.[1] It was frustrating to see leadership and group strategies squandered on intragroup conflict that seemed as rife as ever given the community's increasing heterogeneity. It was equally angering that mainstream recognition of issues important to the Asian American community seesawed between ignorance and apathy or suspicion and panic but never seemed to diminish.

However Asian Americans were viewed politically, in the end not much seemed impressive about pan-Asian political participation and empowerment except the constituency's usefulness to mainstream political structures as a cash cow, and even that backfired in 1996 with the Democratic National Committee fund-raising scandal (see Chapter 5). On the whole, so many political issues still needed to be addressed, and I thought sadly that not much had changed since I wrote that documentary in the 1980s. Were you to watch it today with your eyes shut, you might think it had been produced last week. So I said, why not keep *Chinese* in the group's name, and why not continue to be ethnic specific? Why shouldn't Chinese Americans, who now compose the largest part of the Asian American community, independently seek their own agenda and be open about it?

In framing the answers to these questions and more, this ethnography combines an anthropological and an Asian Americanist approach by tacking back and forth between several major paradigms in both disciplines. Such theoretical synthesis brings together history and race, not only in time and space but between differing imaginaries of community that both delineate and extend beyond borders. This is indicative of current anthropological frameworks that are attentive to constructions of identity that occur with the movement of capital and people in the context of global and transnational discourses (Brodkin 2000; Smith 1994). Moreover, I give special consideration to the transformation of space and place that occurs "from below," that is, social actions that privilege the agency of individuals and groups in altering and reifying larger structures of power (Guarnizo and Smith 1999). In this case, I focus on the narratives of post-1965 Chinese immigrants whose lives unfold as the newest additions to the collectivity known as Asian America. It has been a breathtaking change.

In little more than 150 years, beginning with a community of primarily segregated male laborers, Chinese immigrants from all over the world have been transformed into heterogeneous, multigenerational Americans. In this diversity, post-1965 politically involved Chinese activists in Southern California constitute new elites in the Chinese American and larger Asian American communities. This should be taken not as an assignment of valuation but only as recognition that the choice to take advantage of U.S. immigration and recruitment policies afforded them benefits that gave many an essential head start in their new *American* lives.

Their active participation is visible at every level of civic engagement, from the purely local to the national and beyond. From immigration to citizenship, they have embraced national discourses about the responsibility of participating in a democratic society. However, if current mainstream attitudes are any indication, the day when new Chinese American activists no longer have to pay attention to inequalities of opportunity is a long way off. A poll funded by the Committee of 100 shows not only a disheartening ambivalence toward but deep-seated suspicions about Asian Americans and in particular Chinese Americans.[2] White respondents seem to buy into the myth of the model minority, that is, that Asian Americans are hardworking, family oriented, and don't cause trouble. At the same time, these "positive attributes" also translate into a view of Asian Americans as ambitious, clannish, two-faced, and non–English speaking. Those polled could not distinguish between ethnic groups, and many did not want Asian Americans as bosses or neighbors. A media release from the Committee of 100 about the results expressed surprise: "We were startled. We thought that the findings would indicate some prejudice . . . but the findings reflect highly negative attitudes and stereotypes among a significant group of Americans. These results should serve as a wake-up call to the community" (Committee of 100 2001). The paradox is that while racialization continues, "color-blind" American pedagogies service "the almost complete theoretical silence concerning the state" and the issue of race (Goldberg 2002, 2). What follows here is not color-blind research; it interrogates racial paradigms with an anthropological desire to rectify a silence engendered by the discipline's failure in past years to more fully participate in the ongoing intellectual debates surrounding concepts of race and racism (Shanklin 1999).

The more recent return to discussions of race and racism is centered on the investigation of race as a social construction and is indicative of all that the term *social* implies. Theorizing naturalized Chinese activism falls squarely into this analysis, a liberal anthropology that instantiates racial epistemologies as necessary to the discussion of the persistence of race and racial categorization (Harrison 1995). Moreover, in order that anthropology become an indispensable discussant in racial discourses in this country, I argue for a rediscovered activist role in confronting the enormously complex and lightning-fast changes occurring in these social constructions of race. Anthropology should advocate again for a scholarly and politically committed stance concerning the power of unequal material relations. Firmly anchored in a bottom-up approach, this analysis adds to the conversation about how individuals struggle to create collective histories of shared experience and attempt to alter their life chances within the constraints of global capital projects. Contextualizing the everyday lives of naturalized Chinese activists and their American-born counterparts, assessing the political outcomes inherent in their life choices and social interactions, speaks to the agency and creativity in grassroots political projects and firmly repudiates difference as pathology.

Since the 1960s, Asian American pedagogies have been instrumental in expanding U.S. racial discourse beyond the dichotomous black/white equation. The rapid reconfiguration of Asian America after 1965 aided Asian American scholars, community leaders, and a small but vocal public intellectualism in the discipline. Post-1965 non-European immigration has forced new syntheses and new racial paradigms and has "required a broader conception of what it means to be an American" (Aoki and Nakanishi 2001). Implicit in the national construction of citizens is the integrative process of belonging and its manifestation in social practices such as civic engagement or political participation. As will be shown, broader conceptions of citizenship also require rethinking traditional theories of assimilation.

An Asian American emphasis on the processes of politicization fills in the blanks in mainstream literature, which has regarded Asian American political involvement as, at best, nascent or nonexistent (Massey 1981; Parrillo 1982; Sowell 1981). Although there is discussion of political situations in which Asian Americans have been *victimized*, far less attention is paid to the efforts of Asian American activists who successfully transformed power by creating their own counternarratives (Jo 1980; Turnbull 2003). Thus, Asian Americans continue to be the "done-tos" and not the "doers." More to the point, despite impassioned and sustained critiques by Asian American academicians, dominant narratives of the model minority, assimilation, and a color-blind America are still in play (Kim 2001). The building of a more assertive, politicized community history was left to Asian American Studies, where it still resides as new growth (Chang 2001).

Indeed, there is a new and growing body of research by Asian American scholars on political participation. This is a valuable contribution to the literature, although much of it is statistical and policy driven. During the 1990s, community researchers in ethnic and cultural studies and other social sciences highlighted community transformation wrought by the presence of post-1965 immigrants. Consequences and fallout from transformations in suburban communities have been well documented (Horton 1995; Pardo 1998; Saito 1998). Generally, however, in the discussion of Asian American political participation, there is a relative lack of research directed specifically at *who* these new naturalized citizens are and *how* they construct new identities for themselves, including the specific processes, heavily implicated with power, by which they transform community politics both inside and outside of Asian America. As critical race theorists argue, although power structures that seek to maintain social domination and subordination may still be central, they must share space with the agency of others with less authority (Crenshaw and Gotanda 1995).

I am hopeful that this book will help provide new perspectives. My approach focuses more intimately on the genesis and subsequent maturational processes of politicized identities among naturalized Chinese activists and how these diachronic elements resulted in organizational and collective action. This is an on-the-ground, individual and group integrative process that offers a more nuanced look at how social motivations make history and, individually and collectively, how history informs the production of identity—such as the ways in which *Asian* and *Asian American* have been and continue to be conflated. Naming the past through specific socio-historical schemes allows a look at the ways cultural constructions are negotiated and contested. Theoretically, these historical frames are political acts wherein Asian Americans contest others' representations of and opposition to their integration as participatory citizens. For example, at the beginning of the twenty-first century, dominant narratives portray an ascendant and competitive China. Within this framework, the lives of many new Chinese activists, which include both a grounded citizenship in the United States *and* transnational social practices here and in Asia, have been called into question and viewed with suspicion.

At the very least, I hope that learning more about the activities and motivations of these politically involved American citizens of Chinese ancestry will widen discussion beyond simply acknowledging their increased and visible presence. As for being asked my opinion about a possible name and agenda change for CAUSE, I'm thankful that nobody listened to me.

A word regarding nomenclature. The inability and unwillingness of mainstream society to distinguish nativity or ethnicity has been both a passive and a violent form of subjectification for Asian Americans (Hayano 1981). My aim here is to avoid reifying those discourses that deserve dismantling. Such categorizations minus meaningful explication continue to occupy an especially egregious place in Asian American history. In keeping context always in the foreground, I call activists born in the United States *native-born.* I refer to the post-1965 naturalized Chinese who are at the core of this ethnography *new activists, new Chinese activists,* or *naturalized activists.* The term *new activist* denotes individuals who arrived with the first, large Chinese immigrant cohort to become naturalized and mature in the local, post-1965 U.S. political arena—a watershed year in Asian American history. *New* does not ignore the political activism of a previous generation of Chinese immigrants, for that would abrogate much of the historical foundation of this book. Nevertheless, many post-1965 activists *are* substantially different from those who participated earlier. As part of the so-called transnational Asian knowledge class, new activists are uniquely positioned to utilize their resources within a restructured U.S. economy (Yang 2005). Individually and as a group, their social capital enables distinctive opportunities for political incursions. I will have more to say about this as well as about whether transnational life and the uses of transnational social networks and capital among naturalized activists are new. Suffice it to say here that I don't believe transnationalism per se is a new social phenomenon so much as that scholarly focus on the subject is a new analytical tool that gives us a different perspective in challenging the assumptions about immigration and assimilation (Itzigsohn 2000b).

Regardless of nativity, however, *all* Americans of Asian ancestry participate in identity constructions that are notably fluid and situational in an *American* context. They are naturalized immigrants or they were born here, but they are *all* working out identity projects as citizens of the United States. In this, an Asian American political history has always been one of engagement, of work and participation, albeit oftentimes limited. This speaks to the role of agency and to the behaviors and activities that all of these participants have used in challenging asymmetries of power.

In constructing the histories of the newest political participants, new Chinese activists may begin civic life in the United States as ethnic political participants, but their experiences here have led them to perform as racialized Americans in tandem with other ethnic groups of Asian Americans. This conclusion challenges theories of racialized citizenship that pay attention to socially constructed "differences in the social, economic or political position of a group" but do not fully acknowledge the strength of historically unequal power relationships (Castles and Davidson 2000, 63). As Steven Gregory, whose work resonated deeply during my graduate years, has said: "It is essential that we historicize race and racism if we are to understand and struggle against their continuing significance in the present and the future. We need to understand how and why a ranked hierarchy of races has been put to such destructive uses, been affirmed 'scientifically,' been challenged repeatedly, and yet still dies so hard" (Gregory 1998, 1).

. . .

The narrative structure of this book is primarily longitudinal so that the evolution of a post-1965 new-activist political identity, as well as its inclusion and transformation within existing Chinese American and Asian American political projects, can be more fully comprehended. However, its rough historical and chronological timeline is not absolutely linear but tacks back and forth, paying attention to the simultaneity of events and individuals' memories. Interviews and other ethnographic data are contextualized by subject, not necessarily by time or date. So that the flow of content is maintained, date and place are frequently used as chapter subheadings or stated in the text. My aim is for the reader to visualize changing social and political times and experience the tempo of events as lived by individuals over the past 40 years in the United States and Asia.

Chapter 1 frames a picture of naturalized Chinese activists in Southern California—who they are, some of the activities in which they are involved—and the dialectics of potential alignment with an extant and primarily native-born Asian American political leadership.

Chapter 2 focuses on the construction of a pan–Asian American political identity by investigating the racial paradigms present in hegemonic colonial and imperial discourses even before the first Asian immigrants came to this country more than 150 years ago. This politicized history is a story of agency within a racially ascribed marginality whose roots were recovered by a new generation of Asian American student radicals during the 1960s. From those beginnings, Asian Americans—primarily native-born but joined by a small number of active immigrants who had come to the United States during the 1950s—began to mature and immerse themselves in local political structures. Political identities that coalesced around a progressive, pan–Asian American agenda are analyzed against the backdrop of a political campaign in Southern California. Half a world away, another group of similar age was shaping a different kind of political identity.

Chapter 3 marks the arrival in the United States of tens of thousands of Asian immigrants after 1965. Aided by global economic changes, a cohort of Western-educated students and professionals form the core of a new type of Asian immigrant. Their politicized life histories diverge deeply from the lives of American-born Asian activists. The political outlooks of new Asian immigrants are based on both nascent and marginal colonial or nation-state mentalities. At the same time, they have an overarching vision of what America can provide, not just economically, but in terms of the promise of citizenship and a stake in belonging.

Chapter 4 explores how these activist immigrants have made new lives for themselves and their families. But within these reconfigured communities of suburban Chinese Americans are places and spaces of racialized contestation where they confront radicalizing experiences with racism that do not match the ideals of democracy and citizenship that they envisioned before immigration. In this context, new Chinese American activists begin to be involved in the political process as a way to contest their marginality and seek inclusion and recognition. Their first forays into organized, collective action manifest themselves in ethnic-specific mobilization utilizing transnational networking, a fundamentally different technique by which political identities might be worked that generally is not available to American-born Asians.

Chapter 5 examines the 1990s, and the new-activist political work of the decade, as a time of historic convergence in the Asian American collectivity. After pursuing ethnic-specific mobilization for a decade, some naturalized activists begin to embrace instead the instrumentality of a pan–Asian American identity. Both naturalized and native-born activists have undergone more than 30 years of maturation with common *American* experiences as racialized citizens. At this point in their life histories, they may disagree on some specific political issues, but not on the overall political goal of increased representation and a "seat at the table." The prospects of forging alliances and seeking common ground despite heterogeneity between and *within* each group are explored.

Chapter 6 looks at future cooperative political participation and coalition and consensus building through an analysis of one American-born activist's pursuit of political office and the naturalized citizens who help elect him despite differences in political outlook. Generational issues are briefly addressed. Are naturalized citizen activists one-generation anomalies? Their children are American-born, and although most have yet to reach maturity, the physical fact of immigration, although a vital chapter of family history, is not part of their lived American experience. Will they embrace pan–Asian American-ness or even see a need for political involvement?

Chapter 7 summarizes and offers a response to the questions asked in Chapter 1: Who are these new politically active Chinese Americans, and what do they want to accomplish?

This ethnography investigates the ways in which new Chinese American citizens become participants in democratic structures, and what it means to them and to other Asian Americans who are compelled by an activist agenda and a vision advocating social justice and participatory equality. In constructing everyday lives in neighborhoods all around Southern California, these newest participants on the block have graciously allowed me access and friendship and refreshed hope for constructing a politically empowered future—an Asian American future.

ONE

Transforming the Field

Framing the Rules of Engagement:
Summer 2003, Monterey Park, California

"I don't like all that race-related stuff, give me a better argument."

The room is quiet; the congealing take-out pizza in the center of the table suddenly looks appetizing. The scene is the monthly board meeting of Chinese Americans United for Self Empowerment (CAUSE), a political advocacy group based in Southern California whose membership is over-whelmingly American of Chinese ancestry.[1]

It is early on a weeknight, and other board members have been straggling in after work. Meeting sites shift among the sprawling suburbs rimming Los Angeles to accommodate the group's equally extended membership. To-night the gathering is at the corporate offices of one of the board members on the edge of Monterey Park. The atmosphere is casual and friendly. Board members network personally and professionally among themselves and fre-quently see one another at community and social functions. About a dozen people from Palos Verdes, Monterey Park, West Covina, and West Los An-geles sit comfortably around a long conference table.

. . .

First-generation, naturalized Chinese immigrants founded CAUSE in the early 1990s, having moved to the United States primarily during the late 1960s and early 1970s. They are relatively new U.S. citizens; most have become naturalized within the past 25 years. The level of their political and community participation flies in the face of more traditional narratives that generally portray Asian Americans as rather apathetic bystanders in political and civic life. In particular, much of the existing scholarship, when it mentions them at all, often paints first-generation Asian immigrants as having neither the means nor the motivation to get involved in political processes (Parrillo 1982; Uhlaner 1991). Clearly, the people at this meeting, and those whose lives unfold in the following pages, offer a much more nuanced, activist rereading of that story line. They not only have immersed themselves in local political structures but have actively sought out niches where they can best utilize their extensive transnational social networks, their bi- and tri-focality in social processes—*and* they are doing this all at breakneck speed. In fact, if higher levels of recognition (not always positive) including elective office; greater allocation of government resources; civic appointments; and participation and representation in various levels of formal and grassroots organizational politics, governance, and community life are considered among the markers of success that constitute political empowerment, then this book supports what some have begun to surmise: "Asian immigrants appear to attain levels of political involvement that are the same, if not better, than those of native born Asian citizens" (Ong and Nakanishi 2003, 130).

Political involvement, political participation, and *political activism* as conceived in this book merge with what are considered formal political processes such as electoral politics but extend beyond them as well. Chinese Americans and other Asian Americans take part in a wide range of social practices and relationships in which they negotiate identity and membership. Addressing these activities as political confronts hegemonic asymmetries and power relations. As Steven Gregory (1998) writes, "Politics does not delimit a pre-given set of institutions, relations, or actions, as much as describe a variable field of social practices . . . imbued with power." Social constructions of subjectivities such as racial identity are not just political processes but "the precondition of politics" (Gregory 1998, 13). To gloss political involvement and the inherent social responses that occur outside the electoral field would be to discount the complex Asian American record of civic engagement historically and in more contemporary frameworks including broad global transformations affecting the political economy of the United States and Asia. This supports what Asian American scholars have argued must be a wider theoretical structure for defining what is political in Asian American communities, a wider conceptualization of "potential intersections," relationships, and experiences (Nakanishi 2001, 107).

The dizzying speed and aggressiveness with which new Chinese activists are fashioning politicized identities out of which they pursue collective action have unsettled not just mainstream political structures but those already extant in the Asian American political community. New immigrants' participation in various politically oriented organizations and their attendance at and support of numerous community functions make them politically active. If asked, not many would call themselves activists; many would vehemently deny the label. Yet, when an ethnography of these new Chinese Americans is constructed from their life histories and the flow of the everyday through events, links, and alliances in which they are involved, a picture of activism emerges.

This participation points to the transformative dynamic of a self-inscribed activist identity grounded at the same time in an ascribed ethnoracial assignment (Brodkin 1998). It is the dialectic between Self and Other(s) that impels their participation in political processes. These new citizens of Chinese ancestry have visions of inclusion that insinuate themselves into two existing narratives. The first is an Asian American political sensibility established during the 1970s as a counternarrative to mainstream hegemonies. This traditional Asian American politicized identity translates into a progressivism privileging social justice, racial equality, and the pursuit of a recovered personal and community distinctiveness. The second dominant narrative has evolved out of the nation-state story of national citizenship and belonging, which guarantees citizens full and equal membership (Wang 1991). In this national project, both new Chinese American activists and other Asian Pacific Americans find that the presumption and promise of equal standing—regardless of race, color, or creed—remains largely unfulfilled. Ultimately, it is this dialectic that may have the greatest potential to fashion an instrumental political alliance incorporating both primarily native-born Asian Americans and new-activist immigrants.

These new activists' dreams for inclusion are, therefore, contested visions. As they construct place and space for themselves, their new politicized identities must be understood as an oppositional reading, one that is potentially counterhegemonic to both the existing, predominantly native-born Asian American political identity and the homogenizing imperatives of a national political citizenship. Of course, not all counterhegemonies are resistant all the time. It will be shown that, while not necessarily resistant but rather cooperative or co-optative, a politicized identity project among new immigrants points to the reconfiguration of power relationships not only between themselves and dominant power structures but between the heterogeneous counternarratives that constitute this ethnic subgroup within an Asian American collective.

. . .

At the CAUSE board meeting, the conversation is between two members. The subject of "all that race-related stuff" is Proposition 54 on the October 2003 California ballot. If passed (and at midsummer, passage appeared inevitable before a dramatic shift in voter sentiment led to its overwhelming defeat), Proposition 54 would stop local and state government from gathering racial and ethnic data. The amendment to the California Constitution is the newest sibling of Proposition 209, which in 1996 banned state and local government affirmative action programs. Proposition 54 is already widely opposed by major civil rights and minority groups in the state that believe the gathering of racial data is crucial to political empowerment. But among all voting groups in preelection polling, only Asian Americans support Proposition 54 (Field Research Corporation 2003).

The argument on the table is whether the board should endorse Proposition 54. CAUSE is a nonprofit, nonpartisan community-based organization. Federal regulations do not allow nonprofits to endorse political candidates. Instead, the group's brand of advocacy is geared to taking positions on legislation, propositions, or other ballot measures as well as a wide-ranging number of issues affecting Chinese and other Asian American constituents. CAUSE's positions are performed publicly via outreach and discourse "through education, voter registration, community involvement, research and publication, advocacy and leadership training."[2] There is no animosity in this board discussion, but it is also clear that there isn't necessarily agreement.

One of the discussants is Chinese American, but not native-born. Larry is never comfortable framing debate in strictly racial terms and prefers a wider dialogue. He grew up in Hong Kong, immigrated to the United States as a college student, and was naturalized in his twenties. He left Hong Kong during a period of civil uncertainty and fear. The horrors of the Cultural Revolution to the north were spilling across the border; there were riots and death in the colony. The British had decided that the word *colony* carried negative connotations and had just adopted the more neutral term *territory*, but the mentality remained for Larry and other Chinese living there. Hong Kong Chinese were not full citizens of the realm. His parents decided it was time to look abroad for more opportunities—and safety for their children.

The other person in the Proposition 54 conversation is about the same age as Larry and is also Chinese but American-born. Ric lived in Los Angeles during the radicalizing civil unrest of the 1960s. As an active member of that generation, he both witnessed and participated in the birth of the Yellow Power Movement and the flowering of a pan–Asian American identity. These experiences led him to law school in Southern California and to an evolving personal history of progressive, community-based politics.

Ric looks around the table and says with finality, "Anything that prohibits the gathering of this kind of data or information is really a violation of our civil rights, so it's [Proposition 54] not in our interest." For him, the choice is clear. In quick succession, he ticks off three potential negative results if the proposition passes: there would be less medical research on minority groups, health and safety would be jeopardized by public agencies not being permitted to collect racial data, and the lack of race and ethnic-specific data in higher education would penalize minority students. The points Ric makes are virtually, word for word, the mantra of every progressive Asian American and Pacific Islander organization and individual in the state opposed to the proposition, most of whom also got their political start during the late 1960s and early 1970s. For Ric it is all about "that race-related stuff." He waits for comment from Larry, but the meeting has already gone later than usual and everybody just wants a quick wrap. No one else has any opinions, and by voice count the group supports a "no" vote on Proposition 54. Later, Larry, who complains that he can't get used to eating pizza for dinner, entices a few board members to a nearby Monterey Park Chinese restaurant for noodle soup. Even at nearly 10 o'clock at night, the Atlantic Boulevard restaurant is crowded with new immigrants. Once the small group finds a vacant table and orders, Larry explains that he's not necessarily a supporter of Proposition 54; he just wanted Ric to better articulate why he *didn't* support it—to persuade him that their interests were fundamentally the same.

. . .

At the outset, let me make clear that I hesitate to label Larry's or Ric's motivations or the goals of the respective communities of native-born and foreign-born as antagonistic per se. In the organization both men support—and beyond, in their personal lives—they have common goals, and both search for the common ground that comes from shared meanings of membership and experience. Each wants political recognition and a seat at the table when resources are divvied up, and each seeks validation as a full participatory citizen. And let me also make clear that the purpose of this book is not to simply privilege the issue of nativity but to use dissimilar life experiences analytically in order to tease out the ways in which different political identities and ideologies are born and subsequently acted upon in everyday life. In this way, a more nuanced picture of activism emerges—one that acknowledges the differences but also foregrounds the commonalities intrinsic to Asian *American* political lives. However, as already briefly established, what unfolds in the following pages, and must not be hidden or glossed over within these American lives, is community disjuncture, including both conflict and cooperation over who qualifies for inclusion in an activist Chinese American political arena, who qualifies for leadership, who decides on issues and agendas. In short, who will be considered as representative not just of Chinese Americans but of the wider Asian American community?

Inherent in these broad questions of representation are the overriding problems of increasing heterogeneity within the Chinese American community and the growing differentials of class and gender among Chinese immigrants and, thus, of Asian America. Addressing class concerns has always been part of a radical and subsequent progressive Asian American political project and is slowly being acknowledged by new Chinese activists as well.

The brief and seemingly insignificant exchange between Larry and Ric didn't warrant mention in the meeting's minutes. Such exchange is commonplace in the give-and-take that often characterizes CAUSE meetings, where decisions are usually made without rancor and where later, conversation is parsed. This small bit of ethnographic text between two Chinese American political activists allows for a wider discussion and frames the major themes investigated here about the meaningful ways in which identity is illuminated through life history.

How we identify ourselves and others through ever-shifting, contested, appropriated, structured, and internalized social processes of categorization and the social outcomes that result can be gleaned from everyday events and social interactions. In this view, identity formation, rather than being a static process, is creative and dynamic. Indeed, as has been noted by Kondo (1990), it is a lifelong occupation in which the crafting of self "implies a concept of agency: that human beings create, construct, work on, and enact their identities, sometimes creatively challenging the limits of the cultural constraints which constitute both what we call selves and the ways in which those selves can be crafted" (48). The implication is that humans are not entirely free agents. As will be shown, new Chinese activists have come to realize that much of their own participatory work cannot be separated from the geopolitical and racial contexts of posturing between the United States and China. In fact, to construct and practice an Asian American political sensibility is tacit acknowledgment of differentials of power that continue to exist not just in the United States but in global discourses as well. This, then, is also a story about racial politics in the United States and beyond, including systems and structures of inequality that are defined primarily in racial terms, and how racial privilege within those contours continues to subjectify (Gladney 1998). In this sense, that which is political takes on broader ideological implications—the deliberate efforts of alienated individuals and groups to alter systems of dominance, or what has been called the tyranny of meanings (Sederberg 1984).

In its more quotidian manifestations, political participation is an especially fruitful way of looking at the dynamics of historical transformation in Asian America. Ethnographic constructions of participation are a way of getting at both history and the collective memory of a community. Furthermore, politics—whether electoral or any of the myriad forms of participation in grassroots community activities—constitute unique group and public endeavors that involve a variable and highly fluid field of social practices. It is a means by which Americans perform their public identities.

In the discussion over Proposition 54 at the CAUSE meeting, participants built a shared meaning that became the basis for a collective response. Larry, Ric, and the others performed the rituals and processes of the politically active by staking a claim, publicly declaring their not entirely dissimilar views of the proposition (after the proposition's unexpected defeat, Ric felt the greater measure of vindication). For both Larry and Ric, however, the goal was not revolution but inclusion in the dominant structures of participatory politics. What exists beyond this is a deep and highly personal awareness of the place/space achieved through widely divergent life trajectories. On one hand, there are those like Ric, for whom identity as a native-born American of Chinese ancestry is a lifelong project. Identity-making is rooted in competing metanarratives: unquestioned rights/rites of national citizenship and exclusions from those rights. On the other hand, there is a new group of Chinese immigrants, like Larry, who are naturalized. For them, citizenship has been a deliberate choice, adopted later in life, without the same kind of unconscious rootedness but with a bi- or even tri-focality that crafts its own counternarratives in the global and transnational. It is imperative to point out that although this hybridity is normative among new activists, it is also conceived with a groundedness and a local, place-based *American* identity that is normative as well. The current cachet of some of the scholarship celebrating transnational and flexible citizenships, diasporic identities, and cosmopolitan and global ecumenes must be approached cautiously here lest this positivism becomes complicit with a modern form of Orientalizing (J. Clifford 1994; Hannerz 1996; Ong 1999; Said 1979). That is to say, although this ability to perform beyond borders is extolled, these modern subjects are frequently still seen as foreign, unassimilable, and beyond the reach of civilizing—a view rooted in the enduring belief in ontological difference between Orient and Occident (Jalal al-'Azm 2000). The aim of this book is to articulate a concern for the stereotype of the habitual foreigner and to critically unpack it where it appears both in the literature and in the ethnographic everyday.

The notion that this kind of hybridity is somehow synonymous with postmodernity also must be interrogated. Transnationalism has a deep historical context. More than 600 years ago, scholars and others aboard the Ming Fleets that sailed halfway around the world established enduring social ties between themselves and the numerous new cultures and peoples with whom they made contact (Ma 1997). Three hundred years ago, European and American colonizers who established racialized legal and social structures throughout Asia and the Pacific were involved in worldwide drug trafficking and the movements of 100 million people otherwise known as slaves of the "tropical industrial army" (Mintz 1998; Wolf 1983). One hundred years ago, millions of European immigrants to America maintained networks in and ties to their homelands (Foner 1997). This timeline illustrates the need for attention to earlier transnational histories of race, conquest, and the globalization of labor.

Transnational life is not new, although its dynamics and processes have evolved. In this sense, the activism of naturalized Chinese can be seen as new, having evolved in the context of changing economic and political conditions in Asia and the United States within the past half century. And whereas Chinese Americans have historically displayed multifocal points of identity—of being here and there, Chinese and American—it can be argued that the frequency with which these constructions occur has become intensified and normalized (Basch, Glick Schiller, and Blanc 1994). Again, however, the contemporary condition of transnational life ought not to be overemphasized. New Chinese activists are fully aware of nation-building regimes that create a particular *shared* symbolic place and a sense of belonging that both subsumes and creates difference. Most learn this even before coming to the United States. In addition, transnational social practices are not necessarily antihegemonic. This does not negate the potency of both simultaneity and place-based identities as a means of establishing the rights of full participation. Neither does it imply the dissolution of the nation-state's borders or willingness to weaken its sovereignty over the granting of membership. The nation is not withering away (Hannerz 1993). Efforts by new Chinese immigrants to seek inclusion under the *ideal* of citizenship—that which is liberal, egalitarian, universalistic, *and* fully emancipatory—point to these desires (Giddens 1991; Glenn 2000).

The key questions to be addressed here are, *who are these new politically active Chinese Americans in Southern California,* and *what do they want to accomplish?* Each life history is unique, but threads of commonality can be woven into theoretical fabric. Over a period of 30 years, the warp of their trajectory looks something like this:

- Immigration to the United States during the late 1960s and early 1970s.
- Naturalization by the late 1970s and early 1980s.
- Beginnings of political participation several years after becoming citizens, getting married, and establishing families.
- Collective political organization during the early 1990s.

Filling in the weft, a more personal look reveals the following:

- Immigration primarily from Hong Kong, Taiwan, and, to a lesser extent, Mainland China, though these areas may not be the initial points of debarkation.
- Politicized family backgrounds and networks in Asia.

- Advanced educations, often at European or U.S. universities or at high schools and colleges in their homelands emphasizing Westernized pedagogies; many have postgraduate degrees.
- Mostly middle or upper middle class, with a few considered wealthy.
- Social ascriptions, including self-descriptions, as professionals, managers, entrepreneurs, engineers, scientists, small-business owners, property and real estate developers and brokers, and lawyers.
- Self-made economically. Although it may be argued that new Chinese activists have taken advantage of wider social networks such as university and business connections offering scholarship or work stipends, most come to the United States with extremely limited personal contacts—often with no existing nuclear family network—or financial support.
- Now in their late 40s to late 50s; mostly married men with children in their early teens to early 20s. Married women also have families, and a number are divorced—some more than once.
- Economic and social success, which nonetheless have not spared them racializing experiences in the United States. These experiences have contributed to a sense of group identity and led to their collective political participation.

This last point is perhaps one of the most significant: New activists are coming to realize that what grounds their American identity and frames their U.S. citizenship is the same overarching ideological project that native-born Chinese and other Asian American activists seek to contest—what is described as the *longue durée*, the persistence through time, of racialized exclusion (Sanjek 1998).

The Ethnographic Field

The bulk of this investigation is the result of four and half years—from 1999 to 2003—of ethnographic immersion. Of course, peoples' lives are always changing, so I have tried to update current political positions, demographics, and other professional and personal transitions where possible and appropriate beyond 2003. Equally important to this longitudinal approach are perspectives I gained from field research accomplished over nearly 20 years from the late 1970s to the late 1990s. This research was framed within the parameters of my news reporting, as news events and subsequent coverage frequently led to both on- and off-the-record conversations and participant observation. Until the political field began to change during the 1980s, the focus was primarily on American-born Asian political actors. By the early 1980s, I began to investigate some of the naturalized Chinese, primarily immigrants from Taiwan, who were transforming the suburbs of Southern California.

Because of its high concentration of naturalized Chinese activists, Southern California, especially the environs east and south of Los Angeles, was a logical choice for uncovering sites of social interaction. This vast geographic area includes what is sometimes referred to as Greater Los Angeles—Los Angeles, Orange, Riverside, and San Bernardino counties—an area of more than 30,000 square miles and more than 16 million people (U.S. Bureau of the Census 2000b). Theoretical conclusions and the uncovering of a naturalized Chinese political identity are confined primarily to this arena of "local" participation. Comparisons of similarly involved new Chinese activists in other areas of the United States are beyond the scope of this book.

The selection of CAUSE as one of the central points of investigation was not so much due to the group per se, although its uniqueness is a factor, nor does it merely provide a convenient framework around which to explore naturalized Chinese activism, although that is critical as well. CAUSE emerged during the early 1990s at the same time and as a result of a maturing political participation among new activists. Thus, the combination of the appearance of CAUSE and increased participation was not just happenstance but historically significant if political strategies may be viewed as flexible tactics that respond to changing social conditions. Furthermore, "the best strategies unleash the creative energies of people to do things that they have never tried before in their lives" (Omatsu 1990, 71). Like so much else about the construction of political identities, including those of new activists, the historical context created the impetus for new social movements of empowerment. Collective action and the birth of CAUSE merged. It should be noted that there are other primarily Chinese American groups and individuals who participate in organizations in Southern California. Their mission statements include words like *community* and *empowerment*, with goals such as voter participation and voter outreach. Membership in these groups and CAUSE often overlap. However, CAUSE remains unique

in that it is still a grassroots local organization specifically dedicated to political advocacy and empowerment.

All of the people who appear in these pages, regardless of membership,
know about CAUSE. Subjects were selected by what might be labeled a
modified snowball technique. As in journalism, anthropological field methods privilege open eyes and ears. Simply by observing and participating in
events where activists congregated, I was able to speak with numerous individuals and observe those who were most participatory, not only in CAUSE
but in other grassroots activities. I read accounts in newspapers and newsletters and researched my own extensive files of news stories and interviews I
had conducted in order to identify actors.

In constructing life histories, I interviewed and interacted in depth with
nearly 100 men and women, both native-born and foreign-born. Regardless of nativity, most of the new activists are men, who make up three-
quarters of the interviewees in this study. Interviews usually lasted one
to three hours, often over several sessions. At other times, a conversation
might involve a few quick words at a public function along with untold
numbers of phone calls, e-mails, and the like. I availed myself of people's
hospitality and talked with them one-on-one about some of their most
personal experiences. I met them in their homes; in offices, warehouses,
favorite restaurants, and coffee shops; and finagled invitations to family
functions and countless community events. These in-depth interviews
and other exchanges routinely ended up as wonderful, free-association
conversations about events, places, and people that they often had not
thought about for years, thereby bringing seemingly unrelated events into
sharp focus. By and large, everyone was more than willing to be part of the
ethnographic record. They understood what I was trying to do and why it
was important to share their histories. But like any ethnographic tool, the
collection of personal histories is limited by the interpretive, creative, and
ongoing nature of the crafting of self. About this, I can say only that I have
attempted to reproduce what I was told as accurately as possible and, when
time and energy permitted, to assemble recollections of key events from
several different individuals.

Although the initial 100 provided an outline of new Chinese activism in
Southern California, this book concentrates on a much smaller group of
about three dozen foreign-born and native-born individuals who are most
illustrative of the new activism. Foreign-born activists all have family roots

in China, but most eventually left the mainland for either Hong Kong or Taiwan. Twenty were either born or grew up in Hong Kong, five were born or grew up in Taiwan, and the remainder were born in China but grew up in the United States or Europe. Nine native-born Chinese activists include six men and three women.

Since CAUSE was founded in 1993, all of these activists have participated at some level in the group, from subscribing to the newsletter or buying a ticket to the annual dinner or another public function, to volunteering for programs or serving on the board of directors. Their life histories provide the unifying thread in the fabric of this book.[3]

The book also contains selected results of a survey I conducted with more than 300 individuals who attended the 2000 Democratic National Convention in Los Angeles (see Appendix 1). In the middle of the usual cacophony that characterizes such an event, these Democratic Asian Pacific Americans were both interested in and kind enough to take the time to answer my questions. The survey sought to fill in the gaps in scholarship on both the 1996 fund-raising controversy over campaign contributions that Asian American Democrats made to President Bill Clinton's reelection and the 1999 case of nuclear scientist Wen Ho Lee, who was accused of stealing U.S. nuclear secrets. The results should be regarded as descriptive only. As will be revealed in later chapters, participants in Asian American political arenas see both of these situations as watershed events. This is particularly so among the foreign-born ethnographic subjects in this book, who found themselves targets of federal investigations in 1996 and who, three years later, identified closely with fellow immigrant Lee. The Democratic National Convention survey also contributes to a comparative analysis of opinion on why native-born and immigrant Asian Americans become politically involved and how they see political empowerment among Asian Americans evolving. All of this is framed within a larger geopolitical and national narrative beginning in the early 1990s of U.S.–China relations generally and an economic and militarily aggressive China more specifically.

Additionally, I also participated in and observed myriad public political rituals—meetings, small dinners and large banquets, conferences and fund-raisers—attended mostly by naturalized immigrant activists. These events offered moments during which the performance of a politicized identity was on display, although not always in the way organizers had planned, particularly at banquets attended by hundreds of people.

The scripts at these community events are well known to anyone who attends them. Between endless courses of family-style Chinese dinners, multi-ethnic Asian entertainment or speeches—carefully choreographed to pay homage to the various ethnic constituencies present—punctuate the program. At public functions attended mostly by the native-born community, polite and attentive care is paid to such offerings. Waiters are instructed to serve new courses only between speakers and acts. Not so among activist immigrants. Getting the crowd's attention is nearly impossible. Whoever is at the podium and whatever is being said are immaterial. Between food courses, people plunge among tables, dart around heavily laden waiters, or mill noisily in the aisles and pass out business cards. Those who can't find room to stand, shout at each other from their seats. It is all about seeing and being seen, making new contacts and renewing old ones; it is about the work of constructing identity performed in a way unique to new activists. It is a delightful, ethnographic gold mine.

The presence of naturalized Chinese American political activists coincides with a critical juncture in the history of Asian America. In fact, this historical moment was *created* by major changes in U.S. immigration law after 1965, which allowed for a second and much larger wave of immigration from Asia not seen since the days before Asian exclusion of the late nineteenth and early twentieth centuries. The majority of Asians in the United States are now immigrants (Ong and Nakanishi 2003). In the span of just one decade, the 1970s, native-born Asians became the minority, now constituting less than 25 percent of the total Asian Pacific Islander population. The foreign-born will continue to dominate until 2020 and most likely beyond if current immigration numbers are maintained (Ong and Nakanishi 2003). The explosive growth in immigration has made Chinese the largest subgroup among Asian Pacific Islanders, leapfrogging over Filipinos, Asian Indians, Vietnamese, and Koreans (U.S. Bureau of the Census 2000a).

The new Chinese American activists who are at the heart of this book are a specific part of this newer immigrant cohort. They form a core of "the most highly skilled of any immigrant group our country has ever had" (Takaki 1989, 420). By 1990, 32 percent of new Asian immigrants who self-identified as Chinese listed their occupations as either professional or executive/management. This is quite a remarkable figure and nearly equal to the 39 percent of native-born Chinese who similarly identified themselves (Jiobu 1996).

Another key demographic displacement occurred for the first time during the 1980s; Asian immigrants who had become eligible voters through naturalization outnumbered native-borns (Ong and Lee 2001). Asian American community and political leaders have just begun to realize the potential effect of naturalized immigrants. Thus far, that realization has manifested itself in differing levels of discomfort, apprehension, and even anger. In this so-called changing of the guard, no one active in Asian American participatory politics doubts that the community is experiencing a sweeping transformation (Ong and Lee 2001). Longtime Asian American activists polemicize the domination of transnational capital, dispute newer claims of representation of the wider community, and reassert older notions of community border in reifying the notion that "they" are not "us" (Wang 1998).

For their part, naturalized activists are unsparing in their criticism of those who would denigrate their political participation. One new activist, a man now in his 50s, emigrated from Hong Kong as a college student. In 2003, a few years after he was elected mayor in a Southern California city of 20,000, he spoke in a tone bordering on arrogance, his confidence born of the knowledge of his growing constituency: "We're the leaders, not you! And people like me will become leaders of Asian Americans in the next 10 or 15 years. Now the ABA [American-born Asian] is going to look and say, 'Who are those FOBs?'[4] That's conflict!"

TWO

History and Race

Excavating the Roots of Politicization in Asian America

MAY 2003, WEST LOS ANGELES

> Oh absolutely we're not leaders. It's the new immigrants [who are leaders].
> My type of people, the Cantonese longtime Californ', are a dying breed.
> We should accept the idea that the leaders of the community are going to
> be coming from there, accept that the majority needs of the community are
> going to be coming from there. My wife is one of the new breed; she says
> we should let go. . . . *Let go!?*

If there is one subject about which Ronald is passionate, it is Chinese
American history. Right now, he is speaking loudly enough for other people
in this West L.A. coffee shop to swivel around in their booths to look at
him, the only Asian face, other than mine, in the diner.

Ronald is an American-born Chinese. He proudly calls himself a fifth-
generation pioneer Californian, and his embrace of the term "longtime
Californ'" in the framework of Chinese American history is freighted with
symbolic meaning and membership. To deflect harassment or worse, early
Chinese immigrant laborers often asserted in English, "Oh, me longtime
Californ'" (Nee and Nee 1974). During the transformative 1960s, the re-
appropriation of this phrase by young activists spoke to a recaptured and
highly politicized American identity—"not as a microcosm of Chinese society on American soil, but a unique American community with a history,

language, and institutions of its own" (Nee and Nee 1974, xvii). Its localized reimagining became a contemporary site of liberation, resistance, and empowerment among Chinese and other Asian Americans who demanded recognition and new political presence (Dirlik 1996). On a more critical level, Ronald uses the term to draw attention to the difference between himself and new, naturalized Chinese Americans.

The roots of this constructed collective identity are firmly anchored in the 1960s, as will be revealed in the lives of two American-born Chinese who matured during this period. It was a time when authority and dominant discourses in the United States were challenged and, in the process, altered by Asian Americans on college campuses who began to collectively confront historical forces of racism, poverty, war, and exploitation in new and radical ways (Omatsu 1989). Much more than just providing the awakenings of racial consciousness (although this was an important element in that it recaptured a community's history of racial oppression), the 1960s provided a framework for students to analyze power and domination not just in the United States but throughout the world.

The specifics of this analysis led directly to a strategy for social transformation—mass organizing and community involvement growing out of *local*, grassroots struggles. In this sense, the terms *local* and *community* are applied as parts of the same whole. The emphasis on local has to do with ownership of one's own history and a political activism that repudiates what those with power have constructed without one's consent. For reasons that will be discussed, the original impetus of 1960s Asian American radicals was derailed, but its imprint, although vastly altered, is still visible and continues to inform a contemporary, progressive political agenda. Among Asian American political participants, a progressive agenda still valorizes the local; leaders and others who stake claims on Asian American political discourses do so from community-based work, although much of that work has been institutionalized. In addition, this focus on the local essentializes and historically has been suspicious of outsider incursions into the Asian American community, including the manipulations of transnational influence and capital. The "local" is the dominant paradigm by which American-born Asian political activists identify themselves and *against* which they judge the newest actors—post-1965 naturalized Chinese American activists. This Asian American political sensibility forged during the 1960s and transformed during the 1970s and 1980s as a progressive politics has been constructed largely by American-born Asians.

However, this definition of community activism that privileges only the native-born within the borders of the local must be approached with care. Although it may be seen as an overarching theme of identity, a deeper look reveals that American-born Asian activists were not alone in their early activism, nor were they politicized without keen attention to larger global events and history. There were also young, highly radicalized Asian immigrants, among them students and working-class youth (Ho 2000b). Their politicized participation also focused on issues that transcended nation-state borders, was transnational in practice, and was instrumental to informing global constructs of a racialized identity among the native-born.

During the 1960s, because of immigrant quotas that had been in effect since 1924, new immigration from Asia remained at a standstill. Among the few who had gained entry were university students, refugees, small numbers of reunified families, and diplomats (Ma and Cartier 2003). Many of the foreign students were highly informed politically. During the early 1970s, groups such as the overseas Chinese Students of America were active on U.S. college campuses. These students organized so-called Defense Action Committees and, in concert with other student radicals, held national rallies and teach-ins in major cities such as New York, San Francisco, and Los Angeles.

In Los Angeles, there were protests against Japan's attempts to annex the Tiao-yu Tai Islands in the East China Sea. Foreign student radicals construed U.S. backing as evidence of U.S. imperialism in Asia (National Diao-yu Islands Action Committee 1971). Chinatown was the starting point for marches in Los Angeles. Foreign students invited their native-born Asian counterparts to join them, and many did, identifying this cause with their own concerns about U.S. imperialism in Southeast Asia and the right of self-determination among people in the Third World.[1] Awareness of this kind of historical precedence is vital in understanding how politically active Asian Americans have come to see themselves as racialized citizens within global discourses and how it has shaped their activism.

POWERS OF REPRESENTATION, POWERS OF CAPITALISM

Activist Asian Americans came to keenly understand that their place in America existed within structures of inequality and could not be fully understood without first paying attention to history, an *Orientalized* history that preceded the appearance of the first Asian immigrants in the United States in the mid-1800s.

As Edward Said (2000) has theorized, the immutability of the "great Asiatic mystery" continues to frame Western imaginaries of Asians and Asian Americans and significantly predates colonial/imperial designs on Asia. These "dogmas of the West" include absolute and systematic differences between the West (rational, developed, humane, superior) and the Orient (eternal, aberrant, inferior, and in need of scientifically objective Western description). The Orient is a place to be feared or controlled—preferably both.

Racial typologies placed whites on top and, in this case, Asians on the bottom. Colonialism's authority and the establishment of "canons of taste and value" institutionalized power as well as a systematized racism that followed Asian immigrants to the United States (Said 1979). Asian immigrants were designated the Other, and this racialization became part of capitalism's rationale for labor (Roediger 1991). Capitalism has been key in shaping racial orders in the United States (Mintz 1986; Robinson 1983). These categorizations characterized Asian immigration during the mid-nineteenth century and continued to do so when a new generation of immigrants from Asia heeded calls for different forms of labor 100 years later. It should be pointed out, however, that closer scrutiny reveals sharp contrasts in the social terrain; "subjects were not passive, they resisted, adapted, cooperated, challenged and reinvented their disrupted lives" (Asad 1991, 314).

In addition to burgeoning demands for labor and economic opportunities provided in the United States, the first Asian immigrants left China to escape the effects of both imperial/colonial interference and Chinese state policies. The Opium Wars ended in 1860, though not to the benefit of the Chinese emperor, who found out he could not rule in his own backyard let alone the rest of the world (Wolf 1983). The unequal treaties that England forced upon China at gunpoint, with the intent to import massive amounts of opium and tariff-free products, drained the country of its capital. China tried to increase taxes on the working class but instead began losing both its independence and its labor force (Bai 1982).

By 1860, 41,000 Chinese had made the ocean crossing to California to work in the goldfields (Zia 2000). Suffice it to say, Californian hospitality ran out before the gold did. To give this context, it ought to be pointed out that during this same period, *2.5 million* poor and working-class Europeans landed on the other coast, including tens of thousands of Irish who were not considered white but became "whitened" as state-sponsored racial projects and political structures confronted the "mongrel Asiatics." As demonstrated with American Jews, this whitening process is about instruments of control and political order (Brodkin 1998). Thus, although the number of Chinese was a mere fraction of the number of Europeans, "the rise of Chinese immigration made it possible in the 1840s and 1850s for leading Democrats to develop racial schemes unequivocally gathering all European settlers together as whites against the 'colored races'" (Roediger 1991, 141). This had particular resonance among nativist Californians. For each subsequent "wave" of Asian immigration, which found itself in economic competition with the "American race of workingmen," social and legislative exclusion was the order of the day (Roediger 1991, 143).

This is not to imply that Chinese immigrants had nothing to say about their treatment. Chinese Americans who grew up during the 1960s now embrace what alternative scholarship and their own family histories reveal—the agency, fervor, and organization with which early Chinese immigrants fought for inclusion and against racial categorization. Although they came from disparate parts of China, those first immigrants learned early that subsuming their village differences was necessary for gaining more political clout. They formed group leadership drawn from the family associations transplanted from China, began keeping records of hate crimes perpetrated by white miners, and hired white attorneys and lobbyists to fight anti-Chinese legislation. That the Chinese fought so strenuously against institutional racism even though their successes were minimal indicates their viewpoint not only on their economic losses but on themselves as active participants in the new society. Chinese immigrants fought to change their marginal political status by filing more than a dozen lawsuits on labor and civil rights issues between 1881 and 1896. And unlike the myth of the sojourner, many did become U.S. citizens in California before exclusion.[2] Early immigrants believed that the "United States, whatever its faults, was a country devoted to the rule of law" (McClain 1994, 279). But the right of participation did not extend to them; instead, they were accused of being *hyperpolitical*—fanatically seeking power and influence (Chang 2001). It is ironic that this insinuation of being *overly* political persists to dog many new Chinese activists in the twenty-first century.

Acknowledging the activities of early immigrants in contesting their subalternity is an important part of Asian American history even if this agency was primarily reactionary and defensive. Moreover, this alternative and re-captured view of Asian American history is now visible and accessible. Its inclusion is made possible by the political transformation of Asian America that took place during the 1960s.

RADICAL MASS: THIRD WORLD ALIGNMENTS

In the broadest terms, mid-twentieth-century Asian America comprised a numerically small group of primarily second- and third-generation American-born Asians, first-generation, foreign-born grandparents, and a smaller group of foreign-born college students and immigrant workers. Attempts to carve out meaningful social space for themselves were predicated on a conservatively constructed identity of common experience as a marginalized racial minority that was confined within prevailing racial ideologies whose "outcomes were not always of their own choosing or liking" (Takahashi 1997).

By the late 1960s, the so-called changing of the guard had begun with confluent events that would forever change the face of Asian America (Ong and Lee 2001). First, massive new immigration from Asia resulted in large demographic shifts; there were dramatic transformations in many U.S. communities, particularly those in metropolitan areas. Second, new immigration coincided with the maturation of the postwar baby-boom genera-tion—the largest group of young adults, including Asian Americans, to ever enroll in colleges and universities.

Asian American students became core participants in contesting political and racial inequality. They joined other Americans of color in their unwill-ingness to accept the larger society's view of minority Americans as subalterns and formed new social movements in "a paradigm shift [of] the established system of racial meanings and identities" (Omi and Winant 1994, 96). The bitter experience of those first Asian immigrants was not forgotten; during the 1960s and 1970s, it formed the basis of a politicized group identity whose outlines called for a more powerful pan–Asian American racial experience. This included social and ideological ties that transcended borders to forge partnerships with people of color in the Third World (Iijima 2001).

The term *Asian American* was born on West Coast college campuses as a means of resistance, a radical self-inscription and departure from the domi-nant, baggage-laden word *Oriental.* Its use critiqued the existing frameworks for analyzing Asian Americans and served as a basis for group mobilization. An *Asian American* identity spoke to the collectivity and communality of shared historical experiences of Western colonialism and imperialism. Categories of race also pointed to continuing racial exclusion and exploitation in the United States as it infused the terrain of everyday life.

The parameters of this identity are foundational to a *politicized racial project* that negates seeing asymmetrical social relationships based on race as mere psychological constructs (Omi and Winant 1994). Rather, critically assessing how race is defined in the social construction of place means uncovering how it is also constitutively organized into structures of inequality (Bonilla-Silva 1996; Takagi 1996). This overarching structure forms a collection of ideological themes, many of them legalized and codified, that legitimizes and "maintains the social, economic, and political advantages that whites hold over other Americans" (Gotanda 1995, 257). In other words, the racial project is identified by its system of ideas, thoughts, institutional practices, and behavior that "deterministically ascribe fixed roles and negatively evaluated group characteristics (moral, intellectual, cultural) to peoples on the basis of selected physical attributes whereby their oppression and exploitation are legitimized and perpetuated" (San Juan 1992, 2).

Some scholars privilege ethnicity over race (Barth 1969; Espiritu 1992; Steinberg 2001). But eliding race for ethnic difference "entails blindness to white racism as a causal/historical force in the shaping of U.S. policy and a justification of economic and political inequalities sanctioned by 'color-blind state policies'" (San Juan 1992, 33). Take, for example, the internment of Americans of Japanese ancestry during World War II. Progressive scholarship now sees the suspension of civil rights and the federalization of camps as the nadir of an *institutionalized* racism beginning with exclusion and culminating in public discourse fueled by, among others, "the vicious Hearst newspapers and the long-standing resentment of Japanese Americans' modest economic success on the West Coast" (Matsuda 1995, 67).[3]

The so-called model minority myth, which sets up Asian Americans as possessors of positive values such as family solidarity, diligence, and economic and educational success, is another example of a racial project. This "mastery" of American social forms continues to promote social difference by glossing over intragroup differences and questions of true racial equality and opportunity. It speaks to "a safely sequestered vision of Asian America" in which Asian Americans have been properly taken care of through assimilation (Palumbo-Liu 1999). However, this myth, precisely because it relies on cultural essentialism, is simply a newer version of the Asian American as foreign and therefore unassimilable. More to the point is the inference that Asian Americans are "too busy getting ahead and making money" to worry about issues like politics, thus echoing the old cliché of Asian American apoliticalness. Once again, relative valorization is "inextricably linked to civic ostracism" (Kim 2001). For other people of color who have "failed" to live up to the Asian American example, the myth points to their categorization as deviant citizens.

BLACK POWER/YELLOW POWER

Activist Asian Americans were involved in some of the earliest student radicalism of the 1960s—the Free Speech Movement at Berkeley in 1964 as well as the Student Nonviolent Coordinating Committee and Students for a Democratic Society—and they marched with civil rights protestors in the South. The influence of Black Power, which afforded Asian Americans a sharp recognition of pride in physical and cultural heritage, was seminal for the Asian American left and the Yellow Power Movement in building momentum for rearticulating community and self (Uyematsu 1971). More specifically, a separatist nationalism residing within black communities spoke to the reclamation of both imagined and real territory. Promoted by early leaders such as W. E. B. DuBois, core ideas of group solidarity based on racially common interests are a way of achieving autonomy and social justice (Shelby 2005). Furthermore, black nationalists saw the correlation between the struggles of black Americans and liberation movements in former imperialist colonies around the world, including Asia. This "international solidarity among all 'dark peoples'" resonated with activists (Shelby 2005, 105). Through these African American political ideologies, Asian Americans connected the dots between their own marginalized status and those they saw as equally oppressed in other parts of the United States and the nonindustrialized Third World.[4] Global influences were key to their constructing an Asian American identity. Seemingly unconnected events such as the exploitation of Asian immigrant garment workers, international corporate redevelopment in Asian American communities, and the Vietnam War were all related to broader projects of racialization, imperialism, and genocide (Louie and Omatsu 2001; Omatsu 1989).

Asia, of course, has always been part of an ascribed identity for Americans of Asian ancestry, and activists have always been aware of the tension and conflation of identity between themselves and Asia. One of the benefits of the social transformation of the 1960s was that, for a time, it was possible for activists to appropriate and embrace symbols of Asia as a repudiation of the social projects of integration, assimilation, and disidentification (Hayano 1981). An analysis of this racial position was often found in a revolutionary, socialist Asia. For young Asian American female radicals in particular, "holding up half the sky" had meaning not only with Marxist-Leninist ideologies abroad but with political work at home, in their own communities and among their own peers—Asian American men (M. Y. Chen 1978; Lum 2006).

Shared experience, however, did not always mean inclusiveness. Pan Asian–ness has been and continues to be problematic for Americans whose ancestors called Asia, South Asia, or the Pacific home. Asian cultures and histories are too heterogeneous, and the record is replete with examples of belligerency, imperial conquest, and racial ideologies *between* Asian countries. For example, the uncovering of histories of validation, the stories of the Chinese railroad worker and the Japanese American concentration camp inmate, also needed to make space for other experiences, such as that of the Filipino immigrant worker. The primary role that Filipino farmworkers played in forcing Cesar Chavez's hand in the first Delano grape strike in 1965 is also part of an Asian *Pacific* American history (Ferriss and Sandoval 1997). A pan–Asian American identity is highly political and, for all its warts, was conceived as an instrument of political power and empowerment of community (Espiritu 1992).

And exactly where was the "community" to be found? For many activists of the 1960s, the answer lay in the geographical boundaries that marked the ethnic enclaves—the Chinatowns, Manilatowns, and Little Tokyos. For Chinese Americans, whether or not they actually grew up there, had family there, or spent time there as children or young adults, Chinatown provides a strong, though not always visible, narrative thread in their life histories.

During the 1960s and 1970s, Chinatown and other ethnic enclaves existed as sites of political involvement and consciousness-raising, as arenas where politicized identities framed by dominant racial ideologies were contested and reclaimed from the prevailing tropes of exotic danger and tourist mecca. The enclave symbolized a protected zone where a community could "own" its past. Chinatown was a real social space where people lived everyday lives and had problems that power structures had ignored. Activists working out of numerous storefront social and community service organizations put "serve the people" into practice. The threat of displacement was both real and emotional for American-born Asians (Gee 1976). This approach to a grounded, American historical experience and recruitment by local government of transnational corporations and foreign capital made enclaves highly contested spaces. Redevelopment and expanding development in these areas came to represent the incompatibility of transnationalized investment with the interests of local community (Wang 1998). In 1980s Southern California, this politics of location would reappear in newly configured ethnic enclaves in the suburbs—the ethnoburbs (see Chapter 4).

Despite radical activists' deep commitment to social upheaval and revolution, their notions of community change differed. Some involved in the Yellow Power Movement maintain that the radicals' primary interest was in the more anarchical aspects of social change rather than in real community-based outcomes (Espiritu 1992; Nishio 1982). Radicals point to this view as the result of hegemonic co-optation: "[We] saw that many community groups were starting to transform into social service organizations . . . many of the leaders became sell-outs . . . they no longer focused on social change" (Tasaki 2001, 85). Or more bluntly: "We were seduced by the power as gate-keepers. We liquidated, i.e., gave up, Marxism, socialism and revolution . . . subsumed into electoral politics and mainstream acceptance. . . . How could this happen to so many people with decades of history as revolutionaries?" (Ho 2000a, 12).

It might also be acknowledged that the failure of the left, if it can be called that, was also rooted in community heterogeneity and class differences. Working to "serve the people" didn't always make sense to those served (Kwong 2001; Nee and Nee 1974). Vanguard politicking, Third World unity, and other radical socialist views held by college students were not always supported by immigrant residents or foreign students. This was especially so among those who arrived during the 1970s and had experienced the effects of vanguard politics in China firsthand. Their accounts in the following pages center not on ideological political struggle but on the struggle to escape.

A radical politics began to morph into a more progressive identity and agenda (Takahashi 1997). The emphasis was on working "in the system" to take care of social needs on the ground. It meant dealing with problems such as drug abuse, health, housing, welfare, and political representation; getting rid of height requirements for police officers; protesting a local radio station that wouldn't hire Asian Americans; demonstrating for the inclusion of Asian American history in local high school textbooks (Der 2001). These rearticulations of racial identity that began with movements for social change and coalesced around a progressive agenda were successful if success is defined by government allocation of monies and other rewards. Some radicals were irked, however, because, aside from nonrevolutionary advocacy, it was just another way for dominant structures to co-opt and reassert power.

By the mid-1970s, as power structures began to regroup and respond to the remapping and transformation of racial and political terrain initiated by new social movements a decade earlier, co-optation was well under way. The term *Asian American* became bureaucratized in public agencies such as the U.S. Bureau of the Census and other official power structures that had to monitor new antidiscrimination and equal opportunity laws. The U.S. census became the de facto statement of who's who. State racial definitions utilizing terms like *Asian American* and the more recent labels, *Asian Pacific American* (APA) and *Asian Pacific Islander* (API), are particularly illustrative of the fluidity of and contestation over nomenclature—that is, how racial definitions are socially constructed. "Official" racial categories have changed at least nine times in the past 10 U.S. censuses.[5] In other words, both for the counters and the counted, census taking is a supremely political act. Co-optation also means that whatever racial struggles were raised during the 1960s have now been acknowledged and integrated at the discretion of dominant structures. Established webs of power reasserted ideologies of equality in what many believed was a "color-blind" America.

The foundational efforts of the 1960s, however, are still highly visible and still inform the ways of doing and being a politically active Asian American in the twenty-first century. There are still conscious efforts to widen the national discourse *beyond* simply a black/white paradigm. Asian Americans continue to have specific histories and memories that are not addressed by a narrow discussion of racialized dichotomies. There is still a valorization of what constitutes the place and space of community within wider global contexts. And there is acknowledgment that this local community rootedness in the United States lies at the nexus of a constantly shifting local/ global terrain that exists both in the imaginary and in more direct, on-the-ground, and place-based everyday experience.

Chinatown and Beyond

Ronald and his acquaintance Mike Woo are both American-born Chinese men and members of the 1960s baby-boom generation. Ronald was born and grew up in San Francisco's Chinatown. Mike was born in the Crenshaw area of Los Angeles, a postwar Japanese American community on the edge of downtown. Each has taken the path of professionalism, with college and graduate degrees, but each has also pursued lifelong commitments in the Asian American community. While members of CAUSE, they have guided and spoken for what they believe is an activist political agenda for Chinese Americans in Southern California. Within this crucible, both find the performance of community work a rooted reification of their identities as Asian Americans. Woo has approached his work for social change as a publicly elected official. Ronald has taken a different path, mostly away from the spotlight, but has no less a commitment to social change based on concepts of justice and equality. They would not have considered themselves radicals in college, but both say they were influenced by the social transformations of the 1960s. However, peeling back the layers of family history reveals an even earlier activist model that frames each man's politicized identity and racial position.

Ronald has achieved a sort of elder status, one he is not averse to utilizing. He is perceived as a valuable community resource, someone who has a rich, contextual knowledge of Chinese American history—one that is his own lived experience. Even as a younger man, he was always ready with a thoughtful, well-researched answer on the Chinese American "condition" and amenable to putting himself in the public arena of the mainstream press and media when required. Ronald's birth at St. Francis Hospital on Nob Hill and youth spent near the main cable car barn on Washington Street in Chinatown marked the borders of his world. Like the majority of Chinese Americans, Ronald says he always knew the difference between *us* and *them*:

> Oh yeah! A strong sense. Instilled in you from the time you're born. You gotta realize that in order to make it in this world, you gotta be twice as

good as the other guy, twice as good at school, twice as good at work, twice as good at everything—that's your standard. . . . Other guy? Well, who else is he? In our language we call him the *bakguei*—the white ghost—the *lofan* [white person]. Yeah, that's the culture I grew up in.

That's probably why I spend so much time in the community. As a fifth generation I should be ignoring everybody [who's Chinese American]! I should have a blonde wife, kids with blue eyes, and all that kind of crap, but I don't. I can't get away from that because I grew up in Chinatown—but I'm American!

His Chinatown experiences are representative of his politicization as a minority American. More to the point, by eschewing the trappings of what he views as assimilative "crap," he is valorizing that which he "can't get away from"—his roots as a racialized American.

Initially, many active American-born Chinese do not necessarily think they have had a politicized upbringing. Upon closer reflection, however, they realize that pushing back racial boundaries has been a vital part of the family's historical dynamic and that family members before them fought against hierarchical divisions of social space and actively sought to reconfigure their subalternity (Gupta and Ferguson 1999; Spivak 1988). Furthermore, many of these family relatives—mostly men—chose to do so in highly public roles. During the 1940s, one of Ronald's paternal uncles was among the first Chinese to get involved in Democratic Party politics in San Francisco.

He started to talk to me about how you actually did things politically as Chinese in those days. Power was basically hidden, and you had to find out where it was and deal with it. It doesn't take long . . . for you to see how tough it is. And you see you have to rise up and deal with it—that's where the big battles are. I just watched my uncle operate.

Both sides of Ronald's family came to the United States during the 1860s, not as unskilled laborers, as did the majority of Chinese immigrants from southern China, but as experienced boat builders. His ancestors lived a few miles from Macao and worked on the docks in the colony. The imprint of the West was all around them. Macao had already been Portuguese for more than 200 years, a busy crossroads for Western powers where Chinese were exposed to the mercantilist and subsequent capitalist schemes of Westerners who saw the Chinese as one more commodity. Ronald says his family came as an entire unit including wives and children and settled in Monterey in northern California. Ronald's American-born parents were also politically active. Deeply rooted as U.S. citizens, their political view also accommodated a much broader transnational focus.

The 1920s and 1930s were a period of nation building in China. Sweeping labor strikes against the British in Hong Kong during the mid-1920s and the Sino-Japanese War in 1937 mobilized nascent national sentiment, shaping a new ideology intent on repelling foreign aggression. Newspaper reports, in community-based newspapers and mainstream sources like the *New York Times*, kept overseas Chinese American communities informed about developments in China (Kwong 2001). Chinese in U.S. communities found themselves drafted by supporters of this nationalist discourse, and many responded by establishing local relief and patriotic efforts. Ronald's parents did take part initially but were soon caught up in these transborder political projects where the dystopic effects of the transnational altered their views of participation. "Oh they talked about community activism—*yes*—they said stay away from it!" Ronald says. "Don't ever go into it, it's bad for you. They saw the corruption . . . they realized where the money was going—into local pockets! They realized the money was never going to get [to China], so they quit and decided to raise kids."

Despite the negative experience, their participation in grassroots organizing also speaks to instrumentalities of collectively building identity closer to home. Community leaders reasoned that a stronger China was vital to a more positive reception and acceptance of Chinese in the United States. Community leaders used Japan, at least until World War II, as an example of a stronger country, one better able to intervene in matters affecting Japanese immigrants as it did routinely, albeit with mixed results (Kwong 2001; Zia 2000). Clearly, however, although identity construction and group action have very often manifested themselves in localized response and political organization from below, Asian American lives have often transcended national spaces; identities have *always* been tied to wider world events (Guarnizo and Smith 1999).

For Ronald, his own politicization came full circle in the early 1970s when he began working as an engineer after earning his doctorate at Stanford. A close friend persuaded him to join a new association of Chinese American engineers and scientists. These highly educated workers were part of a larger project, the maturation of the progressive Asian American movement in the workplace. During the late 1970s and early 1980s, many Asian American employees had forged alliances at all levels of government and in private industry. Still within the corporate framework, engineers began contesting the dominant management narrative that Chinese Americans were excellent drones but unsuitable bosses. The drones, mostly young American-born Chinese, appeared by all economic parameters to be on the path to successful careers. Instead, their lack of job advancement brought burgeoning awareness—and radicalizing anger. They began agitating for equal job opportunities, including management-level positions inside Southern California's dense web of government contract, private aerospace, and engineering corporations.[6]

Having the right credentials didn't guarantee inclusion. It did, however, reify stereotypes of a good follower, not an innovator, and, perhaps even more insidious, not quite being 100 percent American. As Ronald points out, their collective action was the result of a bitter realization that being "twice as good" counted for little.

> There are a lot of subtle hints [of job discrimination]. You want to move up the ladder, but right away you hit the ceiling—*really hard*—and that's the biggest motivation. Now there are a lot of engineers and scientists who solve this problem by going out and opening up their *own* companies. . . . But others realize, wait a minute, *hey*, let's not leave, let's fight and take a look at the problem, and *oh my god*, you realize there are other things that aren't right, either. (Cose 1993, 1)

In many ways, the resentment that middle-class American-born Chinese experienced echoes that of middle-class African Americans. Ellis Cose describes it as rage: "I have done everything I was supposed to do. I have stayed out of trouble . . . gone to the right schools, and worked myself nearly to death. *What more do they want?*" (Cose 1993).

The same types of racializing situations form a core of lived experiences for new, post-1965 Chinese American activists. The outrage and shock that ensue are quite beyond anything most would have envisioned in their dreams of America. In this they find commonalities with American-born Chinese like Ronald, who had the sense of being different "instilled in you from the time you're born."

. . .

In recent years, Mike Woo's interests have run more to the culinary than the political; he and his wife enjoy cooking in their home northeast of down-town Los Angeles, and he has produced a guide to Los Angeles' Chinatown restaurants. But his involvement with addressing social injustices through political means has not waned. It is still a passion and perhaps the one thing he knows really well. He is a past board member of CAUSE, among other community organizations. During the 1970s, as an intern for a politician who was elected to the California State Senate, he found himself in Sac-ramento in his first paid job. He has been a candidate himself, running in local races in Los Angeles and for statewide offices in California, where he has won some, lost more. In 2001, he hung his political cap at his campaign headquarters in the Silver Lake area of Los Angeles and ran again for a city council seat. One day, after precinct walking with the candidate, I watched his mother stuffing campaign envelopes at a folding table and listened to Woo as he mused about his political beginnings and his awareness, as part of a generational cohort, that politics could effect social change.

> I was an idealistic student, I grew up in the sixties and seventies at a time when there were big issues facing the country, where there was a civil rights movement, the role of Asian Americans, the Vietnam War, and I think I was one of many members of this generation who felt that something ought to be done to address these injustices and wrongs and that it was natural to become political.

Woo's experiences in electoral politics in Southern California illustrate the intersection of the global with the local and how events far beyond the borders of local community forge on-the-ground strategies for inclusion. These tactics are not always successful. Woo's electoral odyssey began in the early 1980s when the 30-something candidate decided to tackle big-city politics. As a television reporter and graduate student of similar age, I spent time whenever my haphazard off-hours would permit, "deep hanging out" with him and trying to construct ethnographically "thick descriptions" of him and his campaign for city council (Geertz 1973). It was the beginning of a long political career for Woo in which his widening sensibilities as an Asian American politician were forged. His political identity was negotiated through his perceptions as an American-born Chinese, but it is also shaped by his family's deep roots in political activism. At the same time, however, one's identity is never entirely of one's own making. Close attention must be paid to other, overarching discourses that influence individual negotiation. This then, is a cautionary and contradictory story for those who would celebrate transnational linkages and the possibilities of new positionings (Mitchell 1996).

JANUARY 1981

At a cozy neighborhood restaurant in the Seinan area of Los Angeles, more than two dozen community workers from Asian American social service agencies sit three or four to a booth. *Seinan* means "southwest" in Japanese, and for hundreds of Japanese Americans returning from World War II internment camps and trying to rebuild interrupted lives, the blocks surrounding West Jefferson, Arlington, and nearby Crenshaw Boulevard southwest of the Santa Monica Freeway represented a way out of the crowded living conditions of prewar Little Tokyo or Boyle Heights. Restrictive housing covenants were declared unconstitutional in 1948, but that didn't mean they had disappeared, and vast tracts of the Southern California real estate map were still red zoned for anyone of color. Areas like Seinan were one of the few places where Japanese and Chinese Americans could buy homes. For the Japanese, sociality created spaces wherein the everyday enactments of a Japanese American sensibility played out against the backdrop of a politicized group identity forged behind barbed wire.

In Seinan and the nearby Crenshaw neighborhood known as the Westside, dozens of businesses were owned by Japanese Americans, mostly lower-middle-class and working families with third-generation, or Sansei, children. Most were born during the postwar baby-boom years and filled the area's schools. There were social and political clubs and lively debates on important community issues. During city elections, lawn signs for favorite candidates and issues sprouted among the bonsai shrubbery. It was a place where Japanese American identity could be performed in any number of public arenas.

The arenas began to change during the late 1960s as the Sansei grew up and left the neighborhood. Working and middle-class African Americans began moving in. Japanese and Chinese were already pushing farther out, west to Mar Vista, east to Monterey Park, and south to Torrance. Into the 1980s, Seinan and Crenshaw remained vital communities and, it might be argued, even precursors to the new suburban enclaves of Chinese immigrants, although with far less transnational networkings.

On this sunny winter day, the mood in the café is glum. A number of the social service people at this meeting are activist products of this neighborhood. Mostly college graduates now in their early 30s, they had also seen and participated in the campus unrest during the 1960s, not all as revolutionaries but as progressives. Instead of insurrection in the streets, they believe that working within state structures, albeit difficult, ensures more access and therefore more means by which to effect community change.

Ronald Reagan has just been elected president and takes office in a week, so today, they talk about possible cutbacks in government funding and how this could affect their program agendas. The conversation is angry; these community activists are determined to organize against the new fiscal and social conservatism in the United States. Talk turns to the perennial lack of Asian American representation in local government. Los Angeles city elections are coming up, and they had been told that a candidate for city council was going to drop by.

Midway through lunch, we all look as the bell over the front door jingles. Someone is trying to get in, but the door is stuck. It's the candidate, a very young-looking Asian American man dressed in a dark suit. Somebody lets him in. He is introduced as Mike Woo, and he tells everyone that he's running for city council and would like their support. He shakes each person's hand and spends a few minutes talking about being born in Crenshaw before his family moved to Monterey Park and explaining the importance of having someone from the community represent them at city hall. He capitalizes on commonalities of belonging: the group's sense of estrangement from local power and the "problems that are important to us" (Sanjek 1998, 257).

Woo's progression from campus civil rights activities to electoral politics seems natural (he was never a revolutionary and would describe himself as more of a progressive who believes public service can be transformative). Although he acknowledges his college years as grounding for his politicized identity as an Asian American, this period in his life might be seen as processual, a time of growing tension between what he idealistically believed the United States represented and what he had begun to more fully understand was the reality of injustice and social inequality. Yet these tensions also clearly predate the 1960s. Like Ronald, Woo has a highly politicized family history that influenced him early. In addition to raising five children, his mother worked in the family produce business and volunteered teaching English to immigrants. His father, Wilbur, eventually became an executive at a bank with headquarters in Chinatown. Wilbur's political clout in Chinatown afforded his son front-row seats at an ongoing performance that included the major actors in Los Angeles city politics during more than 30 years. Wilbur was one of the first Chinese American graduates of UCLA. Educational credentials and English-language facility made him a broker beyond the boundaries of Chinatown. Woo says "it was normal for him to be a kind of intermediary between Chinatown and the outside world." The younger Woo saw this everyday parade of mayors, council members, and key businesspeople through his father's office as unremarkable: "Contrary to stereotypes of Asian families not being supportive or being involved in the community, of not getting involved in politics, at least in my family it was very different because there was a history of the adults being involved. To me it was very normal."

But even before his father, Woo's paternal grandfather was another, equally influential example of what he describes as a strong tradition of "being involved beyond one's work and beyond one's family." In fact, it may be said that Woo's coming of age during the 1960s *allowed for* and *created* the political space in which familial/generational convergence occurred. His involvement in redefining ascribed roles and pushing for political equality echoed the earlier efforts of his father and grandfather. His political activity builds on this credibility and continues to resonate in his own generational striving.

Like Ronald's family, the Woos have a long and complex history of transnational connections and participation in wider world events. Wilbur Woo was educated both in Los Angeles and in Guangdong, where his father, Kitman Woo, sent him to escape the Depression in the United States. The family was briefly reunited in China when Kitman Woo lost his farm in Stockton, California, and returned to work with the Kuomintang in Nanjing. The 1937 Sino-Japanese War forced another family split. Wilbur fled first to Guangzhou, then to Hong Kong, and eventually back to the United States to finish his college education, leaving a young, American-born Chinese wife and children who didn't join him until after World War II ended.

Kitman Woo, an early supporter of Sun Yat-sen, escaped China when the Communists took over but did not desert the cause in his new home in Los Angeles. Sun was a world traveler, raising money for the revolution from overseas Chinese communities, and Mike remembers hearing stories from his grandfather about Sun's numerous trips to Southern California. In the process of advocating for the Nationalists, Mike Woo's grandfather also became a leader in the city's Chinatown, displaying a collective identity that informed local ideas of belonging among other immigrants with similar life experiences and political leanings. Growing up, Mike understood that this imaginary of community, which superseded geographical borders, served his grandfather well in public articulations and demands for recognition (Billings 2000; Fink and Dunn 2000). "By the time I became political and ran for city council in 1981," Mike says, "my grandfather still had the touch. He could walk about the produce mart and talk to old friends of his and ask for contributions for his grandson, and when they would give him a check, he could joke with, 'Oh, isn't there a zero missing?'"

Through this fashioning and refashioning of memory, activists construct personal narratives about the past that lend new meanings to current circumstances and serve as idioms for articulating experience and identities in the present. As an instrument of public identity, Woo has always parlayed his immigrant history in celebratory terms. One of his campaign mailers features old sepia-toned photos from a family album. The edges of the pictures are faded and show him as a baby, sitting on his grandmother's lap. The copy reads, "Like many Angelenos, Mike Woo's parents came to Los Angeles seeking a better life. . . . I will never forget how Los Angeles welcomed my family when they fled hardship in China."

In February, five weeks after Woo spoke to the diners in Seinan, more than 600 people pay $50 to $100 to crowd into the Golden Dragon restaurant in Chinatown in support of Mike Woo's candidacy for city council. It is perhaps the largest Asian American political fund-raiser in L.A. history. Although he says he can't win with just Asian American support, he is pragmatic enough to realize that the bulk of his campaign money will most likely come from the Asian American community. The dinner's venue is no accident. During the 1980s, the place and space of Chinatown still beckoned both as bounded community and borderless imaginary tying Southern Californian Americans of Chinese ancestry together. Like the Crenshaw area or Seinan, Chinatown is a site of cultural practices, symbols, and patterns of sociality that shape identity and experience, even though most American-born Chinese do not live there. Tonight's attendees are from all over Southern California. Many are "old-timer" Chinatown residents and the political elite from Chinatown's family associations, including the Chinese Consolidated Benevolent Association, a conservative umbrella organization.[7] Many more are young activists in the Chinese and Asian American communities. Dressed in business and cocktail attire, they are progressives who have been working for a decade in civil service, community grassroots organizations, civil rights, antipoverty legal centers, and Asian American Studies programs at local colleges and universities. The dinner theme is "Asian American Unity." It is a way for the participants, a coalition of Asian and Pacific Americans, to share in the construction of an Asian American political identity. As public memory, as a tradition invented and reinvented in everyday life and less an essentialist view of cultural origins, this evening and others like it become a transformative recollection of common histories of struggle (Gregory 1998). The instrumental use of public events in helping to forge community identity will be revisited.

Tonight at the Golden Dragon, the candidate shares his political dream with the audience. It is a familiar story with which many can identify. He talks about how Asian Americans have been successful in business and now must translate that success into political power. One of the most appealing parts of the evening is the introduction of the candidate's 90-year-old grandfather, Kitman Woo, who speaks in Chinese: "When Michael decided to run, he first talked to me about it, then he talked to his father, then his family, then all the cousins, and then the family association. We all said yes, so I back him up!" It is touching to see this very small man standing next to his much taller grandson, their arms around each other. Later, representatives from major Asian American groups speak in support of the candidate. They are introduced by the emcee, *Star Trek* actor George Takei.[8]

Woo's Asian American Unity dinner and its public performance of collective identity galvanizes the audience. The level of excitement and commitment is unprecedented, as activist Asian Americans cross both ethnic and party lines to support him (*Rafu Shimpo* 1981). Woo is seen as a mobilizer, a real chance for a piece of the action and an effective alternative to rising political conservatism.

In the primary election, Woo forces the incumbent into a run-off, but in the bitter contest that follows, he is unable to capture the seat. Months after the run-off, Woo is stunned and depressed by his defeat. But perhaps not too stunned. His incumbent opponent had succeeded in portraying him as the "outsider," a thinly disguised codeword for his Chineseness and for the other Asian "foreigners" who backed his candidacy. In hindsight, Woo says he didn't know what he was getting into. He clearly knows about the discrimination that his parents and grandparents faced in the United States as well as his own racialized identity, but he is nevertheless surprised.

> Until you're publicly attacked in a campaign, it's hard to know what it's like. [The other candidate] put out a piece of mail that raised the question about why so many of my donors were from Chinatown and I was being backed by all these rich Chinatown bankers, which was obviously an indirect allusion to my own dad, and suggesting that anybody who had so much support from Chinatown couldn't possibly understand the needs of the people in the . . . district.

From the beginning, Woo and his supporters celebrated a constructed pan–Asian American identity publicly in campaign flyers, speeches, and events. He was thus unable to deny the importance of this coalition, the majority of whom lived outside his district. City council candidates generally raise money beyond district boundaries without much scrutiny, but whereas Woo's racialized funding sources became a campaign issue, his white opponent's own outside sources did not (Michaelson 1981). That these tactics resonated with voters in the district reflects some of the ups and downs of stumping for votes. On the up side, some voters saw Woo as the personification of the model minority myth. He says, "Well, I wasn't a straight-A student . . . but I didn't object to them thinking that." The down side was that voters also saw him as someone who was not an American. Woo was greeted with comments like, "I won't vote for no foreigners, they shouldn't be in this country" and "Why should I vote for you? The government is giving away millions of dollars to immigrants from other countries who aren't even citizens and they don't deserve that money!" One man asked Woo whether he was the Chinaman gardener. Woo found these experiences eye-opening.

> I realized that although I barely speak enough Chinese to order food in a Chinese restaurant, [I was] the embodiment of these newcomers who were changing the neighborhood and who may have been a threat.
> It became easy for a lot of these voters to assume the worst about Asian Americans. You know, "Oh, they only care about themselves, they don't care about me, they don't really understand me." I would trust an Asian American to be my dentist or my accountant but not my city council member.

Nothing occurs in a vacuum. As has historically been the case in the social construction of Asian America, Asian Americans have been caught in wider global economic and political issues in which identity and citizenship have always been reduced and conflated as foreign. For Woo, the superimposition of a number of global issues during the 1980s had a direct effect in precluding an effective *local* political strategy for counteracting negative stereotypes of the Asian Other.

A principal issue was the perception that Japan, Inc., was taking over the United States. It was not the Reagan administration's willingness to tolerate high interest rates in order to attract money flows from abroad and eventually sacrifice the country's manufacturing sector that captured headlines (Brenner 2002); it was the far sexier story of foreign takeover, direct financial investments by Japan in prime U.S. commercial real estate, that got everybody's attention. Encouraged by the falling dollar, a *fifth* of all Japanese real estate investment in North America was flowing into Los Angeles by the early 1980s (Davis 1992). In one highly publicized two-and-a-half-month period, the Shuwa Corporation snapped up nearly $1 billion worth of downtown L.A. skyline, including the twin towers of Arco Plaza. Responding to the ensuing public outcry, mayor Tom Bradley, who liked to promote the possibilities (economic) of the Pacific Rim, labeled the most frenzied reactions racist. Shuwa subsequently donated generously to Bradley's failed campaign for California governor and gave $1 million to the Reagan Presidential Library (Davis 1992).

Simultaneously, the effects of another oil crisis following the Iranian revolution in 1979, the return of long lines at gas stations, and massive layoffs generated by the initial collapse of the auto industry in Detroit precipitated a climate of fear—and worse for those perceived to be Japanese. Journalist and scholar Helen Zia wrote that the Japanese became "easy to hate. Anything Japanese or presumed to be Japanese, became a potential target. . . . It felt dangerous to have an Asian face" (Zia 2000, 58). Finally, in June 1982, Vincent Chin, a young Chinese American celebrating his upcoming wedding at a Detroit bar, was beaten to death by two automakers who mistook him for Japanese. Witnesses heard one of them say to Chin, "It's because of motherfuckers like you we're out of work" (Zia 2000, 59). Nothing occurs in a vacuum.

Woo's initial foray into elective politics was discouraging to many hopeful Asian Americans. He underestimated the level of deep-seated bias, but he did not go away. He continued to live in the district and do his homework. His became a familiar, and it might be said, less threatening face at neighborhood meetings. He took the time to build ties with various district constituencies. In 1985, he ran again against the same incumbent. He continued to rely on Asian American contributions and support but was less openly celebratory about his Chinese American roots. His opponent was less openly anti-Asian and more defensive about *her* weak record in the district. Equally important, the short-lived Japanese economic juggernaut had run aground by the late 1980s. The backwash was already morphing into the well-documented bubble economy as Japan was "subjected to great political pressure . . . and constant attempts by the US to interfere with its internal social relations of production" (Gowan 1999, 46). Mercurial U.S. public discourse turned triumphal; the Japanese didn't really know how to run the world after all. Woo won with 70 percent of the vote and served two terms as a council member before deciding to run for mayor of Los Angeles.

MARCH 1993

A year has passed since the acquittal of Los Angeles police officers charged in the videotaped beating of Rodney King sparked civil unrest. Television images of the violence broadcast around the clock for four days are still fresh. The rioting resulted in the deaths of 51 people and a billion dollars worth of property damage. Twenty-three hundred Korean American businesses that went up in smoke or were otherwise destroyed sustained more than a third of all the damage. Complicating the acquittals story was the highly publicized case of liquor store owner Soon Ja Du, who shot and killed a black teen after an argument.[9] And once again in popular discourse, a portrait of foreignness marginalized an Asian American group. Korean Americans served as scapegoats—liquor store owners cum gun-toting vigilantes whose failure to understand their mostly African American customers was the enduring image of the riots (Lee and Liu 1994). This marginalization resulted not only in massive property damage but in power structures like Rebuild L.A., the civic group coordinating the reconstruction process, falling far short of expectations (Cannon 1997). The television images made a more commanding impression than any kind of reasoned dialogue about the failure of the city's political and business leadership to address more deeply rooted causes of the riots (Ong and Hee 1993b).

In the primary race for mayor, Woo finds himself vulnerable to attacks on his record as a city councilman. But more insidious are the connections made, once again, to his funding sources in the Asian American community—shorthand for "Chinatown money and Chinatown bankers." The charges this time are more specific and straightforward. Woo's father's bank is accused of making the bulk of its loans only to Asian Americans (Schwada 1993). Again, this plays on the notion of Asian insularity and, to reiterate Woo's comments about how voters perceive Asian Americans, "Oh, they only care about themselves; they don't care about me." Woo has never been a bank officer and has no say in banking decisions.

In the general election, Woo battles neophyte candidate and multi-millionaire businessman Richard Riordan, who continues to tie Woo to Chinatown money. Despite the endorsement of the city's leading newspaper (or perhaps because of it), Woo loses. For the first time in 30 years, Los Angeles' liberal coalition of ethnic groups and labor is unable to pull off a victory. Maybe Woo was not the best candidate, maybe Riordan outspent him two to one, but Woo is also frank in addressing the racial aspects of the campaign and how global events shaped the race: "It echoed things that I had to deal with years earlier. I had a hard time believing it would influence voters. And people even asked me . . . 'Do you remember the *Golden Venture*'? They asked me would that incident have some subliminal effect on the voters."[10]

Equally important, Woo believes, people were "scared out of their minds" after the riots (Ha 1997). Analysis of the postelection voting patterns shows a city deeply divided by race. Woo got the majority of the vote from Asian Americans, blacks, and Latinos who saw him as someone who understood the multiethnic diversity of Los Angeles. But Riordan got the majority of the white vote in a city where more than 60 percent of the registered voters at the time were white (F. Clifford 1993; Simon 1993). Woo believes that the heavy minority endorsement for him may have turned off white voters who did not want to see Los Angeles run by a minority coalition.

Conclusion

The 1960s provided the historical moment in which primarily college-age American-born Asians constructed a new, activist identity. This political project was one of ownership and agency in which they captured historical antecedents that contextualized their status as racialized citizens. Activists saw their individual ethnicities subsumed by broader racial categorizations in the United States; they worked at overcoming intragroup ethnic divisions to emphasize a history that made space for a dynamic and alternative narrative centering on the commonalities inherent in their American experience. As radical intellectuals, they aligned themselves firmly with other peoples of color here and around the world and drew upon the ideologies of radical politics practiced by immigrant workers and students from Asia who also populated community politics. They creatively enlarged the discursive terrain by employing other political frameworks and ideologies such as socialism by which to contest their marginal status.

The major sites where this new identity was enacted became the *local* and the *community*. This foregrounding—both as an imagined site of resistance and as a racially bordered enclave within which new social movements could be practiced—valorized the meanings of local. The Asian American local highlighted direct, on-the-ground work in ethnic enclaves. It addressed social justice issues, such as labor organizing and workers' rights, political education, and access to social services. The local community was reconfigured as a space and place of both tradition and contemporary change, a repository of genuine cultural retention and rediscovery. These consciously selected markers and embodiments of identity grounded community activists.

Strictly speaking, however, what was local never really existed. In the nexus of highly charged political interactions, activists performed a local identity as a counterbalance to what they saw as the negative penetration of global and transnational projects that weakened their concept of community. The attention that power structures paid to these postmodern, global projects resulted in the denial of place, and therefore a political presence, in metanarratives (Dirlik 1996). The manifestations of modernity were not confined just to this time frame but, under other names, have always played a part in wider categorizing schemes that subjectified Asian Americans. Asian Americans in turn also made use of global events such as the Vietnam War, the Communist revolution in China, and the wars of independence in Africa as themes of resistance.

However, as Asian Americans tried to solidify a pan–Asian American identity and transform from a radical to a more progressive politics, they faced challenges from government and other structures of power such as media, which appropriated both leadership and symbols of activism as a way to reassert authority. At the same time, economic restructuring in the United

States and new divisions in international labor began to alter the local into communities of new immigrants and thus also tested an activist community agenda. Although some have portrayed the radical response to these challenges as a failure, the subsequent crafting of a progressive Asian American politics can also be interpreted as successful adaptation to changing social and economic conditions and continuation of an identity committed to the ideals of social justice and the furthering of community-based projects.

The life histories of American-born activists frame the boundaries and borders of late-twentieth-century progressive Asian America. The ideological heart of this American identity continued to pulse in a localized harmony whose beat still sustained ways of mobilization and political action directed at achieving inclusion in the mainstream. By the mid-1980s, a new group of Asian immigrants began to play a somewhat different tune. Their presence was not entirely disharmonious and enlarged the ensemble.

THREE

Envisioning America

Leaving Home

Immigration is once again the dominant factor in reconfiguring Asian America, but instead of the few thousand Asian immigrants who came to the United States at the turn of the twentieth century, *hundreds* of thousands began arriving in the late 1960s. There has, in fact, been a transformation of space and place in Southern California so radical that Asian America has been rendered virtually unrecognizable in less than 30 years.

While Asian American community activists worked to craft a new, politicized identity during the 1960s and 1970s, on the other side of the Pacific Ocean a new generation of Asians unlike any seen before was preparing to move to the United States. The confluence of political and economic events behind this latest phase of immigration had already been foreshadowed during the 1970s, in the first contestations between foreign investments, community redevelopment, and the preservation of Asian American ethnic enclaves in major U.S. cities. The manifestations of animosity and resistance were directed primarily at transnational corporations and other "faceless" international business entities. In tandem with local and federal authorities, overseas corporations reconfigured local spaces in Little Tokyos and Chinatowns. Community activists interpreted these incursions as economic schemes for profit in the guise of community redevelopment. It was still too early to think that this same discomfort might apply to a new group of Chinese immigrants who often practiced transnational modes of living that most American-born Asians did not practice and often had the education, accumulated capital, *and* desire to insert themselves into participatory politics. It has been the addition not just of larger numbers of Chinese immigrants (Chinese now make up the largest group of legal immigrants from Asia and the Pacific) but of a *specific* group of Chinese immigrants who are unsettling established narratives of Asian American political identity. Their arrival has posed a number of new challenges to existing frameworks of immigration theory, in particular the celebratory characterizations of this group of Chinese immigrants as transnational subjects with free-floating bodies, economic capital, and the flexibility to take advantage of it all (Ong 1999; Portes 1997). A portion of their lives *is* given over to transnational social practices, and many do take advantage of strategies allowing for new economic opportunities; however, it is important to understand that among new Chinese activists who are also part of this specific cohort of immigrants, it is the overarching sense of belonging and entitlement as U.S. citizens, a grounded sense of permanency and stake in their adopted homeland that compels their transnationality. It is not the other way around. Transnational social practices form a portion of a wider repertoire of citizenship instrumentalities.

Before these new immigrants established new lives in the United States and achieved U.S. citizenship, they had to take that first step—to decide to leave Asia. Three broad themes were behind those decisions and contribute to the transformation and fashioning of politicized identities among new immigrants:

- Homeland political turmoil
- Nation-state policies in the United States
- Changes in global economic and labor requirements

POLITICAL TURMOIL AND NAME-CALLING

Numerous terms by which to call people on the move have sprouted from ethnographic fieldwork in postmodern times: *immigrant, migrant, transmigrant, diasporic, exile, refugee, sojourner, cosmopolitan*. The choice of expression depends, of course, largely on why they are moving. Rather than being free-floating tycoons and accumulators of flexible capital, new Chinese activists have roots/routes of migration that are much more complex

than such characterizations would imply and that very often assume ex-
ilic proportions. The beginnings may be traced to the political instabilities
brought on by the Communist revolution in 1949. The cataclysmic forces
surrounding the revolution affected virtually every naturalized activist family in this book. Regardless of their previous class or economic positioning,
they became *refugees* fleeing chaos, first from Mainland China and then
from supposedly safer areas like Hong Kong. Theirs is a story of family
survival against the background of war that figures in the early development
of what, in later life, would inform their activist identities. Almost without
exception, it may be said that in this context, naturalized Chinese activists
have highly politicized premigration identities. The costs of this politicization are extreme—in the lost lives of family members and in the bifurcating
paths of activists and their parents that often lasts for years. Recalling these
life-altering early experiences renders many of these normally well-spoken
individuals inarticulate. The danger of politics is never far from sight.

Thus, for many activists, who first escaped Mainland China for other
regions in Asia and then felt compelled to relocate once again, the decision
to move to the United States may be their second or even third point of departure from Asia. Perhaps they can no longer be seen as refugees fleeing the
ravages of war, yet political uncertainty and other hostilities are still important motivators. Safety continues to be an important factor enfolded in opportunities for a better life provided by the United States. And before a reading of refugee is too swiftly dismissed, closer attention needs to be focused
on the forces of politicization and what constitutes "voluntary" displacement
(Malkki 1999). It should also be noted that generalizations and comparisons
of the new activists in this book with politically active Chinese immigrants
in other overseas communities or even other parts of the United States must
be made with caution. As with other forms of social relations, political participation is a qualitatively different experience in each community.

The terms *migrant, transmigrant,* and *sojourner* call forth images of tran-
sitory and temporary legions coming to a host country to work and then
returning to their places of origin (Basch, Glick Schiller, and Blanc 1994).
For the most part, new Chinese activists have no intention of returning permanently to Asia. Their homes and lives are grounded in the United States.
Their children are born here. Their experiences of leaving Asia create a fine
layering of subjectivities that perhaps makes the term *diasporic* a better fit
in the sense that a diasporic community may be defined as people living

outside their homeland whose initial uprooting was coerced to some degree (Tololyan 1996). But even this term reflects impermanence; there remains a residue of longing and hope for eventual return (Ma and Cartier 2003). The familiar term *immigrant* implies a permanent rupture in both space and place and the pulling out of old patterns of sociality and the planting of new ones. This continues to apply to new activists to some degree but does not fully encompass the outline of transnational life, the formation of new patterns of social connections and networks that span borders.

Equally important in the multisituated maneuverings of new-activist families is the need for nuanced awareness of the distinctions of place/space among the so-called three Chinas. The wider political and economic projects of Mainland China, Hong Kong, and Taiwan and their intersections have been seminal in framing identity construction. Adding to this is the hegemonic position of the United States and the complexities of "dual domination" that have always existed across borders (Wang 1995). For a young generation of Chinese who would later become activists in Southern California, it is not enough to simply say that they grew up in Asia. *Where* in Asia they grew up has made for dramatically different experiences.

For many new activists, growing up in Hong Kong meant subjectification as a member of a long-standing extraterritorial project. Chinese were colonial subjects of the British Empire, not full citizens. Despite the praise of some scholars for the legacy of British rule of law, a system of racially based discrimination was in fact created.[1] More recently, the discursive terrain surrounding the return of Hong Kong to the mainland generated new instabilities and another exodus of Chinese.

The Kuomintang's retreat to Taiwan in 1949 fashioned its own set of complex subjective positionings layered upon existing narratives of Qing and Imperial Japanese hegemonies. In the case of Japan, this took place despite rhetoric on the oneness of Japan and Taiwan (*nittai ichinyo*) (Ching 2001). Coupled with the post-1949 state-building apparatus of the Kuomintang, these discourses became triangulated with an emergent nationalist China. This was made more explicit after Richard Nixon's trip to Mainland China in 1973 and culminated in U.S. recognition of the People's Republic of China in 1979. Taiwan's increasing global marginalization fueled not just political volatility on the island but the flight of more people and capital. As in Hong Kong, the politics of identity formation were thus imbricated and fashioned within numerous hegemonic sites.

As ethnic Chinese, however, migrants still have collective memories of homeland and connections that transcend borders. Within this nexus naturalized citizens continue to perform beyond territorial borders, as seen, for example, in their raucous local participation in presidential elections in Taiwan (Pierson 2004). Perhaps as important, they possess an ethnicity as Chinese that becomes more *racialized* as they are transformed into essentialized minority citizens in the United States. More recent diaspora scholarship appears to minimize ethnic and racial paradigms, but in the case of naturalized Chinese activists, the opposite is true (Anthias 1999; Hall 1990).

CHANGING NATION-STATE POLICIES

Political and economic instability in Asia most likely would have had little effect on legal immigration were it not for major changes in U.S. policies that facilitated new immigrant strategies and sweeping changes in Asian American communities, especially in global cities like Los Angeles. The Immigration and Nationality Act of 1965, also known as the Hart-Celler Immigration Act, was in part a by-product of the transformative 1960s. Acknowledging racial discrimination at home also meant extending the same equality to those seeking entry to the United States regardless of national origin. Before this, nothing much had changed in a mostly native-born Asian America since the first exclusion laws in the 1880s virtually froze Asian immigration.

Major provisions in the Hart-Celler Act abolished the national origins quota system and expanded family reunification rules to include immediate family members—spouses, minor children, and parents of U.S. citizens. Nativist groups wanted to know exactly *who* these new Americans might be, so governmental and media discourse had to sell the American public on the idea that even though immigration would increase, the arrivals would look like most of the people already here—white Europeans. Most assuredly, there would *not* be more Asians since they had fewer family ties in the United States (Takaki 1989). Clearly, although the intent of the act as presented in this guise was perceived as a noble gesture by mainstream society, its implementation backfired.

Before 1965, the national annual quota for entering Asian immigrants was barely 2,000, and in 1970, Asian Americans constituted less than 1 percent of the total U.S. population. But by the early 1980s, Asians made up more than *40 percent* of all new immigrants. During the next 20 years, the population is expected to exceed 20 million—8 percent of the total U.S. population—with the majority of these new immigrants settling in either California or New York (Ong and Hee 1993a). The momentous changes in Asian America, specifically as a result of the Hart-Celler Act, have made for a strikingly different community composite profile. From three "official" Asian ethnic groups recognized by government structures, the list has expanded to more than 50 (U.S. Census Information Center 2007).

Another significant part of the Hart-Celler Act in reconfiguring Asian American communities was the result of worldwide economic restructuring and the concomitant global repositioning of the United States that necessitated taking advantage of new requirements for labor. The United States was dismantling its manufacturing/industrial base to develop instead "strategic nodes with a hyper-concentration of facilities" (Sassen 2000, 1). New forms of centralization, higher technology, more skilled jobs in management and control, more service jobs and a de-territorialization of all economic activities were markers of the new economy (Bonacich et al. 1994).

In its zeal to attract new forms of human and financial capital, the United States competed and shopped for different kinds of labor by making it easier for certain types of immigrants to gain entry: people classified as professionals and artists or those with skills needed for the new economy. Whereas many new Chinese activists arrived as foreign students, others won temporary visa and "backdoor" entry as skilled workers that afforded a faster track to permanent status. Of particular importance were the wider definitions of "professional" and "exceptional ability." By the early 1970s, more than 20 percent of Chinese immigrants qualified under these guidelines (Louie and Ong 1995). This group of post-1965 Chinese is more urbanized, wealthier, better educated, and highly mobile.[2] Among new activists and their families, trajectories of movement are very often a dizzying itinerary of comings and goings that do not diminish after citizenship is attained.

The majority of immigrants in the professional and skilled categories continue to be men, but for the first time, figures also show numbers of equally well-educated, entrepreneurial women (Hing 2003). New, gendered discourses of political activism among these women are altering the male-dominated terrain in the Chinese American community. A number of these women are as professionally and politically active as men, even while raising children. They serve on boards of community and political organizations such as CAUSE and frequently run for local political office. (More about this later.)

In terms of gender, however, the same need that compels recruitment of those with more social or economic capital must compete with the economic imperative to provide the lowest possible labor costs in the form of disciplined and unorganized workers. Economic restructuring has also meant the feminization of the workforce, which now includes vast numbers of mostly young, underpaid women, not just in the United States but in globalized economic centers around the world (Constable 1997). The presence of large numbers of Thai garment workers and Indonesian housekeepers in Southern California are but two examples (Kang 1999). For the first time in the history of Asian immigration to the United States, these labor disparities have created substantial heterogeneity in class. Among post-1965 naturalized Chinese activists, social class, and for that matter the ability to use social capital, is *the* defining difference between them and other Asian immigrants both past and present. It is what has allowed them to reconfigure space and place in such dramatic fashion, as will be explored.

Social capital is defined here, not so much in the instrumental Bourdieuian sense of actual resources and benefits an individual or group might possess, but as the process and "ability to secure resources by virtue of membership in social networks or larger social structures" (Bourdieu 1977; Portes and Landolt 2000, 532). Most new Chinese activists do not have large amounts of money when they come to the United States, although a few do tap family capital in the homeland. Like other immigrants, they often pool resources to establish themselves in businesses once they complete their educations here. Many have limited personal or familial ties in the United States before arrival and are frequently the first or perhaps second in their families to make the move. They may join an older brother or sister and will often assert "I didn't know anybody," meaning they didn't have an extended family network in this country to use as a springboard. What they do have is the ability to access and use existing structural resources and networks through language facility, higher education, and professional employment. They take advantage of professors, scholarships, professional mentoring, and soon a widening pool of nonfamilial contacts. Family reunification occurs after they have been here for several years and after they have gained U.S. citizenship.

The larger issue in contemporary immigration and settlement frame-works involving naturalized activists is not so much how they do the work of building social capital but the degree to which social capital and the resulting class status allow them to instrumentally incorporate. In other words, what the neighbors think of them is important. And although ethnicity still functions as a key identification marker, their primary goal is not getting acquainted with native-born Chinese or other Asians but immersing themselves in mainstream white social networks. However, the *ability* to construct and use social capital to achieve status, recognition, or economic gain still cannot guarantee positive outcomes. The most obvious example during the 1980s was the dramatic reconfiguration of place that occurred first in Monterey Park and surrounding suburbs where Chinese immigrants settled, and the anger and white flight that ensued (see Chapter 4).

In contextualizing homeland political turmoil, changing nation-state policies, and restructured labor requirements, I add a fourth overarching subjectification to the motivations of these immigrants for leaving Asia. Safety and opportunity come with a broader vision of hope, hope for the offer of citizenship within an emancipatory democratic ideal that they believed the United States practices.

ESCAPE: IMAGININGS OF THE WEST

Lena was one of the first women to work in television in Taiwan. She was born in Xi'an, China, although if you don't probe too deeply, she won't volunteer that fact. Xi'an is a more distant memory than Taiwan, where she spent her childhood and where she made her mark as a young professional woman proud to be part of Taiwan's modernizing project. Lena's earliest childhood was framed by the violence of civil war and escape. Her father was a Nationalist army general and an intimate of Chiang Kai-shek. His decision to follow Kuomintang leadership in 1949 likely saved the family from imprisonment and execution. Building the new Republic of China (ROC) capital in Taipei brought in the Americans. Lena's father worked with the U.S. military and consular advisors, and although he had never been to the United States, he read widely about U.S. history and politics.

After the United States defeated Japan, U.S. foreign policy during the 1950s was focused on Communist containment and wresting control of what was left of colonial Asia from France and Great Britain. U.S. involvement in Indochina had already begun. Taiwan was a vital linchpin, and by the late 1960s, U.S. economic aid exceeded $4 billion and the United States continued to back both economic modernization and martial law on the island. For Lena, an American imaginary—one of opportunity and difference—always seemed just on the periphery.

> When I was very little, seven years old, me and my dad were sitting outside in the yard . . . the weather was very hot. My dad points to the moon and he says, "Fifty years from now, a man from the U.S. is going to walk on the moon." That opened my mind! Oh gee! I liked this, something that will benefit all people, something beyond the reach of average people. I think this was very exciting for me—gee—the *United States.*

Lena is an intense and focused woman now in her late 50s. She is self-confident, nurtured both by indulgent parents and by the sense of privilege that her father's political activities bestowed. She majored in theater at a Taiwan university and was the well-known host of a TV entertainment program she calls a Johnny Carson–type talk show. During those early days of the 1960s when Taiwan television first began broadcasting, TV was a trope for the modern nation that the ROC hoped to emulate. Discourses of contemporary mass consumption with distinct American influences pervaded the airwaves, enabling Taiwanese audiences to appropriate burgeoning global forms (Miller 1992). Lena participated in this transformation and was one of its keenest observers. An American movie crew complete with a cast headlined by actor Steve McQueen came to Taiwan in the mid-1960s to shoot *The Sand Pebbles.* Lena interviewed the cast, and her realization of the differences between Taiwan and the United States are still writ large in her mind: "Immediately, oh I can feel—the actors, the way they dress, even the way they wear their suits, the cut, the fit, very nice!" she says, raising her eyebrows and smiling. "You can immediately tell the difference. I'd *never* seen this before in Taiwan even though through magazines, TV, and radio, and I listened to the Voice of America, I'd get information about the United States."

A few years later, Lena's imaginings of the United States were replaced by actual experience. She had quit TV and was working at China Airlines in the overseas executive offices. Another model for a modernizing Taiwan, the airline was a choice opportunity. "Overseas" was limited to Vietnam until the airline got permission from the United States to inaugurate its first transpacific flight to Los Angeles. The destination had less to do with global or business considerations than with the fact that her boss's family had already moved to Los Angeles. It was 1969 and she was on one of the first flights. While in Los Angeles, Lena began dating one of the boss's nephews, an American-born Chinese. She says she saw coming to the United States as a way to increase her educational and career opportunities—"What else am I going to do in Taiwan?" After she got married, she never thought about returning to Taiwan. She didn't have to. She took advantage of the new immigration laws to reunite her family. Within five years, she was a new mother and a naturalized citizen and had brought her father—now retired from the Nationalist Army—mother, brother, and sister to Los Angeles.

· · ·

Winston was born in Shanghai in the 1950s but grew up in Hong Kong. He is a meticulous dresser who appreciates finely made clothing. From his father, a tailor, he learned the clothing business inside and out—everything from designing, to cutting and sewing, to pricing and selling. Now in his 50s, he is an attorney and will laugh heartily about his continuing ability to wield a needle and thread. Winston says life was so uncertain in China that his parents decided they would be better off in the safety of Hong Kong. Unlike Chinese immigrants at the turn of the twentieth century, whose knowledge of the West and Westerners was often filtered through and made myth by others' imaginations, many new Chinese activists like Lena and Winston spent most of their early lives surrounded by Europeans and Americans. In these formative experiences lay the basis for modern subjectivities. For those like Winston, the possibility of working and living somewhere other than his birthplace, somewhere that transcended national or colonized space, was routinized by everyday experience (Appadurai 1997). The spaces were filled with models of Western consumption and authority but at the same time were appropriated to forge a distinctly local form.

> My dad learned tailoring from the Brits and the French who colonized Shanghai back then. He became very successful in Hong Kong and had more than 100 tailors working for him. All of his customers were American and most of them were wealthy. I learned about Bonwit Teller, Saks. The best designer clothing they would bring over. My dad would copy them for one-third or even one-tenth of the price.

One of the very famous American designers would use my father as her own personal tailor, but she wouldn't let my dad use her name. Yeah, you're an American designer, but you have a *Hong Kong tailor* do your stuff!

We always had a car and I would just chauffeur everybody around. I got to know Americans, and I really liked them. Brits don't appeal to me.

During the 1960s, Western music became popular in Hong Kong. As a high school student, Winston played and sang in a band he formed with a group of friends. He laughs, recalling that they all sang Simon and Garfunkel lyrics with Chinese accents. For Winston, the sense of agency in appropriating symbols of the West was more about informing his own identity as a young man, but it soon became clear that others had ideas about co-opting the same symbols.

His celebrity as a musician grew, and he remembers being driven in a government car to "gigs" around the city. Hong Kong, of course, has a history of internationalization and Western influences, undergirded by a paternalistic colonial government. Hong Kong during the 1960s was a mecca for manufacturing. The only resource this city on the rocks possessed in abundance was cheap labor. By the 1960s, however, another layer was added over the city's manufacturing base; new forms of concentrated economic activity and the growing demands of multinational finance markets and transnational corporate capital made Hong Kong truly global (Sassen 2000). Winston and his band benefited from this globalization and its attendant iconic, Western cultural forms. Of the five original band members, two eventually moved to the United States, and a third migrated to Canada.

In 1967, the government vehicles were replaced with unmarked cars. Rioting and rebellion broke out in the city. Winston found himself a pawn in a much larger political battle, with the band morphing into a not-so-subtle form of social control. Rock concerts were aimed at pacifying young adults who might otherwise be engaged in making Molotov cocktails and confronting colonial police. Fallout from the Cultural Revolution north of the city hit Hong Kong with widespread labor unrest. Many of the rioters carried Mao Zedong's Red Book. It is a period Winston still cannot recall without difficulty. He forms his thoughts carefully, trying to summon up the disturbing images.

Cultural Revolution [*he speaks as though there are quotation marks around the phrase*] was a nice term—it was a civil war! The Chinese are so good at euphemisms. People were dying all over. *Hundreds of thousands of people died! Can you imagine?*

I remember there were bodies all the way down the Pearl River to Hong Kong. They'd float up to the piers. Bodies all tied up like lotus leaves. All of Hong Kong shut down. One of my neighbors was doused with gasoline and burned alive and we were living in a very nice neighborhood. It was bad.

As in Shanghai, life in Hong Kong became too risky. Both his mother and his father decided to send Winston and his siblings alone to the United States. His sister came first as a college student, and the rest followed, also with student visas, including Winston, who enrolled at a small college in the Midwest. Eventually their parents joined them, with Winston's father using transnational social connections among his clothing clientele to help in the transition. Many clients then made the much shorter trip to a downtown L.A. hotel where the family had set up shop. The United States became a safe haven and realized dream for Winston. "America—that's the future," he says. "America is hope, there is prosperity, democracy, freedom. It's clean, no graffiti—not like now! And of course, we watched all those movies. Movies at that time were not like today, all sex and violence. They gave you a very wholesome view."

. . .

Leonard, another naturalized Chinese activist who later became very involved in local Southern California politics, arrived in Canada as a college student during the early 1970s. He joined a sister who was also a student. As the child of yet another family forced out of China by revolution, he, too, is reluctant to talk about what he went through in Mainland China and later in Hong Kong and the sadness he harbors for relatives in China who didn't make it. Now he only offers that they all saw "dirty things."

As a youngster growing up in Hong Kong, Leonard was extremely inquisitive; his particular interests were history, political science, and current affairs. He was the only one in his high school class who liked politics. "A lot of people told me, 'You're crazy,'" he says. He was a voracious reader, and it didn't take him long to realize that whatever Hong Kong books had to offer about Chinese history stopped in 1949—and it didn't pay to ask questions about what had happened after that. "Everything was still too sensitive and the revolution was still going on," he says. "It was too controversial." He finds it ironic that he didn't learn more about Chinese history until he went to college in Canada. From there, he kept going—to England and the London School of Economics—before coming to Southern California to begin doctoral studies.

> You know, deep down in my heart I always wanted to come to the United States. When I was growing up, I saw this Pan Am Airline ad. They were showing this little girl on a swing and they had this song, they would sing, "Pan A-a-a-m-m can fly the world, fly you to the United States!" It always struck me that the U.S. was a country of opportunity. This is a country I always had good feelings about. It's a powerful country, a big country.

. . .

Kenton has been in the United States since the late 1960s when he was admitted to a small college in a Southern California suburb. His only family here was an older brother who was also a foreign student. Like other naturalized activists, Kenton was already predisposed to have positive imaginings of life in the United States through his Western-based education in Hong Kong.

> My impression of this country? Oh! That place is like a golden state! Plenty of opportunities—democracy—you go there and there's *freedom*! You learn about this when you went to high school, bit by bit, reading newspapers and magazines. Sometimes it was taught by the teachers. So you just pick up all this knowledge. And remember that Hong Kong was a very international city, so American people were never strangers to us.

After college, Kenton went back to Hong Kong, married his high school sweetheart, and, in 1976, temporary visa in hand, returned to Southern California where they could begin family life together. He says his wife "loved it, thought it was [a] really beautiful . . . stable environment. You have a nice house, a backyard, a husband who always comes home after work—not quite like Asia. In Asia, if you are a businessman and always go home by five o'clock, there's something wrong with you!"

Actually, Kenton still doesn't get home before five o'clock, even now, nor does his wife. Both work in the family business, a U.S.-based wholesale industrial clothing business with manufacturing in Hong Kong. The business qualified Kenton for fast-track permanent status. He wasted no time in capitalizing on post-1965 special preference changes in immigration law. "There was a window," he says. "My lawyer called me up and said 'we want to take advantage of that.' One stop—'exceptional ability.' I put all my papers together, and I make myself the expert in industrial [clothing]. It worked!"

. . .

Lynn's parents were living in Shanghai when the revolution forced them to flee to Taiwan. Born there, she remembers the political turmoil and the fears engendered by the Kuomintang's zealous efforts to root out Communist sympathizers. During the longest stretch of martial law in history—nearly four decades—tens of thousands of people were imprisoned or worse. Lynn is unable to characterize or talk about what she saw growing up beyond describing it as "a big mess."

Lynn's parents planned meticulously to ensure the family's safety abroad. They realized that speaking English was indispensable to successful resettlement. Most naturalized activists do have common experiences as limited English speakers, even in the context of primarily Chinese-influenced educations. English serves as a marker of the mastery of Western forms both in Asia and in the United States, where political space is negotiated among other naturalized Chinese.

In addition, upon arrival in the United States, most Chinese political activists choose English first names for the same reason they learn English. It signifies membership and a willingness to participate as Americans in the social processes of the new community, where, for example, it is much easier to conduct relations with power structures (white) if your first name is pronounceable. In everyday conversations, activists often make considerable mention of their own facility (or lack of it) with English. Intragroup differences are not based on whether one speaks English; all the activists described in this book do. Many of them are, in fact, multilingual, speaking English, Mandarin, Shanghainese, Cantonese, and perhaps Korean or Japanese. Instead, major differences are based on the degree of one's accent. For example, at a city council meeting one evening, in a small suburb east of Los Angeles, a naturalized Chinese American council member introduced a motion for a vote. The white and Latino council members sat mute for several long moments before someone realized what had been said and quickly called for a seconding motion. The incomprehensibility of the council member's English is a source of comedy among other naturalized activists. In more private gatherings, when someone says something that nobody understands, the speaker is often told, "Oh, you just pulled a [name of individual]" or "You sound like . . ." No matter the degree of accent, however, speaking and comprehending English is a key determinant not only of the type of educational and business opportunities new activists seek but of their subsequent political participation in the United States.

Lynn's parents decided that, as the eldest child, Lynn would learn English and be given a Westernized education. Needless to say, it changed her life. They saved money to send her to a private school filled with international students. Lynn was just seven, but still old enough to realize her own marginality. "There were lots of Americans," she says, "but after school we went back to our own neighborhoods. There wasn't a lot of socializing. I never knew there were such different people."

When the opportunity came in the mid-1970s, Lynn's father used his transnational connections in New York's wholesale clothing business to obtain sponsored work visas for his family. With everyone settled in New Jersey, he traveled back to Taipei to oversee his business. They would never be all together again. In her new home, Lynn's fluency in English did not make life that much easier.

> We only had friends here, we didn't have relatives, and it was really difficult. I had to be spokesperson for the family. . . . I was kind of like *pushed* out there! I had to talk to everybody, about living arrangements, going to the grocery store, talk to people about service hookups.
>
> Looking back now, I wouldn't want to expose my kids to that! For me, I would not uproot and move to a country where I couldn't communicate well. The courage [my parents] had . . . it's amazing.

Taiwan continues to remain rooted in her family's history. It still informs a profound transnational imaginary, particularly as Lynn and her mother continue daily conversations about the island through Taiwanese television and newspapers.

. . .

Sam and his brother are import/export wholesalers in Southern California. Sam is much more outgoing and politically involved, doing 90 percent of the talking while his younger brother listens and usually nods vigorously. The two are virtually inseparable, showing up at political fund-raisers and community events together but never with their wives or children. In this, they are typical. With few exceptions, spouses, whether male or female, rarely make public appearances. When asked, the spouse will say she or he isn't interested or that "one in the family is enough!"

Sam came to Los Angeles from Hong Kong during the 1970s on a student visa, graduated from UCLA, and became a citizen after a few years of working. Another brother was already at UCLA. For the brothers, the prospect of optimizing their life chances in the United States did not include eventual return to the colony: "We came here to stay; we never thought about going back."

. . .

Attending an elite educational institution is very important for any naturalized activist contemplating success in the United States. Like other new Chinese activists, Franklin's family gave him the opportunity on both sides of the ocean: "I went to a top private [high] school in Hong Kong," he says. "Most of the people were doctors or lawyers. I wanted to come to the U.S. I didn't care whether I liked it or not. I came for the education. It's not that you can't get a good education in Hong Kong—your *potential* is better if you go somewhere overseas. So I went to UC Berkeley."

After Berkeley, Franklin went to work for a Southern California company that paid for him to complete a master's in business administration and then attain a law degree. Franklin is grateful for the subsidy that allowed him to stay in the United States. He talks about college friends who returned to Hong Kong armed with U.S. diplomas and became quite successful. He will say only half jokingly, "Look where I am now!" It is about as far away as one can get from a traditional, newly arrived immigrant enclave. He lives more than 30 miles from downtown Los Angeles, due east on the I-10 freeway, in a new planned community where the average yearly income exceeds $80,000. There is still a numerically small Chinese American population here, adjacent to the Inland Empire, but it is unlikely to remain so. In the span of a few short years, more than 100,000 people moved to the area, lured by more affordable housing. Now in his late 40s, Franklin practices business law in a new professional center. The office where he hangs his shingle has the requisite book-lined library and high-backed leather chairs. On clear days, he has a glorious view of the San Gabriel Mountains.

Narratives of Democracy and Modern Subjects

Within the gaze of globalizing discourses, naturalized activists have already been subjectified both racially and through their continuing cultural membership in countries and areas formerly on the periphery of capitalism but now drawn into global economic projects. As previously mentioned, key aspects of a politicized identity exist even before these activists come to the United States. For those who migrated from Hong Kong during the 1960s and 1970s as subjects of a colonial present, their feelings of political membership are especially revealing and indicative of a systematic discipline of accumulation—an accumulation of both bodies and territory (Said 1979). As subjects rather than full citizens of the British crown, they find the American ideal of democracy to be a vital imaginary that enables them to provide a contesting framework from which to view both their current and future politicized identities. The dialectic between the reality of everyday experience in Hong Kong and democratic ideals in the United States allows for agency in confronting and evading nation-state political projects. They are quite frank in describing their preimmigration subjectification.

Veronica was born in Guangzhou, but war uprooted the family, and they moved to Hong Kong. At age 17, Veronica realized that Hong Kong would never offer the same opportunities as the United States. The possibility of living under Communism was equally unappealing. "My parents said if I wanted it that bad, they would let me go, they were very supportive," she says. "Gave me a chance at a new life." She began attending seminars for students who wanted to go overseas. Veronica left Hong Kong in 1969 as a foreign student, enrolling at a state university in northern California. She was virtually alone; she had no friends and only a distant aunt and uncle living in San Francisco. She says now that she would have been "scared stiff" if she hadn't been so "dumb." After graduation, she sought employment in medical technology; she got her citizenship in the late 1970s by qualifying in a professional category and now works in Southern California. Veronica draws a distinct line between the ideal of her grounded U.S. membership and her "floating" life in Hong Kong.

> In Hong Kong you're not really a citizen . . . you don't belong anywhere. You're not Chinese, you're not British. It was all in limbo. You're a British

subject, but you don't have the same rights as a British *citizen*. You have no rights, period. We weren't Chinese either. It was not Chinese land; it was a colony.

This problem with identity—you're British, but you're not China Chinese, you're not Taiwan Chinese. No identity. A lot of people feel that way. So you're sort of floating around. I *never* thought of *country*. I never had that feeling that I belonged to any one country.

Sam's laugh is loud and derisive when he says he didn't think twice about shedding his British citizenship. "So *what*, you *renounce* your British citizenship? We were British *subjects*," he says. "Oh, they give you a British passport—it *looks* the same but they know it's not. It's not like you could stay in Britain. You could only stay in Hong Kong. Did I feel like second class? *Obviously*, yeah, sure! Of course!"

The strong attraction of educational and business opportunities in the United States comes as no surprise. Naturalized activists like Kenton and Franklin took full advantage of what reconfigured U.S. immigration laws offered. However, for those like Winston, what cannot be ignored is the emotional desire that a sense of belonging can bestow. "Back in the early days I *felt* like a foreigner," he says. "But as my roots sank in here, I don't like people thinking I'm still a foreigner. Kind of funny, you know," and now his tone becomes measured, "but you *really* want to be an American." This is not achievable as a colonial subject. Kenton says it didn't even occur to him that political life outside Hong Kong could be different. The rupture becomes clear when preimmigration imaginings turn into reality after residence and naturalization. For Franklin, it was key to his becoming a new American citizen.

> We don't have a country to belong to. When I was growing up, I was not Chinese, I was not part of China, I was not part of anything! We weren't consciously paying attention to political matters because that was, quite frankly, none of our business. We couldn't do anything about what was going on in the colony.
>
> That was such a refreshing situation and feeling when I became a U.S. citizen—a real sense of belonging. Now, I really belong to a *country*! I never had that feeling before.

Despite the palpable sense of relief and pride of membership that appears in their narratives, the fact that new activists are products of competing projects of colonialism and nascent nationalism in Asia, neither of which allows for dissension, has created political subjects who have been taught to stay as far away from political participation as possible. They have been excluded, but they have also learned that quite simply, nonparticipation is a matter of physical survival. It is better to focus elsewhere, on one's family and one's own business. "You stay away from politics and you stay away from trouble," Veronica says. "Everyone was so afraid . . . just don't get into trouble!" Sam was interested in politics, but this meant tacking back and forth, sailing a neutral course between both the Communists and the Kuomintang.

> People used to be so passionate about politics in the thirties and forties, but they found out it doesn't matter what you do in politics. You either get killed or locked up. But we *all* quietly read the newspapers, and we are all very well informed politically. But as a bystander, not as a participant. It's like watching a movie; you know you're not going to be the star.

Leonard says that his interest in current events and politics frightened his family. After experiencing the Communist revolution in China, his parents' reaction to his desire to study political science was not supportive, to say the least. "They would tell me to stay away, study science, be a doctor or a lawyer," he says. "I told my mother I wanted to major in political science. She almost fainted! Letter after letter from her, 'What are you going to do?'"

For other new activists who were born in Taiwan, there are other hegemonizing narratives that they cannot evade. As Lynn's life history reveals, homeland political issues are never far from sight. Cross-strait hostilities are a contentious part of the local in Southern California's Taiwanese American community—the largest outside Taiwan. Although not necessarily vocal, many naturalized Chinese activists continue to be politically active transnationally via dual citizenship, which allows them to fly to Taiwan to vote in local elections (Kang 2000). This localization of the global has created cultural subjects whose grounding as *Taiwanese* American is complicated by larger political projects. As one activist born in Taiwan relates: "I don't feel Taiwanese. I feel like I'm Chinese. Taiwan is just a province of China. I don't agree with the fact that Taiwan should have its independence. It's really complex because you have all these factors . . . geographically, historically, no matter what angle you look at it, just because you have a self-ruling government or party doesn't mean you have the right to be an independent country."

Modernizing Chineseness

A last layer of subjectivity needs to be peeled away for a fuller understanding of politicized identities among naturalized Chinese activists. Its current seeding in the landscape of cultural subjectivities speaks to an older and overarching paradigm of racial essentialism and exclusivity.

As China tries to reposition itself globally, its presentation of alternative modernities also creates new notions of what it means to be Chinese. In the past 15 years, major themes have included China's embrace of marketization and capitalism socialist style and the formation of overseas Chinese as a model for so-called Confucian capitalists (Dirlik 1997). These narratives, subsumed under "modern political sovereignties," bind all Chinese together no matter where they are and assume a universality of cultural essence, a primordiality unbound by the fetters of Western imperialism (Anagnost 1997). Naturalized activists also co-opt and appropriate their "Chineseness," invoking it as a way to evade and reconfigure subalternity. They will often talk about being Chinese first without necessarily tying their ethnicity to territory. And as will be detailed more fully in the next chapter, cultural essentializing can encompass superiority or self-defense, as this comment from Lena illustrates: "We have a certain pride that no one can take away from us—no one can take it away. No matter how they think or see us differently, we always have our pride, and in certain things we are better than you, especially in [Chinese] philosophy."

Stanton was born in Taiwan and is very active in U.S. political projects. His Shanghainese father left the mainland with the rest of the Nationalists to become part of the new ROC government. After Stanton was born, the family came to the United States when his father was offered a university teaching job. They were admitted as refugees. Stanton was naturalized when he was 23 years old because he says he felt he owed something to the United States for taking in his family. He finished graduate school in the Midwest and was one of the first to do postdoctoral work in computer research. If asked by another Asian American, he will quickly say he is Chinese American; otherwise, he sees himself as Asian American. His transnational networks range far and wide in China and Taiwan. He is now engaged in a startup company based in Southern California, with technology from China and funding from Taiwan. Stanton sees his roots firmly planted here, yet he simultaneously fashions an edge he believes uniquely positions him in a larger Chinese imaginary. "A friend of mine had an interesting metaphor for us overseas Chinese," he says. "She said, 'Oh, you guys come from China and go to America. I know you're not Chinese citizens, you're American citizens. You're like the married-off daughters who come home to visit!' Good analogy. You're married off to America, but you're still part of the other family, too."

Although a nationalizing discourse in China is instrumental in creating new subjectivities among a wider collectivity of its cultural citizens, it is not enough to simply say that this is the result of modernity or contingent only within emergent nations. A Chinese nation-state may be a modern form, but tradition remains a second, closely related order of knowledge, which posits that the potency and continuity of a Chinese identity and cultural core predate the birth of Confucius. In common with other contemporary nation-state projects, Chinese nationalist discourse takes advantage of this by constructing new categories of essentialized narratives for more modernist ends (Duara 1991).

As has been noted, not without some humor, "educated Chinese know reflexively what China proper refers to; they may not be clear about the periphery but they know for sure that the center of China . . . is north near the Yellow River" (Tu 1994, 2). By the late nineteenth century, a master narrative had been reworked to mold kinship and social status into a racialized rhetoric favoring a narrow reading of Han as the dominant group over others who were not descendants of the Yellow Emperor (Dikotter 1990). To be Chinese, then, is to be Han. The crafting of a modern nation-state and a subsequent national identity must be contextualized and conditioned by a shared sense of cultural commonality focused on the practice and rituals of everyday life. This orthopraxy existed in late Imperial China and provided a basis for marking not only difference from the West but, more importantly, advanced Han Chinese from the country's internal barbarians, the *xiao shu minzu* (uncooked minority peoples) (Watson 1993). With the unraveling of Qing epistemologies and foreign colonial and subsequent imperialist projects, Chinese discovered that others saw them not just as un-Westernized but in all likelihood not even as superior.

This notion of cultural exclusivity has never entirely disappeared from the Chinese imaginary and has once again been called forth to service the new Chinese state. Its most modern incarnation is the government naming of minority groups, giving each official status and continuing differentiation from Han in much the same way as the U.S. census reifies ethnic and racial difference. "Hanification" has been successful in creating an officially sanctioned diversity in China that presents many of the same problems as it does in the United States. The Chinese state's efforts to contain and name heterogeneity outside Han parameters is often embedded in commodification and, more recently, transnationalized social practices (Ong 1999; Schein 2000). Like the U.S. government–sanctioned Asian Pacific American Heritage Month each May, ritualized cultural revivals and other enactments of Chinese minority tradition become "authentically" appropriated by the state in its role as a promoter of cultural "essences" (Schein 2000).

The touristic gaze of the majority authorizes the Other's participation and validates an imaginary of Chinese (Han) as "modernist subjects par excellence" both in Asia and overseas, as people capable of building bridges and negotiating the diaspora with flexibility in creating transnational solidarities and networks (Ong 1997, 334). However, being that modern subject carries enormous risk for new Chinese activists who publicly acknowledge and celebrate their ethnicized political identities in the United States and who do so in traditional arenas of political participation and daily life. And, whether they like it or not, new activists are also caught up in a complicated choreography that involves two wary superpowers, the United States and China, and their own groundedness as citizens of this nation-state. Criticized by mainstream discourse, targeted for not being "good immigrants," for being too outspoken or aggressive and having questionable loyalties to the nation-state, new Chinese activists rework this assignment as a politically salient statement of negotiated identity in the United States.

Reifying tropes of Chineseness does have its advantages in localized experiences of simultaneity. New activists like Kenton are frank about the edge he believes this gives him in his political activities in the transnationalized community of the San Gabriel Valley. In his import/export business, Kenton is in daily contact with clients, suppliers, and salespeople not only in the United States but throughout Asia. He is quite literally here and there. "I can go to the Chinese papers and talk to them in Chinese—can you?" he asks. "You cannot. I can go to the majority group of immigrants and mingle with them in Cantonese and Mandarin, but you cannot." The tacking back and forth, whether by choice or for survival, has historically always been the case with Asian Americans, but global restructuring that has made for a qualitatively different type of immigrant in the naturalized activist marks a new and heightened awareness of what it means to be both Chinese and American. Coupled with China's economic repositioning, new Chinese activists are keenly aware of the tenuous position they occupy and the fact that they are often looked upon as brokers.

Stanton says he now realizes that the personal and the professional are tightly bound to the political. U.S.–China relations occupy much of his thinking and motivation. At community functions, he is often seen button-holing people to talk about U.S.–China issues. He and other new Chinese activists were part of a larger group that successfully lobbied Tournament of Roses officials in Pasadena to allow a parade float from China. The 2008 New Year's Day event, watched by millions around the world, and just before the Beijing Summer Olympics, marked the first time a float from the People's Republic of China traveled the parade route.

Stanton's usual meeting place is a back booth in a coffee shop just off the freeway in southern Los Angeles County, where he regularly mentors a handful of young Chinese scientists and technicians who work in the South Bay. After hours, they gather for burgers and chat with Stanton acting as de facto headmaster and counselor. Experiencing China's economic expansion from this side of the Pacific, Stanton sees it as a source of pride and hope. "I think never in human history have so many people been elevated from poverty," he says. "In the past 20 years they have lifted such a large group from poverty. It makes me proud. China has so much to contribute in science and technology." But with the pride comes worry. How relations between the two superpowers manifest themselves will be an important part of an Asian American political identity in the future, as other, similar global events have been in the past (see Chapter 6).

NEITHER POOR NOR HUDDLED MASSES

In the interstices of the migration histories of naturalized Chinese activists are glimpses of overarching ideologies of power and modernity within which Chinese immigrants fashion rationales and motivations for leaving Asia. The simple fact is that with the lifting of U.S. immigration restrictions after 1965, Chinese come to the United States because they can. Again, this is not to place valuation. The decision to move to a foreign country is never easy, even under the most propitious of circumstances. Traditional approaches to immigration scholarship still hold true; it is a rupture that requires elaborate preparation, much expense, and the loss of personal relations at home in order to go somewhere else to live and learn a new culture (Portes and Rumbaut 1990). As one new Chinese activist reflected on his choice to come to the United States, "For me, it was a very stressful life event, but if you cross that hurdle, you believe you can do everything."

On the other hand, a closer reading reveals that new activists' motivations for immigration are more complex in ideological perspective and incentive than traditional immigration scholarship emphasizing economics has theorized. In that traditional view, the basic reasons for immigrating are the consequences of poverty and unemployment in underdeveloped countries (Portes and Rumbaut 1990). Economic approaches see migration as the result of differences in demand for labor and structural imbalances between core and periphery. Theoretically, this can't be dismissed entirely for many immigrants. Deindustrialization in more developed countries has contributed to new, reconfigured areas of production in both core and periphery with the attendant "race to the bottom" regarding labor requirements (Ong, Bonacich, and Cheng 1994; Sassen 2000). But economic factors are not entirely predictive of movement among new activists. "[They] do not emigrate because they cannot survive in their home country but because they dream about America" (Park 1997, 29). The example of the naturalized Chinese activist takes into account avenues of agency in interpreting choices within the framework of overarching structures. Significantly, these new migrants are more skilled in using social and economic capital as means for accessing resources. Once established, they are able to construct and use transnational social networks. Their migration "corresponds to the increasing integration of peripheral societies into the global economy and their populations' growing awareness of opportunities abroad" (Portes 1995, 21).

New activists see in their migration not just safety or opportunities in the United States, but qualitatively *better* opportunities to maximize their abilities in capturing more social or economic capital. And as part of the scheme to utilize better opportunities, the larger structures of U.S. society, such as education or the technical and professional industries, take on key symbolic social and political meanings. The achievement of U.S. citizenship, educational credentials, or professional success is confirmation of status and progress.

This growing awareness of additional life chances must be historicized in the context of power and spheres of influence—centuries of contact, colonization, and intervention that continue to characterize the hegemony of modern structures of globalizing capitalism.

Conclusion

The outlines of a reconfigured Asian America were discernible in the late 1960s. While a core of college-age and primarily native-born Asian American activists was engaged in the largely parochial project of redefining and rediscovering a community's historical roots, another parallel project of Asian American identity—one with a much different trajectory—had begun within a group of new Asian immigrants. As the routes/roots of their life histories illustrate, the contexts of their post-1965 exit from Asia and their reception in the United States coupled with their expectations for their new lives here problematize and call for a rethinking of migration theory beyond simple push–pull economic factors. In addition, the Eurocentric ethnic model of immigration and assimilation that framed pre-1965 migration to the United States has been categorically and dramatically upended.

Significant structural changes in postindustrial economies like that of the United States and the concomitant legal modifications of immigration policies are even more profound. Recruitment of immigrant labor from Asia has deep historical roots. Now the parameters of this historical model must be expanded to include a new type of Asian labor: Western-educated and professionalized Chinese. For this emergent group of naturalized citizen activists, the choice to emigrate from China was initially framed by family histories of unpredictability and the fear for personal survival. In this sense, they can be seen as refugees. The decision to undertake yet a second migration from other parts of Asia to the United States is made up of a more complex combination of reasons, including survival and the maximization of life prospects they believe the United States affords (Giddens 1991). "One thing they are certain of is freedom to choose a way of life and the opportunity to live up to one's expectations" (Zhou 1992, 61).

Life expectations become a defining foundation upon which these new U.S. citizens construct their American identities. The internalization of these hopes begins years before they move to the United States, through firsthand Western cultural and media exposure and education in Asia. Their ability to benefit from the resources that these types of social capital provide in the homeland also allow them to take advantage of establishing and expanding on new social relations when they migrate to the United States. With the right schooling and the right professional contacts and positions, they see themselves achieving the social and economic status necessary for full participation in American society. The focus on family and business before extensive civic participation is not rooted in deterministic notions of Confucian capitalism but rather can be interpreted as a means of both legitimization and survival in new circumstances.

To reiterate, new activists are not apolitical or apathetic about participating in political or civic life. They are, in fact, *highly* politicized in their awareness of the dangers that participation posed in their countries of origin. Seen from this perspective, their desire to become involved in what the ideal of American democracy and citizenship offers is all the more remarkable. The emancipatory nature of democratic freedoms available to them in the United States provides a clear alternative to homeland political nullifications and marginalities. This more nuanced reading allows for critical understanding of one of the bases upon which future political participation in the United States is constructed. In the next chapter, the expectation of democratic participation and the yearning for inclusion collide with the harsher realities of everyday new American lives.

FOUR

California Lifestyles

Grounding Places/Spaces of New-Activist Experience

By 1985, naturalized activists were no longer new immigrants. They had finished schooling, gotten jobs, married, started families, and become U.S. citizens. Their trajectories were similar to those of many Americans the same age, but beyond that their life experiences had been decidedly dissimilar. For many of these activists, the 1980s was a defining decade during which they fashioned new identities as U.S. citizens, but in that fashioning, there was disjuncture. They began to see themselves not just as new citizens but, unexpectedly, as racialized members of the community. This chapter looks at how that happened—in the selection of a profession and a place to call home—and how these experiences transformed individuals politically to undertake their first, collectivized action. New activists who were business entrepreneurs would call this period the "startup phase."

Racialized Places and Spaces

When the National Civic League named Monterey Park as one of its "All America Cities" in 1985, it lauded the city's record of community and government working together. The phrase "All America City" started appearing on everything from billboards to office letterheads. The designation not only fostered community pride but, beyond bragging rights, meant possible economic stimulus and job growth. Long before the ink was dry on the stationery, however, things started to fall apart—actually, they had been falling apart for some time. Even though the social changes wrought by the presence of thousands of new Chinese immigrants seemed to have occurred overnight, the transformation began shortly after the Hart-Celler Act was passed in 1965.

Barely a year after Monterey Park's All America designation, Lily Chen, the first Chinese American mayor of any city outside Hawaii, was voted out of office. An immigrant from Taiwan, Chen was distressed to find herself the object of a nativist backlash thinly disguised as antidevelopment and slow growth. Monterey Park soon became better known for its ethnic upheaval and community discord where egregious stereotypes about Chinese immigrants were circulated. For Monterey Park, it was "the invasion of their small-town America by mini-malls, condos, congestion, jumbo signs in Chinese, fancy cars erratically driven by arrogant newcomers, and foreign stores" that led some there to believe that they "did not need or want the business of established Americans" (Horton 1995, 84).

From its incorporation in 1916, Monterey Park has been a multiethnic community.[1] This city of about 60,000 is a short 10-minute drive east of downtown Los Angeles, and in its land boom days Anglos, Latinos, and Asians settled the area. Early Hollywood film producers used the Monterey Hills for making Westerns, and Japanese farmers improved the old Monterey Pass Trail into Los Angeles so they could truck their produce to market. Real estate investment and development are not new phenomena either. During the 1920s, numerous subdivisions advertised the genteel country life, including one, the Midwick View Estates, that described itself as "a proposed garden community designed to rival Bel-Air and Beverly Hills" (Monterey Park 2004). The latter appellation stuck, although not exactly the way earlier developers had envisioned. A half century later, Chinese newcomers came to know Monterey Park as the "Beverly Hills of *Chinatown*."

During the 1970s, the Chinese American families who lived in Monterey Park were mostly pre-1965 immigrants or American-born, as were the numerous Japanese Americans who had begun to buy homes in the Monterey Hills after being freed from the internment camps. Lily Chen, her husband, and two young children moved to the area in 1979. Her husband is also a naturalized Chinese American who has largely stayed out of the political limelight but is a longtime member of the Chinese American Engineers Association and other groups organized to promote Chinese American issues. The family was drawn to Monterey Park by images of a suburban American life with good schools and quiet neighborhoods. And for a time it was. No one was prepared for the social and economic changes that swept the community with such cyclonic force.

Monterey Park was the first suburban city in the San Gabriel Valley to undergo radical transformation. It may be considered the beachhead. However, a broader look shows that Monterey Park was actually only one of at least *two dozen* cities also in the process of being reconfigured by new Chinese residents during the growth of the 1980s with equally significant social and political implications in each. The entire San Gabriel Valley was the new center of a triangulated vortex of Asian immigrant transformation resulting from the three points discussed in Chapter 3: changes in immigration policy, labor requirements in the United States, and homeland political and economic turmoil. In the past two decades, other suburban areas even farther from the downtown core of Los Angeles have shown significant gains in Chinese populations.[2] San Marino, known as a primarily wealthy, white enclave where the median home price is now seven figures, went from just 4 percent Chinese in 1980 to nearly 42 percent by the 2000 census.[3] Out of an Asian Pacific population of 1.13 million in Los Angeles County, Chinese are now the dominant ethnic group, constituting more than 28 percent of all Asian Pacific residents in the county (Garoogian 2005, 7).

In other cities in the San Gabriel Valley, concentrations of Chinese immigrants with capital and transnational networks may not have been greeted with the same degree of overt and organized animosity they experienced in Monterey Park, as will be shown, but that does not mean they were welcomed with open arms either. Ever widening pools of immigrants radiated outward to find newer neighborhoods in which to live and raise families or to invest, thus expanding the transnational economic node into which Monterey Park had morphed. It is through the lens of the globalizing economy, the speed with which this new articulation of territory occurred, and the new competitive labor positions in which nation-states find themselves that this transformation can be critically analyzed.

The term *ethnoburb* is an apt description for this new model of suburban, ethnic settlement where new Chinese immigrants become part of an already diverse neighborhood. While sequestered in what has normally been thought of as suburbia, the ethnoburb also functions "under the influence of international geopolitical and global economic restructuring" (Li 1998, 481). It is in fact a tentacle connected to major globalized economic areas of cultural and social heterogeneity. By the time Chen decided to run for her first Monterey Park elective office in the early 1980s, the Los Angeles regional area was already the leading Chinese business center in North America, surpassing both San Francisco and New York (Horton 1995).

Restructured social and economic frameworks coupled with advances in transportation and communications technology have been instrumental for new activists. Many new immigrants who possess more educational, professional, and managerial skills than previous Asian immigrants have constructed social and professional infrastructures of transnational banking, real estate development, technology, and international trade. With accumulating capital and transnational networks, they have been able to create new entrepreneurial ventures for themselves and their families. This has enabled many of them to leapfrog traditional ethnic settlement patterns and, in the process, challenge accepted modes of immigrant community formation. They maintain multistranded social relations, practices, and imaginings beyond national borders, all of which constitute what has been defined as transnational. To reiterate, however, this quality of being in between is not their definitive subjectivity, and new Chinese activists do not entirely fit the label "transmigrant" (Basch, Glick Schiller, and Blanc 1994). Rather than a continuing in-transit impermanence, naturalized activists are set apart from a narrower focus on a transmigrant experience by the fashioning of a model of participatory citizenship that includes the transnational but, more importantly, also insists on activist political projects that privilege what is grassroots and *local.* Although new Chinese activists are uniquely positioned to benefit from macroeconomic and political transformations, they don't reside in some imaginatively unbounded, abstract third space. Their social collectivities and connectivities are unequivocally local. Transnational social practices and spheres are still bounded by and performed where they live in local suburban Chinese communities.

It has been popularly assumed and academically theorized that settling and blending in, including eventual social and economic upward mobility, are associated only with succeeding generations of American-born. The "sudden" appearance of professionalized Chinese immigrants, many of whom are new activists, in upscale, primarily white enclaves has challenged these "acceptable" routes for integration and assimilation. By 1990, the imprint of the professionalized immigrant was inescapable (Hing 2003). As Kenton put it (see Chapter 3), it is the American Dream—"a nice house, a backyard, a husband who always comes home after work"—fulfilled. The traditional Chinatown enclave populated by a disciplined class of working poor, or the crowded conditions that exist in most major cities in Asia, offers none of this.

But make no mistake. Also obvious is the new class diversification within both the Chinese American population and the larger Asian American community. Aside from the focus on professionalized immigrants, a closer reading of global economic restructuring shows a burgeoning Chinese immigrant labor class with less education and economic success. The unskilled and semiskilled working class still constitutes a large part of the post-1965 Chinese immigrant community in the ethnoburbs as well. And as was the case in old Chinatown, workers still depend on businesses in these areas for their livelihoods, albeit in an increasingly transnationalized atmosphere. (For a more detailed socioeconomic comparison between Chinese immigrants, native-born Chinese, and whites, see Appendix 3.) Furthermore, in global cities like Los Angeles, the less skilled now find themselves competing with ever greater numbers of similar immigrants from other parts of Asia, the Pacific, and Latin and South America.

To look at new activists' incorporation—the ways in which they can live here and there—is to give attention to an unconscious simultaneity of thoughts and practices. Again, however, characterizing this as a continuous circulation of people, money, goods, and information into what has been called a "virtual single community" is simplistic and not fully descriptive of the lives of new Chinese activists in Southern California (Rouse 1991, 14). A reformulated analysis of the dynamics involved in (dis)integration, (un)assimilation, and (non)incorporation reveals new social practices, including the transnational, that occur while people are still firmly anchored in bounded communities. It must also be remembered that immigrant social practices qualifying as transnational often perform important survival functions because of preexisting and embedded racial structures that carry differing memberships and access in the new homeland (Basch, Glick Schiller, and Blanc 1994; Pedraza 1996). New Chinese activists were already marked by U.S. social and political narratives, which historically viewed Asia and Asians with fear and suspicion.

Not Quite American

Lily Chen's personal and political life history mirrors almost exactly the social and economic changes that transformed Monterey Park and soon affected other nearby suburbs. Among the earliest of the new Chinese immigrants in the San Gabriel Valley, she considers herself an old-timer. She has moved away from Monterey Park, retiring to the hills above Glendale, but remains an active participant in community groups and still attends political events and fund-raisers. Now a grandmother, she continues to look the part of a well-groomed politician. Chen has been surrounded by some sort of political activism for most of her life, but she didn't go public until 1982. To the consternation of more than a few people, she ran for and won a seat on the Monterey Park City Council.[4] Like most new activists, Chen has had to develop a thick skin. One of the first things she told me shortly after being selected mayor by the city council more than 25 years ago was, "We're here to stay!" Her political mantra has not changed.

Heading north into Monterey Park off the Pomona Freeway, east of Los Angeles, the first shopping center you see is Atlantic Square Mall. It is filled with Vietnamese and Chinese restaurants, a Chinese grocery store, trendy boutiques, and the inevitable Starbucks. Across the street is a local branch of the East-West Bank. In late spring 2001, a big plastic banner floats off the second-story balcony. Its red and blue lettering reads "Judy Chu for State Assembly." The banner is in English, but nearly all the signs are written in a combination of Chinese and English characters. In the shadow of the mall, just up the street, is a nondescript self-serve gas station. Twenty-five years ago, this was ground zero for the anger and fear directed at new Chinese immigrants who moved into Monterey Park—in particular, those with financial capital to invest in or develop property. A poster, supposedly put up by the then-owner of the gas station, was aimed directly at Chinese immigrants and became the focus of a Los Angeles County investigation.[5] A county official commented, "We've heard of signs that say 'Will the last American to leave Monterey Park please bring the American flag?'"

Nobody driving by on Atlantic Boulevard, including Chen, missed seeing that poster. When I asked her in 2000 what it was like 20 years earlier when she campaigned for city council, she remembers the animosity as if it were yesterday: "*Ohhh*—it was s-o-o-o *strong!*" she says, her angry voice dropping to a deep whisper as she carefully enunciates each word. "At my swearing-in ceremony, English-only proponents came to city hall. I remember [an English-only supporter] said, 'You *stole* the office!' *You people, you people*—how many times he repeated it!"

Like other new activists, Chen's family was forced to leave China because they supported the Nationalists. Her deeply politicized family history, influenced by her father, who was a professor, has always placed heavy emphasis on ground-up participation. "My father was elected to become a member of the legislature, the first ever election in China in the late forties," Chen says. "He was elected simply because he had so many students supporting him. My father had his grassroots, I remember that!" As an interested young daughter in a family with no sons, Chen was encouraged by her father to take part in her community.

> He would take me to the legislature, and I would observe. . . . I told him one day, "One decision you make can impact so many people!" There was a drought in China, and I saw pictures of Chinese dying of hunger—so tragic. There was a dinner party, and I brought some pictures and showed them and said we ought to have a fund-raising drive. They're human beings and they're all Chinese—we should help them! And I actually collected money.
>
> I remember one birthday he gave me a mirror, a life-size mirror. I was learning to make speeches. He said, so you practice in front of the mirror before you come to me.

Chen came to the United States on a student exchange program sponsored by the U.S. Embassy in Taipei. At the University of California, Berkeley, she met her husband, whose engineering job eventually brought them to Southern California. She remembers vividly an aggressive sales campaign by Chinese American real estate agents who had begun advertising Monterey Park as an upscale Asian American community. The agents also capitalized on transnational social networks in Hong Kong and Taipei, marketing properties by shuttling between Los Angeles and Asia. The promotional materials boasted, "In Monterey Park you can enjoy the American life quality and Taipei's convenience at the same time" (Tseng 1994, 172). Thus, much in the same fashion as labor contractors of the mid-nineteenth century recruited workers with promises of Gold Mountain, real estate agents recruited new immigrants to Monterey Park. The land rush was on. Chen says that is when the backlash began: "Old-timers really like the idea of their property going up, but they did not like the look of these people. They looked strange, they act[ed] differently, they changed the signs, they built condominiums. It's not that the Asians *chased* them out. They sold their property for a good price and moved on to other places."

Shortly after that, English-only supporters began organizing against the use of Chinese in business advertising. Notions of community membership and entitlement became unmoored. White residents complained that "jumped up" Chinese immigrants did not settle in "traditional" ways; they were not poor and appeared neither grateful for new opportunities nor eager to "fit in" (Horton 1995).

As a new city council member, Chen tried to defuse racial tensions by ordering that city signage (which had become heavily Chinese) carry at least 50 percent English, but it wasn't enough. As mayor, her idea of printing part of the city newsletter in Chinese, to help bring the growing Chinese community into the political process and encourage them to become citizens and vote, also backfired. Her inbox overflowed with hate mail. In 1985, Chen and two Latino council members lost their reelection bids to three white residents, putting city government firmly back in white control. The events are bitter memories for Chen, who realized she was a lightning rod. "I was representing my whole race as well as the city," she says, "but it was such a struggle. No matter how hard I tried, I was always reminded that I was an outsider. How did I feel? How did I *feel*? I was furious. I was emotional because I felt that when I'm being told I'm not exactly an American, that really hurt, that really hurt."

Despite being intimately involved with city politics, a naturalized U.S. citizen, and a longtime resident, Chen was unable to overcome her perceived foreignness. Instead, community conservatives saw her as part of a marked category of outsider. "You people" lived beyond the dominant discourse of preservation of community. Some might see these racial constructions as eliding more potent political and economic issues from contestation. But there doesn't appear to have been much elision in Monterey Park. Race was at the root of the degradation of community, posited directly through an economic issue—commercial and residential development that "old-timers" thought included too many strange new businesses, garishly designed condominiums, and unreadable signs. Nobody was fooled into thinking this had nothing to do with race. *New development had a Chinese face.*

The imposition of a different culture and language in the span of a few short years became part of the history of racialized politics in Monterey Park. However, the neighborhoods where new Chinese activism has flowered cannot be considered unique exceptions or anomalies of immigrant settlement but must be seen as *integral* to the larger phenomenon of new flows of global capital and labor within a reconfiguring, deindustrializing U.S. economy.

During the early 1970s, U.S. business had to relocate capital and the means of production to cheaper areas of the world in order to maximize profits. What began as exploitation of manufacturing in underdeveloped countries evolved into fierce competition from those countries in other areas of industrialization. The so-called newly industrialized countries—China, Taiwan, Korea, Singapore, and Malaysia—became cheaper sources of both labor and capital investment (Brenner 2002). This has evolved into new divisions of labor, with the United States focusing on supplying technological and business skills to service global enterprises (Ong, Bonacich, and Cheng 1994). Again, it is no coincidence that economic restructuring, the arrival of new, more skilled Asian immigrants, and the transformation of previously undervalued areas of Southern California real estate into transnational economic nodes *all* occurred during the same time frame.

It bears repeating that transnationalism is not an entirely new phenomenon. As discussed in Chapter 2, it has always existed in ethnic enclaves and is a part of the life histories of Chinese Americans like Ronald, whose parents sought to become involved in overseas nationalist Chinese fund-raising during the 1920s and 1930s. Sun Yat-sen's world travels to raise money for the Chinese revolution are well documented (Chong 1984; Wilbur 1976); his visits to Southern California beginning in 1910 and the support he got from Los Angeles Chinatown leaders like Kitman Woo are part of grandson Mike Woo's memory. However, there is no precedent for the new flows of capital, technology, information, and people experienced in the San Gabriel Valley during the late 1970s and early 1980s. Realtors and others were able to capitalize on luring these new immigrants to Southern California, but this would not have been possible without the wider global events and resulting national policies that specifically targeted these new economic recruits.

Thus, many new-activist Chinese have benefited from the transnational aspects of entrepreneurial membership. Their politicized American identities took shape as the direct result of experiences they had in their businesses. Charlie Woo's life history exemplifies this equation between business and politics.

August 2001

A midweek service club business luncheon at a Pasadena hotel is similar to thousands of lunchtimes across the country. This group of about 150 people is mostly composed of white men, with a sprinkling of women and people of color, who have come to hear the weekly inspirational speech from another successful local businessman. He is introduced as an empowering and supportive individual—the "personification of the American Dream." Charlie Woo is in his mid-50s and the wearer of many hats—father of Los Angeles' Toy Town, former chairman of the Los Angeles Chamber of Commerce (the first Asian American chair in its 114-year existence), and the current chair of CAUSE, to name a few. He is, in fact, so indefatigable and omnipresent at virtually every major political and social event in Southern California—Asian Pacific and otherwise—that one wonders how he has any time to spend with his family or to run his large toy import/export business from Los Angeles and Asia. Woo's speechifying at various events is a political statement for recognition and inclusion. It is a way for him to define his being both a successful businessman and an American citizen.

In this regard, Woo's life history plays to familiar new activist themes, yet it transcends this experience in significant ideological aspects that are coming to be shared by a small handful of other individuals in the activist circle. It is a core transformation that is manifested in a slow but growing realization that as an instrument in gaining political recognition and empowerment, *ethnic specificities must make room for a larger and more inclusive pan–Asian American political identity.* This is a direct by-product of the racializing personal and professional experiences that these activists have shared in the United States. Like others of his foreign-born generation, Woo did not have these sensibilities as a new immigrant. His priority as a newly arrived 17-year-old from Hong Kong was finishing his education at UCLA, earning a doctorate in physics, and bringing his parents and brothers to the United States—certainly not participating in Asian American issues. "I was aware of the Asian American community in L.A. but that was not my interest," Woo says. "I wanted to learn everything there was to learn about *mainstream* America."

Woo usually pulls few punches. Every so often he will say something and then add quickly, "Oh-oh, that's going to get me in trouble!" Beginning in the late 1990s, when I became interested in studying CAUSE and some of its more active adherents, Woo and I spoke frequently about politics and participation. He is straightforward about his first thoughts on meeting American-born Asians and his evolving identity as a member of something called the Asian American community.

> In the Asian American community, they call us new immigrants "FOBs"— fresh off the boat. In Chinese, we call those born here "bamboos" [canes from the tree]. Bamboos have sections and partitions so you can't really see from one side to the other no matter which end you look at.
>   You have a community of people here that are not quite Asian. They don't really understand Asian culture, but they don't quite understand Western culture either, so they're halfway in between and they call themselves Asian Americans. That's why the term "bamboo" came in; they don't really get it from both ends! *At least that's what I thought!*

After his parents asked for help in starting an import/export business, Woo stopped writing his doctoral dissertation and started writing spreadsheets. "I remember the very first time I went to the bank to get a loan, and the banker says, 'Do you have a financial statement?' I said, 'What's a financial statement?'"

Gazing east from the high-rises that shape downtown Los Angeles' Gold Coast along Flower Street, you can see Woo's wholesale toy warehouse on the outskirts of Little Tokyo. Look more closely and you might be able to make out the colorful, cartoonish company sign that reads "Megatoys" on the side of the low building. Physically, Megatoys appears superfluous to Los Angeles' corporate heart, but in the restructured global economy in which the city participates, Woo and his company are vital to its lifeblood. Los Angeles is headquarters for the company, which also has key suppliers in Hong Kong and Shenzhen, China. This makes Woo pretty much of an airborne commuter. Equally important, however, he is firmly rooted in the political and civic life of the region and goes to great lengths to immerse himself in what is local. The walls of his downscale offices are cluttered with pictures of him with civic leaders and politicians; news clippings; and city and county plaques and awards for the company, including Top 100 Fastest Growing Companies in L.A., Minority Manufacturing Firm of the Year, and various citations from the Chamber of Commerce.

During the 1980s, Woo struggled to make a go of the family business. He had managed to rent space near the railroad tracks and the Los Angeles

River, an area of industrial streets full of derelict buildings and the home-less where prices were cheap. As he gained a tenuous foothold, other small entrepreneurs from Asia, and also Latin Americans and African Ameri-cans, began to approach him for help and advice on renting space or deal-ing with city business codes and regulations. In the process, Woo learned something he could never have experienced in Hong Kong, something that had less to do with business than with his own position as a person of color in the United States. "I really began to have a much broader perspec-tive of Los Angeles and my own community," he says. "How everybody just wanted their children to be successful, to be better than they are. And I began to get more involved with both Asian American community organizations as well as mainstream organizations. It's really quite differ-ent from Asia." This new awareness of deeper connections filtered into his business and personal outlook.

> I really didn't have a lot of help from government even though it was a
> blighted area. I know the government spent tens of millions of dollars on
> economic development programs . . . but, number one, I didn't know such
> things existed, and, number two, I wasn't plugged into the system.
>
> I learned how to overcome that and started talking to politicians and
> city officials, and that's what got me really interested in politics. Out of ne-
> cessity I got interested, and I've just continued to pay attention.

Entrepreneurial Models of Incorporation

The immigrant with business acumen is a well-known description of Asians in general and, in particular, politically active new Chinese. However, new activists don't fully fit either of two competing theories extant in the scholar-ship regarding Asian entrepreneurs. One model posits that resources from co-ethnics are important in establishing immigrant businesses, while the other emphasizes the importance of class resources (Min and Bozorgmehr 2000). For pre-1965 Chinese immigrant entrepreneurs, reliance on ethnic and family ties was often a key factor in starting and sustaining a business. Support from outside was usually not sought and more frequently not given. Even professionals like Ronald's uncle, who practiced immigration law in San Francisco's Chinatown (see Chapter 2), served an entirely Chinese clien-tele built through word-of-mouth referrals.

Among post-1965 Chinese immigrants, however, new activists use some family ties initially but also tap class resources to establish themselves in businesses and professions in the United States. The most common resource is American higher education, which they are able to achieve because of their fluency in English and Westernized educations both here and in Asia. These opportunities are not available to the majority of Chinese immigrants. The single-mindedness with which most new activists approach an American education indicates the importance they attach to capitalizing on class resources and securing the benefits of social capital. An American education and a degree from a prestigious university bring membership in broader social networks and new ways of accessing resources outside the ethnic community.

Despite these advantages, ethnic resources remain an important part of the formula for success. Activists like Charlie Woo and Kenton, with his industrial clothing company, relied on family labor in their startup businesses. Woo's parents and brothers were also initial partners. Kenton's business is still run mostly by family, including his wife. And although both businesses have been able to penetrate and capitalize on U.S. markets, not just in selling their products but in securing financing, they also have continuing strong transnational familial and business connections to Hong Kong and Mainland China.

New-activist women are similar to activist men in achieving Western educations; although they are perhaps not as highly educated as men, many have college degrees and others have completed some postgraduate work. On the whole, however, activist women are still anomalies among post-1965 Chinese immigrants. Even those who have children pursue professional careers as a conscious decision or because divorce has made working a necessity. They favor work in real estate and property development because such careers have flexible hours that require less personal capital. Among women who remain married, husbands are either extremely supportive of their partner's endeavors, adopt a kind of laissez-faire attitude to their activities outside the home, or are largely absent with careers of their own, which require large chunks of time traveling or living in Asia. Only one or two of the activist men in this study are divorced; most have wives who are stay-at-home mothers or who are involved in some aspect of the family business.

. . .

After Lena's boss at China Airlines introduced her to one of his nephews, she and the nephew were married, and within a year, Lena had a baby. She likes to say she is a traditional Chinese woman, although she was not a stay-at-home mother. A year after her son's birth, she was back at work and going to school. Two years later, she became a U.S. citizen. Like other activist women and men, Lena's initial support network in the United States was extremely limited—two people. She was very lonely, living first in an apartment and then in a newly purchased house in Pasadena. Soon, however, the changes in U.S. immigration law permitted her to bring immediate family to Southern California. Within five years, parents, brother, and sister were reunited—and she had childcare. She went to work as an accountant at the credit union of a large Southern California aerospace company and ran into her first on-the-job racializing experience. She saw herself as well educated, cultured, and ambitious, but her co-workers did not. She was unprepared for the suspicion and stereotyped sexual innuendo she encountered. "He [one of her co-workers] called me a China doll—China something!" she says. "I knew they thought I was different. My attitude is that you're no different. I have a tendency to put unpleasant things away in a box. I don't open it. Maybe one day I'll open it."

After six years, Lena quit that job and went into real estate development, taking a position at a small company in Glendale. She was also in the process of getting a divorce and had two young children to support. She felt her new career was "untraditional" and something she should hide. By 1978, the San Gabriel Valley was going global. She realized that more Chinese immigrants were looking for places to live and property in which to invest. With dozens of new clients, she began brokering deals with mostly white owners who wanted to sell their decrepit warehouses and apartment buildings. She negotiated fiercely for her Chinese clientele and for the overseas capital they were willing to invest. She says other Chinese agents told her that she made deals "just like an American." It was not intended as a compliment.

She has been in real estate development for 25 years now, and it has afforded her a comfortable though not lavish lifestyle. Her white stucco home sits on a quiet street above the din of the 10 Freeway in Monterey Park. *Comfortable* is a word Lena uses frequently. She was not comfortable working at the aerospace company, and she moved to Monterey Park because it was a place where she felt more comfortable.

. . .

Through her father's garment business, Lynn's family was able to capitalize on a network of American contacts to gain entry to the United States during the early 1970s. They were sponsored and had jobs qualifying them as immigrant professionals. The move took a toll, and her parents split—her father returning to Taiwan. She remembers how hard her parents worked so that she could go to an American university. She graduated from a top East Coast university with a degree in business and has been a real estate broker for 20 years, starting her career when her two daughters were toddlers. Lynn bristles when she hears people talking about new Chinese wealth. Her own beginnings as an immigrant and her subsequent professional experiences allow her to see a more complex picture of the post-1965 Chinese.

> That thing about "Oh, all of you are rich, you don't need help," that's a small sector of our community. And you have to remember that most of these immigrant families sold everything they had to come here. They are hardworking people.
>
> They've saved all their money, and the first thing they want to do is buy a house. These are all people who are engaging in their community. Buying property is how you start a network and how you begin to get an understanding of the culture here.

Lynn regards political participation as an obligation that doesn't end with her commission check. As a broker, she says, it's important to educate new Asian immigrants about how democracy works.

> They say, "I'm trying to establish my family and make money. I'm getting my electricity, I have my water, I'm getting my services. I don't need to ask for anything, so why is it necessary for me to vote?" It's important for me to tell them and make them understand why it's important in America to be involved, and why it's important to vote.
>
> Overall, it's a *community benefit* for us to get involved. It's being recognized as a total community and being in the politicians' thoughts, that there is a segment of the population that you need to include in your understanding.

Lynn's husband is heavily involved in his businesses in Taiwan, frequently traveling back and forth. Lynn laughs, saying that's why they're still married after three decades. She says her husband is supportive of her political work, but "he thinks I could allocate my time better doing something else. I tell him this is the system here—the influence of individuals!"

In Pursuit of Democracy

Naturalized Chinese activists believe in the United States as a place of both opportunity and democratic freedoms, a place where they might escape the confines of other subjectifications in order to more fully pursue their social and economic projects. That they have previously been racialized and denied full citizenship in Hong Kong or peripheralized in Taiwan renders the American example of freedom and equal opportunity all the more exceptional. This is idealized through the achievement of citizenship as the necessary condition for full participation in U.S. society and politics, a representative democracy that allocates costs and benefits in the acquisition and distribution of resources. Access to and inclusion in the allocational process are what they desire and what the name of CAUSE confers—empowerment. In simpler political terms, it is the "pluralist wheeling and dealing" by which *any* interest group in the United States protects those interests (Gotanda 2001, 82).

In the United States, new Chinese activists find they are still marginal, but they come to understand that there are also empowering counternarratives of racial and cultural heterogeneity that can create different outcomes. This is largely due to the transformative 1960s and the role that radical and progressive activists of color played in expanding political discourse and interaction on the peripheries of state power. Domination is not absolute, but neither is marginality. For Kenton, this realization became, in itself, an empowering strategy that he had never before experienced.

> I was brought up to think, don't waste your time with politics, because you just listen to the government and the government tells you what to do. And if you're from Mainland China, that's even worse over there! You start to think, what are the major differences between here—now we call it home—the U.S. The differences are very simple. By the people, for the people, of the people.

Veronica also began to realize the value inherent in enactments of citizenship: "When I first became a citizen, I didn't register to vote," she says. "It was a foreign thing. It took me a while to get going. It's like, to me, this is your house. Who wants to run the household? You should have a choice who runs your house. Participating in the whole process is a way of living. If you don't participate, you don't have a right to complain." Stanton took participation as a personal responsibility: "To be a citizen, you get the rules of the game and you get the boundaries, but how you get treated by the rest of society is really up to you. That's why I'm in politics."

Clueless in the 1960s

In the United States, citizenship models and decisions on who qualifies for full participation have always been linked to race (Roediger 1991). American-born Asian activists who honed their political skills and knowledge during the 1960s have had lifelong experiences with the stereotype of the perpetual foreigner. As explained previously, these experiences have allowed for a more inclusive, pan–Asian American identity and sensitivity to the experiences of other Americans of color as well. American-born Chinese, like Brent, did not reach adulthood until after the 1960s. Nevertheless, he is fully cognizant of this ideological legacy: "I'm very aware of being a person of color," he says. "The civil rights issue applies to Asian Americans as much as it applies to African Americans, Hispanic Americans, Native Americans. I have more perspective on that than [naturalized Chinese]. Having grown up in a society where I was always different affects my thinking and affects the importance I place on forming alliances with other Asian Americans."

Brent, in his mid-40s, is a business attorney whose clients are mostly Chinese American businesspeople. He says because he is American-born and doesn't speak Chinese, he focuses on local businesses in the San Gabriel Valley and not on Chinese subsidiaries of transnational companies. Like Ronald's "longtime Californ'," Brent's self-ascription as a "local guy" is further delineation of difference from naturalized citizens. He was born and raised in the South Bay area of Los Angeles County and graduated from a top California law school. He lives with his wife and children in San Marino, although he has mixed feelings about the possibility that his children may get the wrong idea that Chinese are the majority in the United States. More than half of his son's grade school class is now Chinese American. Brent used to work for a major Southern California firm with more than 400 attorneys but left to start his own practice where, he says, he doesn't have to worry about an "unlevel playing field." Despite the alternative discourses advanced by the social movements of the 1960s, Brent is still discouraged by what he sees as corporate racism—the fact that very few

Asian Americans are senior partners in major law firms. He says an Asian name on the front door may look inclusive, "but it's basically to cover up underlying problems" of inequality.

While the 1960s provided American-born activists with new political orientations within a nexus of historical and racial dynamics, new Chinese activists were busy with different trajectories of migration, movement, and becoming. Many were recently arrived foreign exchange students or young working professionals. Many more were still in transit, and none was a citizen. For them, the dynamic process of integrating into a new society, shaped by both structural elements and their own participation as citizens with common U.S. experiences, was yet to come. They witnessed the widespread student demonstrations of the 1960s, but, not to put too fine a point on the discussion, they simply didn't understand what was involved in the struggle for civil rights and racial equality. Sam watched from the sidelines with a sense of bemusement: "It was pretty amazing to me," he says. "I thought, gosh, it was the sixties. I couldn't imagine [that] people, black and white, couldn't go into the same restaurant. I was shocked. I couldn't believe that. I thought America was at the forefront of democracy. I was shocked that there was so much discrimination in this country!" Larry recalls violence on his college campus but had no compassion for students who were squandering a valuable American education—one he felt grateful to experience. "The [police] had riot gear on, and they shot at students; they chased students," he says. "I saw that . . . the actual physical danger. I think they're [students] wasting their time. I take the conservative view—they come to the university, there's this opportunity, why were they wasting it away? I did not get it, and I was not sympathetic. My reaction was, I was lucky to be here and I'm not complaining." Kenton echoes those sentiments and sees elements of disloyalty. "Gee, what's all this rioting?" he asks. "I mean, don't you know what's out there in the *rest* of the world? You're so lucky and you're rioting here. What's wrong with you? It's your country. Why are you doing this? You have a country to fight for. Why aren't you fighting *for* your country? I didn't have a country." For new activist Leonard, his view of an idealized American history and the sense of "belonging to a country where you can build, you can make it prosperous and you can make it strong" didn't fit with what he saw in the streets. "I didn't really understand about civil rights. My idea of America was equality. Movies talk about blacks and their problems, but you thought that was already in the past."

No Longer Clueless

As new Chinese activists and professionals begin to establish themselves, however, they are confronted with their difference. For the first time, they experience group membership and a citizenship bounded by race and foreignness. It is quite a shock. Sam's initially positive vision and expectation of law enforcement helping citizens rapidly deteriorated into cynicism and anger when he began a small import/export business and saw how white police treated Asians.

> It was pretty bad. I'm sure if we were another group, if we looked different, if we looked white, they [the police] would have thought it was a good thing!
>
> [T]hese white motorcycle cops . . . a lot of families come shopping with their kids, and they got their cars towed away! This motorcycle guy was *so* brave! He was speeding from one end of the street to the other just to make sure everybody had a parking ticket! I never saw them so brave chasing robbers!
>
> They didn't care about us. They'd say, "Hey, whatcha guys doing here?" It was too much. They said, "Hey, the civilian politicians are out of town until Monday, and we're going to show you who's in charge now!" They got very hostile. They don't understand what we're doing, a bunch of foreigners.

Leonard's reckoning left him feeling shaken and powerless. "I was walking down Del Amo Boulevard in Torrance," he says. "Two white guys, long hair, dirty, walked by me and bumped me really hard and said some racial epithets. I was so mad! These guys were trying to hurt me. I got into my car and I drove around and looked for them. It really bothered me. I was absolutely shocked! This had never happened to me before."

Nonphysical confrontations are just as numbing. At Lena's first job at the credit union, she became a scapegoat for anything that went wrong:

> I worked very hard . . . [and] after a year got promoted to head cashier. You have to balance things to the penny. You cannot have one penny more or one penny less. When that happens, nobody goes home. You have to find that penny. Now I know it's not my fault, but they *always* tried to blame me, that it's all my fault. They wouldn't have dared say that if I wasn't different.

Franklin found that being a naturalized citizen and practicing attorney didn't stop his being racialized. "The first time I showed up in court," he says, "the judge, *in open court*, said something like, 'What are you foreigners doing here?' I felt *so* embarrassed! So many times, the clerks never thought I was the lawyer; they thought I was the *client*! I mean how many Chinese American lawyers were there [in 1979] who spoke English with accents?" Naturalized activists know that their accents, foreign-sounding names, or appearance are key markers of difference, but they are still unprepared for the consequences of mainstream society's judgments. Stanton says that he learned about people of color in corporate America from an African American boss of his. With his mentoring, Stanton finally broke through the glass ceiling to become one of the first naturalized Chinese executives in his American company.

> He knew what I could do and the story about me getting passed over. He said to me, "When I put your name up, nobody said much, except one guy said, 'Hmmm, well, you're a good engineer, works hard, gets good results, but how about his *presence*?'" And my boss, being black, he really blew up. He knew what he meant.
> He made this guy get the dictionary and look up the word *presence*! That shocked me because he meant that I looked different. It's subconscious racism. This guy had in his mind what a vice president should look like—not like a Chinese.

Stanton took his cue from his boss. He realized he had a responsibility to bring others like himself into the company, but he got minimal support.

> The personnel guy told me we have a hard time recruiting. I said, "But we have a lot of applicants. Show me all the résumés we got." He started showing me résumés. You know what he was doing?
> He said, "This guy is Lo Wen Chang," and he's throwing down the packet. "This guy is C. Fong," and he's throwing down the packet. I said, "What the *hell* are you doing?" He said, "These are foreigners." I said, "How the *hell* do you know they're foreigners?" He said, "Look at the name!"

Marlon is an immigrant from Hong Kong. He finished college and law school in the United States during the 1970s and now specializes in international business law. He is in demand at professional and community events, though his take on global political and economic conditions is not always received in the manner he expects.

> When the Hainan incident happened,[6] I went to a debate in Orange County. I don't know whether she was naïve or stupid or what, but the hostess asked me to put on a *Mao* jacket and Mao cap! I took one look at this and threw them into the trash. I said, "*I'm an American. I'm not kid-*

ding, I'm an American, I'm an American!" After the debate, I had to check
to see if my tires were punctured.

Thus, though new Chinese activists possess degrees from the "right"
schools, have the "right" professional credentials, or live in the "right" neighborhoods, the ideological entanglements of race and citizenship act to marginalize them no matter how much socioeconomic capital and success they
have. And as Stanton's experience shows, they are also subjected to a perhaps
"unintentional but often condescending approach" when they don't fit the
mold of what white America expects from its executives and professionals
(Cose 1993). Similar to the argument that Ellis Cose (1993) makes about
African Americans with similar credentials, naturalized Chinese now occupy meritorious positions and have succeeded in business, so *what* is white
America complaining about? As W. E. B. DuBois said about the twentieth
century, the problem of the twenty-first century is still the problem of the
color line; and in the continuing struggle for equity, a number of naturalized
activists have come to believe that color-conscious social and governmental
policy is still paramount in counterbalancing that which has become color
blind (Appiah and Gutmann 1996; Cose 1993). This borders on familiar
ground already tread by 1960s progressives.

These are new ideologies for many naturalized Chinese activists, yet they
present a major source of commonality with native-born activists. Over
time and through the process of building collective memory and experience, their shared history in the United States is given life and value. In
tandem with the construction of common experiences lies a shared agenda
that can be used to "generate purpose and goals, bind people together and
create a sense of legitimacy for a movement" (Saito 1998, 62). Moreover,
new Chinese activists are very aware of how the politics of belonging ideally
ought to be performed in this country. It is that ideal which propels them
into collective action.

Testing the Political Waters

David Lang was still a graduate student from Hong Kong, finishing his
doctorate at the University of Southern California, when he was introduced
to Mike Woo via some friends who said they wanted to work on a political

campaign. When Lang found out that the candidate didn't speak Chinese, he volunteered to help.

Before the late 1980s, English was the lingua franca at pan–Asian American community events in Southern California. Only rarely would a sentence or two in an Asian language be interjected. That began to change with the influx of new immigrants. Not only that, but ethnic-specific events were becoming more common, as new immigrants tested the waters of political organization where they felt most comfortable—in their own ethnic communities. By the early 1990s, when Woo was running for mayor of Los Angeles and again a few years later for Los Angeles City Council, he was making the rounds of separate fund-raisers in the Korean, Chinese, Japanese, Thai, South Asian, and Vietnamese American communities.

During the 1990s, for example, the Thai American community in Southern California had become politicized over the issue of official recognition of Thai Town, a stretch of mini-malls and businesses in east Hollywood. The combined efforts of a number of Thai organizations and Woo's input finally achieved success in the mid-1990s when the City of Los Angeles erected small street signs designating the area as Thai Town. Thai leaders, including some who lived as far away as Orange County, repaid Woo's help by becoming ardent supporters of and contributors to his political campaigns. During his last, unsuccessful run for city council, Woo held his election night party at a Thai restaurant in east Hollywood.

Lang's ability to speak Mandarin allowed Woo to penetrate another constituency that differed both culturally and generationally from his own roots. Although Woo's grandparents were Cantonese immigrants, they would not recognize the newcomers now populating the political landscape. Lang's role as bridge builder and cultural broker was a life-altering event in his political education. He was part of something entirely new, and he was hooked.

> I had no idea about American politics, about local politics. I got educated very fast. I went to many community events and different groups every night. If [Woo] couldn't go, I'd go and represent him. I remember one of the first was the Asian Pacific American Legal Center banquet. Five, six hundred people! I was shocked! I said, "Wow, there's a big Asian community here in Los Angeles!"
>
> I didn't realize there were so many different groups of active Asians. And very diverse—those who were very successful, and those who weren't, and

those who live at the margins of politics . . . it was just fascinating. I never finished my Ph.D.—I've never looked back.

Lang's focus on international relations and foreign policy melded with his new interest in local politics. After the Woo mayoral race, Lang became one of the founders of CAUSE (see Chapter 5).

Since that first campaign, Lang has worked on a number of different, locally based campaigns. He now has his own business in strategic communications and political consulting. He believes that the power of numbers can effect social change, but the numbers are very complex, with the differences between Asian Americans almost unbreachable.

> We Chinese have so much division. You're from Hong Kong, you're from Taiwan. We speak different dialects. It's Chinatown versus Monterey Park. So how do you bring all these people together? You need some kind of structure, and if you're going to talk about political empowerment, you need that kind of structure and you need money!
>
> And then there's ABCs [American-born Chinese]. When it comes to running for office, ABCs still have the edge. You guys [the ABCs] speak much better English than immigrants, and you can mainstream and integrate much better. You guys feel more at home; you guys have more friends here. Like Mike [Woo], although he has yellow skin . . . I bet 70 percent of his friends are white, 30 percent are Chinese.

Lang's early immersion in the Asian American community gave him a unique perspective on progressive Asian American politics. Although he still believes in ethnic-specific political organization, he also thinks that, in wider arenas, a pan-Asian identity is necessary for attaining recognition and resources. His politicization as an activist was an early call and one not shared by most other new activists, who generally got involved over 20 years or more.

The first step toward individual participation and then group organization builds from the conscious choice new activists make to become citizens of their new country. After that, they focus primarily on finishing university and postgraduate educations and establishing themselves as entrepreneurs or professionals before they become activists. By contrast, many American-born activists were still college students who challenged the nature of university education as an "abstract curriculum that ignored contemporary social issues" (Reuben 1998, 153).

Naturalized activists experienced political processes before immigration, but theirs are memories of politics as anathema. They were not participants as much as they were escapees. They were also observers of the paradigm shifts of the 1960s, but again, not participants. It is their not-so-subtle early experiences as racialized individuals in the United States coupled with the imagined ideals of American freedom that are the catalysts for their future political work. They come to understand that American democracy not only offers the choice of participation but in many cases mandates citizen involvement. Those who don't get involved have no voice. Sam found that the process and the possibility of participation are encouraged in a way he had never experienced:

> This is the idea here—that democracy ought to be brought to the people, to get more and more people involved. In that sense, you don't have to look for politics, politics will be looking for you in ways that can affect your community or affect your business or Chinese Americans. If you know something about these [issues] and don't speak out, and somebody who doesn't know anything makes a decision *for* you . . . then what?

The Basics of Network Support

Two kinds of grassroots networks that are instrumental in framing discussion of "from-below" political organizing—pan-Asian groups and those that are ethnic-specific—emerge in the Asian American community. Neither can be treated independently; together they constitute common experiences that both foreign-born and native-born Asian Americans share and are part of the wider tent under which Asian American political identities reside.

Pan-Asian networks have been common in the primarily American-born Asian community since the 1960s. In their first, tenuous forays into political activity, naturalized activists like Lang seek membership in pan-Asian organizations such as Woo's political campaign. Former Monterey Park mayor Lily Chen remembers what she calls her introduction to Asian American politics in the early 1980s: Tom Noguchi, the first Asian American coroner of Los Angeles County, had been demoted for the second time, and Asian American groups rallied for his reinstatement.[7] Chen says she knew other Asian Americans who were getting involved, so she did, too. She felt kinship because Noguchi was also foreign-born and spoke with an accent. She took part in public demonstrations organized by a pan–Asian American group of social workers. "That was my first introduction to so-called Asian American togetherness," she says, "my first experience about how we could all get together to fight as an Asian group."

By the latter part of the 1980s, ethnic-specific networks were beginning to emerge in the newer grassroots of the ethnoburbs. Started by natural-ized activists, this political activity sprouted in the backyards of neighbor-hoods where new Chinese activists lived and where circles of professional and social networks intersected. After nearly a decade of U.S. citizenship, and perhaps another decade of solidifying businesses and family life, natu-ralized Chinese activists began to challenge and engage dominant discourses in ways that drew on their own brand of agency. Seeing similar work con-ducted by Asian American community organizers was also a way to learn about political participation in the United States.

Naturalized activists worked on projects that were local, with expected outcomes that were also local; but at the same time, and in ways not part of a progressive Asian American repertoire, new Chinese activists capitalized on the transnational. In the same way that transnational businesses became embedded in the fabric of existing communities in the San Gabriel Valley, the new activists utilized their transnational social networks and connec-tions. This was not necessarily to revolutionize dominant power so much as to force inclusion. The grassroots, from-below political work that unfolds in the following pages is performed specifically as a means of decentering, re-sisting, and reformulating the borders of dominant discourse—in this case, in the arena of public education.

South Pasadena via Beijing

A period of breakneck development and settlement begun by Midwestern-ers—many from Indiana—formed the core of the City of South Pasadena, which incorporated in 1888. Advertising from the railroad companies pro-moted "South Pas" as *the* place to buy a home. Despite its proximity to downtown Los Angeles, today it still possesses a small-town atmosphere, with tree-lined streets and Craftsman-style bungalows. For the past 40-plus years, the 25,000 residents of South Pasadena have made national head-lines, united as they are in a political battle to save their town from being plowed under by the extension of the 710 Freeway. Less well publicized is the fact that in the past two decades, South Pasadena has become more than 25 percent Chinese American. Just five minutes away, and along a straight line down Fremont Avenue, is Monterey Park. During the 1980s, new Chinese immigrants began to look for less crowded neighborhoods like those in South Pasadena. Proximity to Monterey Park, good schools, and the suburban atmosphere were high on the list of qualities that defined desirable areas for naturalized activists, many of whom were parents of young children.

Paul Zee and his wife liked South Pasadena right away for its quiet streets, and in the early 1980s, housing was affordable there. But even a new house was secondary to finding good public schools for their children, and South Pasadena seemed the answer. The district was small, with only five schools, including one high school. Parental involvement was an important part of ensuring children's education, so a few newly arriving Chinese parents started joining the town's parent-teacher association (PTA). Through networking, a nucleus of concerned Chinese American parents evolved. Some already knew one another through business contacts, and still others met while shopping at the local supermarket or attending school events. Parents began meeting socially and informally, at a weekend barbeque, for example, to talk about their families and how the kids were doing in school.

In 1988, the district's teachers went on strike. Zee says parents were aghast to see picket lines and children not in classes. It was an event that galvanized the Chinese parents. "A bunch of us said we have to form a group and some kind of organization so we can go to the school district and voice our opinions collectively," Zee says. "And that was the birth of the South Pasadena Chinese American Club [SPCAC]." It must also be pointed out, however, that although the strike provided critical impetus for coming together, more amorphous feelings of alienation had been building for some time. Veronica had also moved to South Pasadena a few years earlier. She became involved in school activities through her two children and eventually joined other friends as one of the original board members of SPCAC, which she calls the "Chinese PTA." Veronica says the teachers made very little effort to include her and other Chinese parents:

> I feel like they [teachers] don't know how to deal with us. We wanted to liaise with the school so we can become part of the whole system. Because we weren't.

I can see it in my kids. When I picked them up or dropped them off, they both told me, "Mommy, don't speak Chinese!" "Mommy, don't wave at us! I know you're there!" I don't know what happened to them, but they felt the pressure, they felt the embarrassment.

Members make it clear that the SPCAC was formed not as a social club but as a means for them to intervene in larger discourses—an eminently political motive. Once the strike was settled, the SPCAC did not disband but became active in the small school district. Initially, group formation was fashioned from two perceptions. First, there was a perceived assault on the main reason that many Chinese moved into South Pasadena—*quality of life* (Sanjek 1998). School problems threatened that. Second, the parents realized that their position, or lack of it, left them excluded and without power to influence any decisions the school district made. Even after organizing, the club existed outside the educational and political establishment of South Pasadena. As in Monterey Park, the infusion of Chinese Americans in South Pasadena's conservative core was an unsettling experience. But club members persisted in attending board meetings and informally meeting with schoolteachers and other officials.

Over a period of a few years, the SPCAC worked its way into becoming a familiar and integral presence in the city's public arena. Its increasing influence also coincided with growing numbers of Chinese American students in the district. This helped to reinforce a negotiated and collective identity that the club was trying to promote. At the same time, the school district and other dominant discourses evolved to make a place/space for these new social interactions. References to the club began appearing with greater frequency in the local newspaper, city council meeting agendas, and city celebrations.

It is also highly significant that the SPCAC used its transnational social networks to penetrate and change the dominant discourse—the teachers' lack of knowledge and ease in relating more fully with the Chinese American community. After the strike, club members met to talk about how Chinese American parents could continue to have access and even greater effect when issues of policy and administration were discussed. Members made the decision to raise funds for the schools. Some of the donations would help provide scholarships, but the club also took a very direct approach to fund all-expenses-paid field trips to Asia for the district's teachers. They labeled the field trips "Dragon Tours." To immerse teachers and even their own American-born children in the Asia that the parents wanted to present, club members called personal and business contacts in China and Taiwan to set up the tours, which would include more than the usual tourist attractions like the Great Wall. Transnational social connections were pressed into service to arrange visits to local schools in China, to meet and talk with Chinese teachers, and to watch student performances. Other acquaintances arranged hotel and hostel accommodations for the California visitors.

Veronica says the Dragon Tour was one of the most important SPCAC programs and, needless to say, was met with great enthusiasm. Parents took turns as leaders on the trips. One year, Veronica found herself shepherding 36 students and teachers. "The teachers, they were all white, had never been to China," she says. "They *loved* it! It really opened up their eyes to Chinese culture. It was a great opportunity for them. We went to Beijing, Xi'an, Guangzhou, Taiwan, and Hong Kong—14 days."

The concept of transnational *life* (R. Smith 2000) allows for an unpacking of what the Dragon Tours meant to these parents and why they saw the trips as an important part of their local lives. The emphasis on *life* makes for a more intimate, lived, everyday experience. In this sense, transnational life is a quotidian affair from below; it is out of sight but not entirely hidden from larger economic or political influences. And although it keeps the focus on local lived processes, transnational life also acknowledges important, ongoing social practices that form links and connections with people in the home country. These practices have significant meanings that embody aspects of identity. While the parents were immersed in the local issues of South Pasadena educational politics, they continued to have common imaginings of China and the important elements of Chinese culture. These imaginings were transformed into concrete travel plans whereby group identity was affirmed.

The teachers who were selected to travel with the club were literally unmoored from their local everydays and transported into unfamiliar territory. Role reversals in Asia about who was teaching whom, who was speaking for whom, and the creation of these roles in public spheres both in South Pasadena and in Asia also afforded Chinese parents a way by which to ground their status as participatory members of their American community. The ultimate goal was for participants to bring knowledge gained about Asia *home* to South Pasadena so that it might be integrated into the local setting. This local setting included not just the classroom but the myriad ways in which the tour became incorporated into the everyday lives of the teachers, who interacted with the wider community upon their return. In this sense, the valorization of racial and ethnic marginality—Chineseness—was an aggressive strategy for altering the hegemonic terrain and relations of power at home, in South Pasadena. Veronica says there is no doubt that the outlook of the teachers—not to mention that of the parents—changed after the tours. "I invited them to my house for a get-together to share pictures and stories," she says. "They were all very excited, and they all talked to the other teachers. I would never have invited them before. They told me, 'Oh, so many teachers want to go now!' And then we had a hard time picking after that! It's very positive feedback, and we really accomplished a lot."

By the early 1990s, SPCAC members had become regular fixtures at school board meetings and other community events, donating time and raising money for various charitable and civic causes such as the South Pasadena Public Library. An invitation to join a Dragon Tour (the selection process controlled by the SPCAC) became a prestigious honor. The club had become institutionalized in the community's educational hierarchy. The major fund-raising group for the area's schools is the South Pasadena Educational Foundation, and it now has formal ties with the SPCAC. By the 1990s, the election of Chinese Americans as members of the school board and even wider civic office had become commonplace.

This look at the underpinnings of transnational community life points to politicizing identities that seek reform, not revolution, in creating new social spaces. For new Chinese activists, political activities are all about contesting space for inclusion and negotiating membership as U.S. citizens within existing structures even if they have to create that first opening themselves. Wing Chung Ng (1999) looks at Canada, which has also undergone a dramatic influx of Chinese immigrants primarily from Hong Kong and Mainland China. Faced with similar cultural and racial obstacles to full inclusion, these new immigrants strategize identities in a fashion similar to those of Chinese Americans by also forging ethnic-specific projects designed to instill a sense of membership and mutual support. And they do so within official government policies that permit enactments of multiculturalism in prescribed contexts.

The activities of groups like the SPCAC inform new ways of analyzing immigrant adaptation. Where the transnational field intersects with this contestation for inclusion shows how one group of post-1965 naturalized

Chinese citizens is incorporating its members into their new American lives. For them, maintaining social networks and practices across borders becomes the normative path to incorporation.

Leveraging Leadership Capital

Another important benefit accrued to naturalized Chinese activists during the fledgling stages of ethnic grassroots organizing. The political work of initially creating group agency also produced enough mutual support for some members to assume leadership positions in wider discursive terrains.

Paul Zee was the first president of the SPCAC, an experience that taught him about the strengths of a collective voice. In 1989, a member of the club decided to be the first Chinese American to run for the South Pasadena School Board. One seemingly insignificant event during a strategy meeting crystallized Zee's thinking about political involvement.

> A middle-aged guy, a third-generation Chinese American—doesn't speak a word of Chinese, doesn't know how to write his name in Chinese—and quietly, he said one thing: "Are you sure we are accepted by the community?" And that thing *really* struck me. I thought, oh my god, one day if I have to leave my home, I can go back to China. I can go back to Hong Kong because at least I speak the language, and I can easily integrate into society there.
>
> But you don't have a choice! You are third-generation ABC. I just didn't realize this. I thought at the time the only thing I should be doing is my business and making money. I should build my sense of security on the zeros in my bank account. [But] what about my grandkids? One day they're going to think like that man, and that's sad. I was so shocked.

Zee's revelation registered on several levels. It clearly delineates the difference between himself and American-born Chinese and the fact that Zee saw ABCs, and therefore his own American-born children, as cultural captives with an inability to negotiate and work in a wider world. Naturalized activists do not consciously flaunt their bi- or tri-focality in across-border social spaces, but it does serve as a political marker and a part of their transnational lives. It is another instrumental strategy that enables them to dynamically negotiate the symbols of identity in the context of other social relations. Like other activists who initially recoiled from political involvement,

Zee focused primarily on taking care of his business and his family. But in fact, as a racialized citizen in the United States, Zee recognized that getting involved politically *is* taking care of family and business.

> I came to one conclusion—that conclusion is, you have to get involved. There are *no* other avenues here. You have to come out and participate so that you get to know each other and get to work with non-Asians, so that feeling, "Are we accepted by the community?" will go away. We are not accepted because we Asians are quote, unquote, *strangers* to them. Why would they trust us to run the schools? Why would they trust us to run the city? You are a foreigner!

Zee redoubled his efforts at community activities, and before long, he got noticed. The Latina mayor of the city appointed him as the first Chinese American on the city's planning board. In 1988, Zee found himself being recruited to run for city council. His conservatism on business issues appealed to the city's traditional political establishment. But even with the backing of city leaders, Zee found he was not welcome on the ballot.

> Every morning I opened my front door [and] there were eggs on my door. And people called me all kinds of racist terms. Somebody called me a Chink, a Chinaman, to my face! When I was walking precincts, "Why don't you go home, Chinaman!" Well, this *is* my home. Where do I go?
> "Why don't you go back to China?" is what they meant. I was afraid for my family. One morning, two in the morning, some guys—I saw their pickup—they had pulled up all the yard signs, 150 of them, and dumped them all in the front yard of my house.

Zee refused to quit. On election night, he remembers, the vote tally crawled. The last precinct to be counted was an area that his supporters called Paul Zee Town, the Monterey Hills area of South Pasadena where nearly two-thirds of the residents were Asian American and mostly naturalized Chinese immigrants like him. Voter registration outreach in the area had been intense, and Zee's candidacy fired up many formerly uninvolved Chinese Americans. It was Veronica's first political campaign. "A bunch of us in the South Pasadena Chinese American Club were all rooting for him," she says. "It was the first time I did precinct walking for anybody. We actually got out and walked around, me and another board member!" Zee won by fewer than 300 votes. He credits his victory to the SPCAC's efforts at getting Chinese Americans not just registered but voting. "Truly, it was touching, very moving," he says. "At 7:45 [polls close at 8 P.M.] people were telling me they were looking at polling places up in the Monterey Hills area—long lines, all Asian Americans. We were effective and drew a lot of attention. Even today, 12 years later, they [city residents] all know it's a group. We are now *the* deciding bloc vote in South Pasadena."

Former Monterey Park mayor Lily Chen has similar leadership training that helped to propel her into local politics long before most other Chinese American women. Although Chen was a social worker and had already been involved in Los Angeles County political issues such as the Noguchi firing, an event closer to home in Monterey Park provided the first impetus for her to participate in the wider community and assume leadership. The issue was also about educating her children. Chen was part of a group of women involved in the PTA; they raised money for a school auditorium through bake sales. Chen says she finally told them she had baked enough cupcakes and it was time to get state funding. "They decided I knew a little more than they did and that was it," she says. "After that, they wanted me to run for city council. They were about a dozen good friends, and among them they said, instead of talking to city council as a parent at the podium, why don't I *sit on* the [stage]? My friends at school were the first people to support me." Chen lost that first race for Monterey Park City Council but developed a web of support that enabled her to run again and win in 1982. Chen, Zee, and other naturalized Chinese activists who were involved in early grassroots organizations came to understand the power of informal sociality. The transformation into a more politicized, structured network and group agenda was not so very far removed from their first social networking.

Not Just Women's Work

It is worth noting that this collective and politicized experience was constructed from the involvement of both men *and* women. Although most naturalized Chinese activists are men, including those elected to political offices in suburban communities in the San Gabriel Valley, more women participate in political activities than might be expected.[8] The stage, of course, is much broader and populated by more actors than just those who are elected. By widening the discussion to include grassroots and volunteer activism, it is possible to see women's work and how their political actions come to be valorized, though not always acknowledged by them or by others around them. What might be considered "public" versus "private" ought not to be overly privileged. The kind of work that new-activist women perform is seen here as part of a much bigger discourse on women's activism that should not be depoliticized as some sort of private endeavor. Early new-activist organizing clearly shows the mutually constitutive aspects of both the public and the private and demonstrates that politicized terrain needs to be viewed as a seamless whole. The totality is not reducible; the constructions of new activists' politicized identities are part of one discourse equally informed by gender as well as class and race. These parameters specify and shape women's personal and political concerns, in the way they perform, and in the types of political activities in which they choose to participate (Bookman and Morgen 1988). The influence of women's political participation cannot be minimized.

In constructing activist life histories, it is evident that women have politicized family roots similar to men's and have been given opportunities by their parents to pursue means of social capital that are similar to if not commensurate with men's. Not a few have been given opportunities by their fathers to participate on an equal footing with sons or, in families without male heirs, to function as surrogate sons.

What is unusual about the activist women in this book is that once their children are school age, many choose a professional path and become involved in some form of real estate or property development. Part of the reason, they say, is that real estate draws more women in general, with its more flexible though not necessarily shorter hours. The flex time is attractive in that it allows mothers to be more directly involved in their children's education. It is also possible that women who want to continue to work find that this career is more acceptable to husbands. Lena's post-divorce embarrassment over her real estate career was perhaps more closely tied to the notion of *needing* to work to support herself and her children. Also, servicing other new Chinese immigrants who are putting down roots and purchasing homes is a way to literally construct community and to be closely integrated with on-the-ground issues such as quality of life and education. The emphasis is on amalgamating both public and private spheres in everyday actions. Women were instrumental in organizing those bake sales and backyard barbeques in a way that transformed the political landscape. Motherhood—and fatherhood—act as vehicles for resistance and social change and provide an important entry point for further participation in their communities.

Conclusion

In these examples of grassroots efforts and building leadership, what emerges first is a picture of new activists who are "keeping an eye on the block" by creating and fostering politicized organizing at the local level, where the ability to network and bring about social change is more easily accomplished (Pardo 1998, 198). Being political is related directly to being good mothers and fathers. Obstacles in the path of good parenting manifested in schooling their children reflect their own life histories in pursuit of all the opportunities offered by an American education. For many, early mobilizing around families and other existing social networks meant a base grounded in naturalized Chinese American neighborhoods as extensions of the family and the everyday actions that constitute family living. These everyday social interactions are really the backbone from which a collective identity is constructed. This truly local, neighborhood focus provides ground-up experiences in a smaller suburban setting quite removed from big city politicking and larger urban issues. Smaller cities have given naturalized activists new opportunities, a way to break in and achieve all-important access and effect that would not be possible in a larger setting. Mobilization can therefore be more finely directed, with results that are more rapidly and readily visible.

Also more visible is the early presence of involved Chinese American women whose roles as mothers and organizers were an important factor in leadership training. As Gregory (1998) and Pardo (1998) have observed, men and women perceive and partake of leadership in different ways. Chinese American women who capitalized on their gendered roles as part of their everyday lived experiences were effective in directing political change.

It is also noteworthy that some of these women have been given opportunities—indeed have been trained in their families and their communities—to fulfill political work as centerwomen. As Sacks (1988) has theorized, these are leadership roles that extend beyond commonly accepted notions of influence such as speaking or holding public office. Lynn's and Lily Chen's parents thrust them into public arenas at an early age to be leaders in their families. Veronica was one of the first leaders in the SPCAC.

The lessons learned during the 1980s are writ large in terms of the life histories of naturalized activists. These activists became aware of how racial differences compounded their status as immigrant citizens in the larger community and how this related to their lack of voice and representation. Action was built around this commonly perceived problem; common goals forged group membership. At the same time, this behavior was also a way to claim membership in community and to ensure that the claim is inclusive of the naturalized Chinese American experience.

In creating agency, the community-based work also led to the production of leadership positions and the social prestige that surrounds leaders. Members began to coalesce around individuals and, in the process, also got exposure and training. In this way, new players were drawn into the process, and the group became more solidified. As social action became more structured, the interjection of competing visions of community began to decenter dominant discourses. This decentering may be viewed two ways. On one hand, organized action accomplished its main goal of inclusion by adding naturalized Chinese Americans and their agenda to the repertoire of community actors. This was done through acceptable structures, and as with American-born Asian progressives, there was never any intent to overthrow existing frameworks of power. On the other hand, it didn't take long for dominant power structures, such as the "old boys' network" in South Pasadena that recruited Zee, to reassert power by plucking Zee from the SPCAC and placing him within the conservative political establishment. This is not unlike what many radical Asian American activists faced during the early 1970s and why they dropped out, criticizing the co-optation of progressives. But since domination is never absolute, these fledgling naturalized activist leaders were now in positions to pull others onboard with them.

In this way, people like Chen or Zee may be seen as catalysts for future organization, people who can carry the banner for other naturalized Chinese Americans. New Chinese activists did not jettison their racial identities in the process, nor would they have been able to do so. Self-definition meant continued reliance on their neighborhood bases and the social practices of other naturalized Chinese Americans even though it might also be argued that this resulted in the continued marking of difference while reproducing the general, hegemonic framework of established community politics.

Yet, in their unwillingness to accept ascribed constructions of identity marking them as racialized outsiders, new activists were aggressive in mobilizing politically over a relatively short time. They used models existing in other community organizations and grassroots causes, including those extant among progressive American-born activists. And, in a departure from traditionally based Asian American political projects, a significant amount of this new organizing relied on transnational networks. The next chapter explores the maturation and institutionalization of these grassroots beginnings.

FIVE

Coming of Age

Maturing New-Activist Political Identities

During the 1990s, the political activism of new Chinese became institutionalized in Southern California, and awareness of these new participants
as a political cohort and interest group grew. They were actively courted for
their personal and financial support, especially in the neighborhoods where
they interacted with local political institutions. Part of the response from
new activists was to formalize political and social ties through the dynamics
of collective action. CAUSE became the first large-scale, nonprofit political group in Southern California organized by a few of the post-1965 new
activists to provide a mechanism through which they and other like-minded
naturalized Chinese could participate politically. The electoral experience
of an American-born Chinese politician provided the catalyst linking their
own racial experiences as naturalized U.S. citizens to mobilization.

SUMMER 2003

Sitting in a downtown L.A. restaurant, David Lang is still second-guessing
some of the tactics in Mike Woo's 1993 campaign for Los Angeles mayor.
More than a decade has passed, but the defeat and the what-ifs are still
fresh. Lang's disappointment centers on the racialization of Woo by the
campaign of businessman Richard Riordan, or, more to the point, the
inability of the Woo campaign to effectively confront it. In particular,

Lang categorizes as dirty tricks the not-so-subtle hints portraying Woo as a foreigner.

> They used a picture of Hong Kong and they [intimated], "Do you want L.A. to be like this?" They used his connections to Cathay Bank. We should have sent a mailer out—let's get the record straight, media! Mike is an ABC, he has no connection with Hong Kong! Cathay Bank is *not* foreign owned; it's a local bank with local investors! I don't think we handled that well.

An uncritical observer picking over the remains of that campaign would see in Woo's continuing quest for public office the cobbling together of his traditional Asian American support and fund-raising base. But a closer look at the ground-level staging reveals that by 1992, a very different cast of characters like Lang and Winston was active. It was Winston's first real experience with helping someone get elected. He says that "Riordan took advantage of the ignorance of citizens toward Asian Americans" and the perception that Asian Americans are insular and don't care about politics.

Winston became a major, first-time fund-raiser for Woo. He wouldn't have done it had it not been for his friend Lang's personal endorsement of Woo. Within a few days, he collected more than $30,000 from among his acquaintances. Most of them were also first-time contributors, and Winston says that as he collected checks, he offered a civics lesson about prejudice and inequality, telling people, "You don't just come to this country and just think its Hong Kong! Here you have the right to vote, and you gotta get involved. You don't get involved, you're going to be discriminated against and you're going to be pushed aside. You know, this is America. You have the *right* not to be discriminated against."

Woo's loss left many of his naturalized supporters embittered and feeling disenfranchised. Fighting against apathy, a few nascent leaders translated the event into a pivotal point reaffirming their own status as citizen-participants, a process that sought common ground as new activists and new political organizers in the naturalized community. The first meeting of a small group at an El Monte coffee shop was fairly mundane, but Paul Zee says there was no denying that they wanted to do something about the Woo defeat and the racial aspects of the campaign.

> It was ugly. We said, "What's wrong?" We don't have a political machine. The original idea was to form a PAC [political action committee], but we

realized that a lot of people don't buy the idea of a PAC, and if they donate money, they want to make sure the money is tax deductible![1]

So, "Let's do a nonprofit first so it's easier to get the contributions to support the organization," and that was the birth of CAUSE.[2]

Lang pays more attention to a diachronic approach in describing the evolving need for a Chinese American political group.

I don't know whether it [the Woo campaign] was a major catalyst as much as it was a natural progression. You need some kind of structure, and if you're going to talk about political empowerment, you need that kind of structure and you need money. Just forming another OCA [Organization of Chinese Americans] wasn't enough.[3]

We were trying to learn our lessons about what went wrong with Mike's campaign, tried to think about how to do things in a more organized fashion. We need to play hardball politics.

CAUSE's overall goal, as is implied by its original name—Chinese Americans United for Self Empowerment—is political empowerment initiated and sustained by Chinese Americans. Its founders felt that collective action would gain them legitimacy, but the early political experiences of those like Zee and Lang also taught them about the importance of money. They believed that if they were to have any effect, they would have to be aggressive and they would have to raise funds. They put together an initial list of about 50 acquaintances—Chinese American activists and naturalized citizens like themselves who would each donate $1,000 for seed money. Thirty-seven people said yes and became founding members. The group was overwhelmingly made up of naturalized Chinese Americans who lived in and around the San Gabriel Valley.

THE BASICS OF A POLITICAL ORGANIZATION

The birth of CAUSE came just two months after Woo's unsuccessful bid for mayor. Within a few months, the organization had become a structured nonprofit corporation with 15 board members—11 men and four women—a mission statement, a newsletter, administrative staff, and temporary offices in Montebello. Ten board members were from Hong Kong, four were from Taiwan, and one was a first-generation American-born Chinese whose parents emigrated from Taiwan. The work of constructing CAUSE's public face went into high gear. Between August 1993 and May 1994, CAUSE and its members were involved in more than two dozen events, including political fund-raisers, news conferences, voter registration drives, educational outreach programs, and political forums.

The CAUSE leadership sought to enter wider discourses of political activism outside the San Gabriel Valley area. Part of this effort is attributable to a larger membership base, but the group also saw its mandate as filling a perceived void in Chinese American political leadership in Southern California. One of its first newsletters staked a claim to the content and construction of a politicized identity and the issue of representation: "We have all contributed a lot of time and money to CAUSE to ensure that CAUSE can truly be a voice for Chinese Americans. Our members, especially our directors, are all very well connected with all levels of government which will allow CAUSE to be more direct and effective in representing Chinese American issues" (D. Fong 1994).

The implication, of course, is that until CAUSE's inception, no one else had been speaking for Chinese Americans or at least not speaking loudly enough or with enough articulation. The historical sweep of Chinese American engagement in the United States had been minimized. Those active in CAUSE represented a new Chinese American interest group with less knowledge about the content of an earlier Chinese or Asian American history. They had fewer ties to American-born Chinese activists and widely divergent life histories even though they had had their own racial experiences. This perspective widened within two years as more progressive American-born Chinese joined CAUSE and added the contextualized voices of several generations of Chinese American experience to the agenda. In fact, broader experiences in mainstream events and activities and a more inclusive approach to American-born Chinese activists would ultimately transform the organization, but that was still several years in the future.

During the 1990s, most new activists were in their 40s and believed that they had the personal and professional acumen to act as representatives of the Chinese community. They were a mix of Hong Kong and Taiwanese immigrants who worked at subsuming regional and homeland political differences. Individually, members and supporters of CAUSE maintained strongly felt personal opinions on issues regarding Taiwan and Hong Kong—views well known to others. However, in public, the spotlight remained steadfastly centered on the local and on politically empowering Chinese Americans in

U.S. political arenas. No CAUSE newsletter mentions the return of Hong Kong to the mainland in 1997, despite the momentous nature of that event. Rather, newsletters highlighted issues such as voter registration, a visit by Vice President Al Gore, a briefing on racism and the continuing Democratic National Committee (DNC) fund-raising controversy (more on that below), and details about a CAUSE campaign workshop. A rare exception to "homeland" politics was the reprint of an article from the *Asian Wall Street Journal* arguing for a more enlightened U.S. policy toward China (CAUSE 1996).

For many early CAUSE supporters, the focus remained on making an imprint, not just within the new Chinese community where they lived and worked, but in numerous corporate and private boards and in organizations outside the Chinese American neighborhood. Then and now, the business and professional credentials of new activists, not to mention their ability to use their social capital to raise money, give them the means to gain access in different ways than radicals and progressive Asian American activists of the 1960s. This does not mean, however, that the playing field is level or that these negotiations are not performed from below within asymmetries of power.

WORKING THE ROOM

Excerpts from CAUSE Activities Reports between spring 1994 and summer 1998 reveal a long list of activities. The group's public face was seen mostly in Southern California. A yearly Celebration Dinner raised the bulk of the organization's operating funds from individual and corporate donations.[4] Individual members also sought wider arenas in the rest of the country and in Asia. CAUSE met with top California elected officials, U.S. Congress members, and presidential candidates. In addition, as the California economy became more globalized and integrated with businesses in Asia during the 1990s, new Chinese activists involved with CAUSE were in a position to utilize transnational networks and connections. They met with congressional representatives to discuss trade and immigration policy or were invited to travel frequently to Asia as members of official U.S. delegations. Some were appointed members of state boards dealing with Asian affairs.

These connections to Asia bring up a question regarding new Chinese activist involvement: How much does an agenda of empowerment such as donating to political campaigns have to do with simply promoting and protecting the entrepreneurial and transnational businesses in which many are involved? For some Asian American activists, this point has created much suspicion and angst about the "true" motives of new immigrant activists and their claims of representation. As L. Wang (1998) writes,

> . . . it becomes clear that they [new immigrant activists] represent the in-terests of a very small class of people within the Asian American communi-ties; a handful of rich business entrepreneurs and professionals and above all, persons with extensive connections to transnational Asian capital and multinational corporations. . . .
>
> This is hardly surprising: the overwhelming majority of Asian Americans do not have available cash. . . . In fact, the majority of Asian Americans fall within the lower and middle classes, desiring only to work hard to make ends meet and above all, to put their children through schools. (8)

The assumption that new immigrant activists and entrepreneurs who en-gage in political acts such as making financial donations have interests only in fortifying transnational economic lives is simplistic on at least two counts. First, the inference that they have no concern for family denies the early po-litical work that the new Chinese activists in this book accomplished. Noth-ing was more important to these Asian American parents than their children's education. Their transnational networks functioned both as an intercession-ary tool for contestation grounded in the local and as a way of successfully challenging tensions between their Chinese American experiences and those of predominantly white school districts. Second, the assertion that the ma-jority of Asian Americans don't have the money to make political contribu-tions and only want to work hard reifies stereotypes of nonparticipation and evades the Asian American political record. In fact, Asians Americans have historically given "more money to political parties per capita than any other constituency group except Jewish Americans" (Wu and Nicholson 1997).

Transnational social connections and the monetary contributions of im-migrant Chinese citizens form a much more complex equation. For this group of naturalized U.S. citizens, transnational life comprises new kinds of performances. These acts occur as part of a "repertoire of identities" and "the full potential of resources they have for constructing social selves" (Brodkin 2003, 57; Kroskrity 1993). The way in which activists exercise agency in fashioning ways of belonging and in legitimizing their citizenship cannot be labeled as either aberrational or dysfunctional. Moreover, transnational social practices are still grounded in the everyday and do not automatically evade the regulatory, taxonomic features and power of dominant structures. While this new American group asserts its citizenship, it also becomes another subjectified, controlled constituent group in wider power schemes.

"Working the room" at fund-raisers and meetings with those in power is, in itself, a contestation of and negotiation over inclusion. Beyond photo opportunities (not inconsequential for new activists who are quite literally making space for their politicized bodies in these pictures), face-to-face interaction also advertises an agenda.

In 1994, CAUSE moved quickly to involve Los Angeles County law enforcement after mailers intended to intimidate Chinese American voters were sent out in Monterey Park. The mailers were eventually traced to "anti-Asian activist organizations, as well as proponents of legalized gambling in Monterey Park" and were one of many "efforts to thwart Asian American political participation" (Shiao 1994, 1). As a new organization, CAUSE was largely a cipher in the wider Chinese American community. To call attention to the mailers, it held its first news conference. Copies of the mailers were distributed to print and electronic media, including Chinese-language news outlets, and sent to the offices of the L.A. County district attorney and the secretary of state, with whom CAUSE staff members had follow-up conversations. The decision of activist leaders to involve news organizations, particularly the transnational Chinese-language media based in the San Gabriel Valley, highlights CAUSE's role among new immigrants in furthering community formation and cohesion. CAUSE activities are routinely covered by Chinese-language newspapers and TV, whose subscribers live throughout Southern California and the United States. In this, the importance of forging the imaginary bonds of community consciousness clearly find purchase (Anderson 1991). (More later about the role of Chinese-language news media in validating transnational aspects of new immigrant communities and the activities of new Chinese.)

GENERAL ADVOCACY

During the past decade, CAUSE's agenda has expanded to include a wide range of issues, which can be divided into three broad categories: general advocacy, voter registration, and training future leadership.

Members have sought to place themselves as leaders in the Chinese American community by positioning CAUSE as the go-to organization on a myriad of Chinese and, more recently, Asian American issues such as immigration reform, affirmative action, and media stereotyping of Asian Americans. Other advocacy subjects include the following:

- Characterizations by white politicians of a naturalized Chinese citizen's understanding of English (1994).
- Letter to the *Los Angeles Times* pointing out that although the newspaper extensively covered the inaugurals of white politicians, it ignored the inaugural of California treasurer Matt Fong (1995).
- Immigration reform provisions targeting legal family reunification (1996).
- Debates on California Proposition 209 outlawing affirmative action programs (1996).
- Briefings on the Democratic campaign fund-raising scandal (1997).
- Stereotyping of Asian Americans by media and politicians (1997).
- Letter campaign in support of the prosecution of Richard Machado, convicted of hate crimes involving his sending e-mails targeting Asian American students at the University of California, Irvine (1998).
- Racial identities and the role of Asian Americans in public life (2002).

The organization is well known in the San Gabriel Valley, but recognition in the larger Southern California region, home to numerous and more established Asian American organizations, has come more slowly. For example, although not a political advocacy group per se, the Asian Pacific American Legal Center (APALC), headed by a progressive Chinese American man who came to the United States from China as a toddler, is seen as a representative of the Asian American community and often appears in media stories on Asian Pacific issues.[5]

VOTER REGISTRATION

CAUSE believes that "through voter registration we are able to involve, educate and enlighten Chinese Americans about the American society, and thus become better contributing citizens to our society" (*OUR CAUSE* 1997). It remains committed to a two-pronged focus on voter registration and education: staff members appear on Chinese-language television to emphasize the importance of voter education and participation among Chinese Americans, and it supports voter registration telephone hotlines in both Cantonese and

Mandarin that are aimed at increasing the presence of naturalized citizens at the polls. One of CAUSE's major challenges is getting those who register to actually vote on election day.

Although most would concede that registering voters one by one is per- haps not the best use of volunteer time, a number of new Chinese activists have spent hours standing outside venues like the busy 99 Ranch Market in San Gabriel where Chinese Americans shop. Lynn was an early CAUSE board member and is a strong believer in voting. She says she was deter- mined that her two American-born children share her belief. "In high school they were both out there in front of the market getting people registered," she says. "They looked at it like I'm forcing them to do it! 'Of course, Mom is *making* me do this!' But over the years, they now recognize the impor- tance of involvement."

During its most successful registration drives, CAUSE has signed up 300 to 400 new voters. It claims to have registered several thousand Asian Pacific American voters. Assuming that those registered get to the polls, they could represent a more than sufficient swing vote in many local races.

TRAINING FUTURE LEADERSHIP

CAUSE's education programs are also ways of contesting place/space. Like the SPCAC and its overseas trips, CAUSE also sponsors trips, albeit closer to home, to Sacramento. The itinerary includes capitol tours, legislative brief- ings, and meetings with lawmakers and other elected officials. Although the field trips are billed as opportunities for participants to become bet- ter acquainted with political processes, a more important goal is "to dem- onstrate to the policymakers, the unity of CAUSE and its strong interest in the well-being of the communities we call home" (*OUR CAUSE* 1995). Paid internships for college students in California are available through the Chinese American Students Internship Coalition (CASIC). The summer stipends range from $500 to $1,000 per student for the eight-week program. Students work in legislative and elective offices that include the California governor's and Los Angeles mayor's offices, the U.S. Congress, and the Cali- fornia State Senate and Assembly. Interns are required to keep a journal of their experiences both to monitor the program's effectiveness and to pro- vide students with an ongoing framework to contextualize what they have learned. This begins the work of mentoring future leadership and "exposes students to a deeper understanding of issues that impact the Chinese and Asian American community" (*OUR CAUSE* 2001).

Although the CASIC program is directed at leadership *development* among college students, the goal of CAUSE's one-day Political Institute is leadership *training*, particularly among those interested in seeking elective or appointive office. But as with most of CAUSE's other activities, the institute's underlying motive is what leaders call *engagement* with institutions and those representing power structures.

Race Trumps Ethnicity

The concept of engagement points to public arenas, where decisions are made about whose opinions and issues get vetted and approved for public discussion and consumption. This is an always evolving and contested site of negotiation both from above and from below. On one hand, the view from above shows how those with power to control narratives perceive Chinese Americans and draw out an essentialized Asian American political identity. On the other hand, the view from below reveals how Asian American political participants respond with their own counternarratives.

A Chinese American focus has begun to transform and reconstruct itself into a more broadly based perspective inclusive of an Asian American identity. In particular, there is recognition of a more progressive approach to social justice and equality that centers on discourses of race and a common racial identity that trumps ethnicity. This is a newer vision and as yet is shared by only some new activists. It has not been accomplished easily, nor is this transformative project yet complete. This newer pan–Asian American approach does not necessarily undermine or negate what is Chinese American. Co-positioning need not occur at the expense of a specific ethnicity but instead can enlarge the means by which multiple ways of resisting and transforming power are envisioned and enacted. And naturalized activists who are able to participate in transnational life find that their repertoires for contesting subaltern images can offer even more choice. "They now wield their power vis-à-vis the state to demand that it attend to their interests" (Mahler 1999, 89).

This development of a broader group racial identity among some new activists did not occur in a vacuum but, rather, as has already been discussed, as a response to an accumulation of life experiences in American civic and political life. It began to simmer during the early 1980s when new Chinese immigrants started to establish careers and families. By the late 1980s it boiled over as backlash in the transforming suburban Southern California communities where many of these immigrants lived. It continued apace during the 1990s. Two events discussed in greater detail below—the DNC fund-raising controversy in 1996 and the arrest of nuclear scientist Wen Ho Lee in 1999—were watershed events for new activists. Both offer further evidence of how racialized ascriptions affect new activists and subsequently determine strategies of empowerment beyond narrowly specific ethnic categories. A critical ingredient in this racialization is the admixture, in the past two decades, of global tensions between the United States and China and corresponding national narratives portraying China as a threat. For activists like Lily Chen, the specter of China as an economic and military competitor to the United States is never far from sight. "Americans are not supposed to look the way we do," Chen says. "Our problems [as a community] are being compounded by the threat of China. If you're Chinese, you must be stealing and spying for China. That's why it's very important for Asian Americans to get involved."

SUPERPOWER HEGEMONIES AND CULTURAL BROKERING

Constructions of Asia have historically marked Americans of Asian ancestry as foreign. Scholars note that this alien status has been a formalized political and legal condition as well as an equally powerful cultural position within narratives of belonging. Each is constitutive of the other (R. Lee 1999). The twenty-first-century incarnation is the growing influence, and potential threat, of a Communist Chinese superpower, whose manifestations are now common fare in mainstream media discourses. As an article in the *New York Times* put it, "The Bush administration can couch Beijing's new role in whatever politically advantageous language it wishes, but ultimately, it comes down to this: China's influence is rapidly rising and America's is rapidly declining" (Shaplen and Laney 2004).

Despite the inherent risk, many new Chinese activists accept and see themselves as cultural brokers and mediators in global U.S.–China relations. Many like Stanton are worried about what could happen.

> I think the U.S.–China relationship is the most important relationship on earth in the next 50 years. If that thing's not right, we're in bad trouble, everybody on this earth. If we ever fight a war with China . . . oh. [*He stops.*]

You cannot change your face. Americans still think you're a foreigner. I believe we as Chinese Americans, especially people with our backgrounds, should be catalysts for promoting understanding. Like a bridge.

At their most cynical, new activists like Franklin are aware of being convenient cultural pawns. "It reminds me of [the film] *The Last Emperor*," he says, "when the guy was made the Manchu emperor and he was in Communist China. He said he wasn't going to be a stooge anymore for the propaganda machine. And he was told, 'Well, aren't you lucky you are still being used?'"

Leonard, who experienced China's power as a teenager in Hong Kong, says Chinese Americans need to be savvy in identifying allies outside the community who also stand to benefit from the relationship between the United States and China.

We need to learn to play the game smarter. . . . "We" meaning Chinese Americans. There's always some kind of anti-Chinese group, but there are [those] who are benefiting from this growing Chinese/American relationship, and we need to identify those people. Companies like Boeing, Johnson & Johnson are big in China. It's a proactive stance.

How many planes does Boeing sell to China? You know, lots of people are investing in China, and they don't want to see deterioration in the relationship. We need to start looking at these things strategically . . . not wait till something happens and we all scramble.

American-born progressives, like Mike Eng, willingly cede the broker's role to those naturalized activists who are able to more broadly strategize. Speaking before the Organization of Chinese Americans in Los Angeles in 2001, Eng talked about the limitations of a strictly local focus.

I'm concerned that some of us, and that includes me, are so local in our scope that we miss the big picture. We need to live locally but think globally. And those of you whose experiences bridge two cultures or more, two continents or more, you take the lead in answering. No one can tell us to go home because America *is* our home now even though we were born in a different country!

Even when American-born activists do not share the same degree of concern over foreign relations, those like Brent are still highly aware of the negative racializing effects engendered by problems between Asian nations and the United States. "My attitude towards China is going to be far removed from [that of naturalized immigrants]," he says. "But do I believe that things can turn in an instant against Asian Americans? I will *always* believe that. Never get too comfortable here while you're a minority." At its most basic, the core of the new activists' perception of their citizenship and their activism is the realization that the geopolitical will always influence how they are seen and judged in American society. And if history is any indication, then future relations between the United States and China will, without doubt, have an impact on the entire Asian American community.

During the 1990s, those activists who got caught in the net of suspicion cast against a geopolitical backdrop were forced to rethink their positions as citizens and to reevaluate strategies of group empowerment.

THE COLOR OF MONEY

Democratic National Committee chairman Joe Andrews is looking around the gathering of Asian American Democratic activists attending the 2000 Democratic National Convention in Los Angeles. He is no doubt wondering what kind of reception he'll get as he tries to mend fences among the political faithful. "Our party has stumbled with Asian Pacific Americans," he says, "but when you stumble, you get up and run again. *We* are America, we welcome everyone. We don't care *what* color you are!"

The loudest applause is from the leaders of the Asian Pacific Islander Caucus, whose job is to rally the troops at the party's nominating convention. There is less reaction at the back of the room, and someone whispers, "Was that an apology?" Andrews has already left the room. Despite the applause, many of the Asian American delegates are far less enthusiastic about DNC efforts to clean up what they see as the inexcusable mistakes of the 1996 fund-raising scandal. Most believe that racial discrimination was at the heart of the controversy. But by the time the Democrats meet in Los Angeles, 1996 is old news, yet another chapter in the history of racialized politics. The focus is on keeping the Democrats in the White House.

. . .

The 1990s will be remembered as the decade during which new activists came of political age and made the leap into the consciousness of larger national political structures. In 1996, the quadrennial U.S. political project was electing the president of the United States. As citizens, many new activists affirmed their democratic right to take part in this national process by making campaign contributions; they had learned that giving money to support issues and candidates is one of the major ways business gets done in U.S. politics and policymaking. For instance, at public functions like the 2000 CAUSE Political Institute in Los Angeles, a California state official told the audience: "You either have to have money or you have to have votes. If you don't have money and you don't have votes, then nobody gives a shit about you, and that's the way it is!" Contributing funds is one method by which a marginal, unacknowledged status can be contested and a new social space/place can be created; many believed that giving to a candidate was another "form of expression and free speech" (U.S. Commission on Civil Rights 1998, 33).

New capital flows and politics create strange bedfellows. During the 1990s, the imprint of new, more flexible regimes of accumulation began to reconfigure traditional sources of Asian American contributions. The imposition of new-activist political players afforded opportunity but also great risk for Asian Americans participating in the 1996 reelection campaign of Bill Clinton. The insatiable beast of campaign finance is always alert to additional food sources; money from new communities of primarily naturalized Chinese Americans was a fresh menu item. Asian Americans became the unlikely new moneybags for national political parties (Nakanishi 1991). If giving money is part of a definition of political participation, then Asian Americans can hardly be considered politically apathetic. But the frustration, well known among the politically active, is that they haven't been able to make their contributions count toward enough recognition or empowerment with dominant political structures like the national parties. "Asian Americans have always been tapped for our financial resources but not for our human resources"—this from U.S. Secretary of Commerce Norm Mineta speaking to a group at the 2000 Democratic National Convention in Los Angeles. A poll of Asian American attendees, aimed at descriptively gauging sentiment on a variety of political issues, found a high degree of dissatisfaction on whether they got their money's worth when they contributed to candidates, political parties, or issues (see Appendix 1, Table 1).

The Democrats were particularly aggressive in trolling for new sources. Instead of tapping an American-born Asian, they picked John Huang, a naturalized Chinese immigrant and mid-level Clinton appointee in the

Commerce department, as DNC finance vice chair. Huang is from China, grew up in Taiwan, and lives in Southern California. His life history mirrors that of many of the constituents he was trying to reach. He was seen as a power broker capable of creating change in political structures and was applauded by community groups. In 1994, CAUSE presented its first annual Citizen of the Year award to Huang, one of its founding members, "who is a role model for all of us. . . . We are proud to have John as our representative of the Chinese American community in Washington" (*OUR CAUSE* 1994b).

Huang crisscrossed the country, mining campaign gold. At one Los Angeles–area event, hundreds of Asian American donors, including many new Chinese activists, responded to Huang's invitation and crowded the upscale Century Plaza Hotel in Century City. Huang eventually raised more than $7 million in "soft money" alone.[6] The problem was that Huang and others, like Maria Hsia, another naturalized citizen, also raised about $2 million from illegal or questionable sources.[7] Embarrassed and in a panic to rectify the situation before the elections, the DNC began auditing contributions from Asian American donors, culling their last names from donor rolls. Although the DNC denied it, Asian Americans believe strongly that there was racial targeting (see Appendix 1, Table 2). According to testimony at hearings conducted by the U.S. Commission on Civil Rights, white contributors with names like Lee were also investigated. In other words, the net was cast far and wide for anyone with an Asian-sounding surname, citizenship aside.

Stanton was a regular contributor to Democratic campaigns and gave generously to Clinton's reelection in 1996. He had finally made it into top management at his company after a protracted battle with the glass ceiling.

> I was a vice president . . . beautiful building, corner office, sitting in there with my secretary outside. *Boom, boom,* on my door! A lady came in and flashed her FBI badge. "Did you contribute to Clinton on this day, on that day there?" It was *crazy!* "And where did *you* get the money?" I said none of your business!
>
>   This is mahogany row at my company. All the senior executives there. This lady is dodging past my secretary. I had to explain to everyone what happened. She just barged in. She asked if I was a citizen. It made me mad! They just looked at my name. She didn't even have the courtesy to give me a call. This was terrible.

Charlie Woo, who has also supported numerous Democrats and eventually became chair of CAUSE, euphemistically refers to his 1996 experiences as "challenging."

> They asked me, "Are you a citizen? How do you make your money? How much is your income? Can you give me your Social Security number so we can verify your financial status?" I said, if you ask Barbra Streisand that question and *she* gives her number, then I will! They said, "OK, if you don't cooperate, we have to release your name to the public, and if the public concludes you have something to hide, then you have a big problem!"
>
> Jesus! This is scary! Pretty soon the FBI came, and then the Senate investigator, and I was subpoenaed for the grand jury. I was worried about my kids, they were eight or nine at the time. An FBI agent called me [at home] and left a message. . . . My kids said, "Dad, are you OK?" I said of course I was OK, there was nothing wrong. [But] they had my telephone records, financial records—all because of my last name.[8]

Presidential candidates like Ross Perot weighed in on the "foreigners": "Now then, Mr. Huang is still out there hard at work for the Democrats. Wouldn't you like to have someone out there named O'Reilly? You know, so far we haven't found one American name" (Wu and Nicholson 1997, 1).

Media agitprop reported sensational stories under headlines referring to "Chop Sueygate," insinuating that the "Asian Connection" favors "hungry foreigners" and "people whose ties to this country are tenuous" (Safire 1996). White politicians were caricatured as "Manchurian candidates" with buckteeth, thick glasses, monks' robes, and begging bowls (Lowry 1997). Those who contributed and those who collected were accused of being involved in everything from breaches of national security to foreign influence peddling and spying for China. In fact, suspicion and concern about China's alleged spying and influence on domestic politics had been brewing a decade before the DNC fund-raising controversy.

Already widely argued by the early 1990s in political and media circles was China's testing of miniaturized nuclear warheads—how and when Beijing had gotten the technology to conduct such testing. Putting aside the more basic question of whether or not Beijing actually had a feasible mini-warhead, the discourse assumed that, at its worst, China had a deep espionage network in the United States intended not just to spy but to influence U.S. policies. At best, U.S. companies were giving the Chinese help in contravention of U.S. laws (Schmidt 1999). The former scenario became the preferred conclusion. On the opening day of the Senate investigative committee's televised hearings into campaign finance in 1997, committee chairman Republican Fred D. Thompson linked alleged illegal actions by China and Chinese Americans' fund-raising for the Democrats. Thompson said that investigators had found evidence of "high level" Chinese officials plotting to "pour illegal money into American political campaigns" to "subvert our election process" (Walsh and Gugliotta 1997). Thompson's statement was disputed by Democratic senators on the committee, as were allegations by other Republican senators that some Chinese American fund-raisers were guilty of spying for China (Walsh and Gugliotta 1997).

Congressional leaders could not distinguish U.S. companies from transnational corporations accumulating capital here and elsewhere.[9] Neither were they able or willing to differentiate between American-born Asians, foreign-born Asians who had become naturalized citizens, and Asians. Without question, Asian Americans saw these characterizations as racist and a painful, frightening reminder about who qualifies as American (see Appendix 1, Table 3).

Asian Americans were not able to control narratives of the scandal. Their collective resistance to these negative characterizations received far less public attention. As posited earlier regarding naturalized activists' vision of democracy and the pact that is supposedly forged with citizenship, the core of this resistance was a contestation over the rupture of the ideal—"the long-standing tension between the First Amendment freedom of expression and the Nation's commitment to equality for all people" (U.S. Commission on Civil Rights 1998, 2). Community demands for public hearings through accepted structures of formalized dissent revolved around a pan-Asian collectivity including ethnic-specific groups like the Organization of Chinese Americans. Press releases and news conferences concentrated on reifying citizenship.

> Asian Pacific Americans are Americans, not foreigners . . . whether they are U.S. born, naturalized citizens or legal permanent residents, [they] have as much stake in this country as any other American. (Asian Pacific American Institute for Congressional Studies 1996)

> When Caucasian Americans raise money from other Caucasians, it is called gaining political power. But somehow, when Asian Pacific Americans begin to participate in providing financial support . . . we are accused of being foreigners attempting to infiltrate U.S. policy-making. (Fletcher 1996)

Indeed, other campaign violations and subsequent fines by foreign nationals from countries such as Germany and Belgium received far less public attention (Lardner 1998; Wayne 1997).

Civil Rights Commission hearings were not held until the following year, and by then, much of the national media focus had moved on to other topics. Many Asian Americans believed Huang was a convenient target, representative of a disorganized minority community whose resistance to stereotypical narratives and discourses could be labeled as "playing the race card." The real focus of the investigation should have been campaign finance itself: "Ultimately bit players in the big drama of America's corrupt system of moneyed politics, these foreign-tinged transnational Asian American fundraisers garnered more than their share of blame and media attention" (Hu-DeHart 1999, 15).

One of the fundamental projects of the modern nation-state is to preserve national unity by resolving or negating contradictions of difference. New-activist Chinese learned about these complexities of power inherent in constructions of identity, and the ways in which identity claims can be manipulated and dislocated to take the focus off racism. They took these experiences with them into the latter part of the 1990s. And as will be seen, for some members of CAUSE, it was another important element of a racialized political identity that allowed them to rethink and enlarge upon ethnic-specific strategies. Many new activists, like Charlie Woo, remain deeply wounded by the experience. "What hurts is that no matter what you've done in this country," Woo says, "sometimes people jump to the conclusion too quick that you're a foreigner. That hurts because we come to this country, we contribute, we come not just for economic reasons—we come here for the ideals and for the equal opportunity."

Asian American responses illustrate the dynamics of agency in which "subordinated populations may utilize their differentiation as a rallying point or even as a battle cry, but the challenge continues to be made within the language of nationalism" (Basch, Glick Schiller, and Blanc 1994, 39). Indeed, it appears that this has been the outcome of the 1996 fund-raising controversy. Initial worries among Asian American community leaders that this racial scrutiny would have a chilling effect on political participation and lessen campaign contributions do not seem to have been warranted, although, as Woo and others believe, 1996 is still a cautionary tale.

Additionally, there are subtle differences between how naturalized and native-born Chinese Americans assessed the 1996 fallout that deserve a more nuanced reading. For many naturalized activists, Clinton's reelection was a political coming-of-age wherein they believed they were enacting a fully sanctioned citizenship—and indeed had been invited to do so by being singled out and courted for their money. As a result, they felt more strongly than native-born Chinese that the federal investigation limited their participation (see Appendix 1, Table 4). Furthermore, these limitations put a damper on their perceptions of a level playing field and their desire to get involved (see Appendix 1, Table 5). Thus, although a majority of both naturalized and native-born activists denied that the investigation made them more cautious about participating, there was also an indisputably high degree of concern about participating (see Appendix 1, Table 6). Whether or not these feelings are permanent can only be guessed.

What has happened among new Chinese activists can be characterized as a political radicalization that continues to be engaged and refuses to accept an ascribed, racially negative identity. Aside from his own personal experiences with racism in this country, part of Leonard's widening reality also comes from exposure to different historical perspectives involving other people of color in the United States.

> You know, I have a lot of sympathy for Muslim Americans now. I see them walking in the street and [getting] called names. To that extent, all minorities should have a common front because what happens to me today can happen to you tomorrow. You have to speak up, and speaking up for them actually speaks up for you.
>
> I never *heard* about the Japanese internment. I heard about Chinese coming here, but you don't hear about the bad times. You do hear that many Chinese were sold, but that was the early days. That was what you grew up hearing. "If you're naughty, you're going to be *sold* as a slave! We'll sell you for a piglet!"

Winston had been making political contributions and raising money for candidates and issues for half a decade. Perceptions of his minority status were also enlarged by this negative experience. He was not intimidated when the FBI called him.

> I told everybody I knew to write and tell them [the media] we're not foreigners . . . just because one Asian American or a foreigner has committed a crime, you can't say *all* Asian Americans are guilty! It was horrible! It was

media, it was congressmen. It was scary. Now I understand why there was [Japanese American] internment! That's why I spoke up.

And I was worried about my children. For the first time I visited the [Manzanar] Japanese American internment camp on the way to Mammoth. I thought it could happen again. But *not* to *my* children, so I had to get *more* active!

Experiences like the 1996 fund-raising controversy forever put to rest any doubts that naturalized activists might have had about how power structures, particularly at the national level, viewed them as U.S. citizens. Like Winston, many of them redoubled their efforts to get involved, especially at the local level. For many naturalized activists, the emphasis on the local was their initial point of entry into participation, where they felt most comfortable in crafting everyday identity projects and a point from which they could make the most difference. And because they had been on the local political scene for a few years, they were better known individually and as an interest group.

Building relationships, of course, is a cornerstone of political involvement in the United States and has been well understood and accepted by new Chinese activists intent on overcoming the perception that "we are strangers to them." Aspects of network ties, *guanxi*, and other forms of reciprocity are embedded in the construction of Chinese personhood—reciprocity that is at once structural, instrumental, and particular (Harrell 2001; Yan 1996). As their education in the United States shows, this group of naturalized immigrants has experience in constructing personal networks. Initially, most lacked extensive kinship ties in the United States; the shift from bounded forms of solidarity, like family or village, to wider, fictive networks created new niches for interpersonal relationships. The pursuit of *guanxi* as a form of social capital and practical kinship and the use of connections that are flexible, situational, and of an individual's own choosing are manifestations of individual agency (Bourdieu 1977). These ties become more salient with shifting borders and notions of "community," especially where naturalized Chinese Americans try to gain space and place as new neighbors.

This may help to explain, for example, why many naturalized activists have several different business cards at their disposal and why their office walls are frequently decorated with innumerable photographs, awards, plaques, and other forms of civic recognition. They will often criticize one another (privately) over the number of organizations and connections printed in both English and Chinese on business cards. One activist, a former San Gabriel

Valley elected official, griped that although embracing activism was a good thing, proof of connections and the attendant ego boost were getting out of hand. "You see on their business cards everything. . . . They will put down past president of this and that," he complained. But then he realized, "Well, I did the same thing"—he had also made use of *his* connections.

In conversations about political empowerment, activists often mention the networks and avenues of reciprocity that can result. Like other natural-ized activists, Franklin came to the United States with an attitude that re-garded political involvement with skepticism. His thinking began to change after he earned a master's in business administration and finished law school and became more familiar with democratic ideals. As an immigration attor-ney representing primarily Asian clients, he says, he saw "a lot of injustice" that didn't equate with those ideals. When he moved to the Inland Empire area of Riverside County, he took with him to this new, predominantly white community a politicized identity honed from these experiences. He plunged into community organizing by building a network among the few Asian Americans in his area. "Everybody's very isolated [here] and doing their own thing," he says. "The first thing I did was to call the presidents of these groups. I said, let's do some functions together so we can get to know each other. We can network and at least give each other our business."

After that, he started showing up at political and civic events, becoming a familiar face among local politicians and getting his name in the local pa-per. Franklin's very public display of networking garnered him recognition, and through that networking and recognition he contested a marginalized status—his and that of others. "I had a Chinese friend who applied for a permit to lease part of his building to Starbucks," he says. "The city turned him down. He was so frustrated, so I said, 'Let me see what I can do.' I talked to the city manager and the planning department. . . . He got his permit. . . . *Me* knowing these people didn't hurt."

SPIES IN OUR MIDST

The Select Committee has received information about Chinese-American scientists from U.S. nuclear weapons design laboratories.

U.S. Congress 1999

Just three years after the 1996 fund-raising controversy, continuing geopo-litical pressures between the United States and China again made Chinese

Americans into suspect foreigners. Wen Ho Lee, a naturalized U.S. citizen from Taiwan and a scientist at the Los Alamos National Laboratory in New Mexico, was accused of stealing U.S. nuclear secrets, presumably for China. In January 1999, the classified Cox Report had been submitted to the U.S. House of Representatives, detailing without ambiguity that the People's Republic of China had been stealing thermonuclear weapons data from the United States for some years and continued to do so.[10] It singled out methods the PRC used, included examples of compromised Chinese American employees at U.S. weapons labs, and recommended that the United States take a hard look at the PRC's efforts "to exploit the open character of U.S. society by penetrating businesses, academic and social institutions, and political practices" (U.S. Congress 1999, 3:176). Leaks from the report preceded a sensationalized page-one story in the *New York Times* three months later that made the case for Chinese spies inside national weapons labs (Risen and Gerth 1999). Although Lee was not named in the initial *Times* story, he was fired and subsequently arrested and indicted, though not for espionage. Once again, celebratory notions of a transnational citizen's ability to navigate freely among "divergent cultural experiences" were also called into question (Hannerz 1996; Glick Schiller and Fouron 1999). Although the Cox Report was widely discredited as biased and alarmist, verging on hysteria, not many doubted that China, as well as a host of other countries, was spying on the United States (McGeary 1999).

Asian Americans have been largely powerless to influence metanarratives because of what some see as a lack of cohesive group organization and a tendency toward reactive rather than proactive response. However, the Lee case presents another angle—as an example of collective action and a sense of common purpose among both American-born and naturalized Chinese activists that can serve as an important alternative reading. With a focus and a specific goal in sight, realignments of power *did* occur, however briefly.

In contrast to mainstream media portrayals about a lack of engagement beyond their jobs, naturalized Chinese citizens in defense and related research industries have become quite politicized over the years (Schmidt 1999). Their life histories in these pages convey some of the reasons, such as a glass ceiling and other discriminatory experiences they had while employed at large private and government contractors despite high qualifications. Both naturalized men and women took their politicization into advocacy, forming and joining Asian American employee groups and some later joining CAUSE. For Stanton, Lee's experience reflected his own. "Wen Ho Lee was a very inductive process and emotional for me," he says. "I read the background and there was no balance. Senior-level management of Los Alamos made many trips to China. That was the policy then! And they took Lee and showed him chitchatting with this guy and they were hugging each other. They were *encouraged* to do that. Now they're holding it against him, and that's wrong!" Veronica, who has worked for large health-care corporations, says she had suspicions about the severity of Lee's treatment. "If he were a white American, what happened to him wouldn't have happened," she says. "I don't know what he did, but I don't rule out the possibility that he was treated differently because he's Chinese. Other people are violating the same policies, and they weren't prosecuted. That sent a message that there is discrimination. It is alive and well." In Lee, Charlie Woo saw himself: "Had I not gone into the toy business, I would have gotten my Ph.D. in physics, probably working on a similar project. Many Asian American scientists really identify with this. That no matter how hard you work, how much you contribute, sometimes people jump to conclusions too quick . . . and treat you like a foreigner."

Lee's supporters were especially angered by the allegation that he had spent $700 on airfare to Shanghai. The implication was that he was meeting with Communist contacts, but it was later revealed that Lee had sent his American-born daughter on a trip to experience Chinese culture. Like other transnational Chinese Americans, the Taiwan-born Lee traveled frequently to China and Taiwan, where he maintained personal and professional contacts. As the example of the SPCAC shows, this is normal among naturalized activists who have American-born children. Stanton believes that such trips are necessary: "I sent my two daughters to China to visit when they were in college in the summertime. I think it's very important for them to broaden their views of different people, to see different places. I think they should know their heritage because they look like Chinese."

A few months after initial media stories about Lee's possible role as a spy, and nearly five months before his arrest and indictment, fellow naturalized citizens including other scientists and engineers began a campaign to counter negative national media coverage. Their behind-the-scenes tactics were much more proactive than anything that had occurred during the 1996 DNC fund-raising controversy. It is also significant that grassroots action initially came not from putative Asian American community leaders but rather from naturalized Chinese (Committee of 100 1999; Associated Press 1999). New activists launched an extensive, coordinated national campaign complete with a website and federal complaints charging racism (Rabin 2000). Their tactics contested the dominant discourse on two levels: first, by declaring that the conflation of China and Chinese American was racist, and second, by stating that the negative political fallout could affect global relations. In a letter to U.S. Attorney General Janet Reno, new activists wrote, "You understand the grave and potentially tragic consequences it may have . . . for the delicate strategic relationship the United States is try-ing to build, [and it] could do incalculable harm to our foreign policy with China" (Committee of 100 1999).

Some of CAUSE's most active members also became Lee's biggest back-ers. And although they themselves did not have direct contact with those in power, they knew American-born Asian leaders who did. They began to work together, first using their resources and networks to approach Secre-tary of Commerce Norm Mineta.[11] Says Stanton, "I know Mineta because he's an engineer, and he said let's get in there and raise the [Lee] issue." With Mineta's help, the group realized its ultimate goal of speaking personally to President Clinton. After the 1996 debacle with Democrats, Stanton was ag-gressive in not wasting his historic moment.

> We talked to Clinton, a one-hour session, and he spent 20 or 30 minutes talking about Wen Ho Lee. Afterwards, I pulled him aside and told him Chinese Americans made a tremendous contribution to the national de-fense but nobody ever publicizes it, and in the case of Lee, I told him he's being treated very unfairly on many of these issues. Clinton didn't defend the government's action, I could see that.

There is no doubt in Stanton's mind that the meeting had its desired effect: "Shortly after that, he [Clinton] gave an interview to *Rolling Stone*. He said, 'I have my Whitewater . . . and we have other cases like Wen Ho Lee.' He was comparing himself and the Lee case. That's leverage."

Widening Asian American protest and a media-savvy legal team were key factors in forcing mainstream journalists to more closely weigh the "facts" of the case and to challenge the reporting done by the *New York Times*, which had broken the story. Although Lee was denied bail and sat in soli-tary confinement in a federal prison, new stories surfaced about widespread problems at the nation's weapons laboratories. Some media coverage began to portray Lee as the victim of a "witch hunt spawned by a political atmo-sphere that demonizes China" (Stout 1999). Additional reports appeared of Chinese Americans being systematically harassed and denied promotions at other national labs, resulting in employee boycotts by Chinese Americans.

Out of a 59-count indictment, Lee was eventually convicted on one charge of mishandling information. The eventual abandonment of the case by federal prosecutors, Lee's release after nine months in solitary confine-ment, no further prison time, *and* an unprecedented public apology from the federal judge were stunning events attributable in no small part to the national Asian American campaign, which provided an alternative narrative of the case (W. Lee 2001; Associated Press 2000; Sterngold 2000). Secre-tary of Energy Bill Richardson, who had fired Lee even before he had been charged, was forced to begin a recruitment program directed at attracting Asian American scientists back to lab work.

The Lee case is significant in that it illustrates agency and coordinated political action. Asian Americans have a long history of such resistance, with varying degrees of success in transforming traditional power relations. The presence now in Asian America of naturalized activists who are capable of effectively manipulating social connections in order to challenge the power of hegemonic structures points to new strategies that will, by virtue of larger racializing projects in the United States, encompass all Asian Americans. Economic capital and transnational networking, though not used entirely legally, as 1996 illustrates, are at the same time a precarious yet potent for-mula that has transformed power relations.

CHANGING COURSE: WHAT'S IN A NAME?

About 100 people are attending the 2003 CAUSE Political Institute lun-cheon at the Biltmore Hotel in downtown Los Angeles. A political analyst from CNN has been invited to answer questions about the Asian American presence on the national political radar screen. "One thing I can tell you is that Asian Americans are not the flavor of the moment," he says. "No one knows what Asian America is."

After the luncheon speech, Charlie Woo comments, "I think [he] made those remarks because he hadn't thought about it beforehand. Had we talked to him before, he would have said, 'Oh, you are growing . . .' and he would have given a different speech. But I liked it better this way. It's a wake-up call!"

Implicit in this "wake-up call" is the use of the term *Asian America* and acknowledgment that a collective identity is the path to recognition. Many activist members of CAUSE had been wrestling with a more encompassing political identity for a number of years. In 2003, a defining moment finally occurs, though without much public fanfare: CAUSE changes its name from Chinese Americans United for Self Empowerment to Center for Asian Americans United for Self Empowerment. This marks the beginning of another chapter in the synthesizing of American experiences and the politicizing of racialized identities among naturalized Chinese activists.

Coinciding with the celebration of the organization's 10th anniversary, CAUSE activists and leaders like Woo pushed the name issue again. Agreement was by no means unanimous, although at meetings where the subject was broached, discussion was fairly muted. The board eventually voted, and most board members went along with Woo. CAUSE public programs also changed their names, such as CASIC, from Chinese American Student Internship Coalition to California Asian-American Student Internship Coalition. For activist leaders, particularly those who have had extensive and racializing experiences in wider social and political structures for at least a decade, embracing a pan-Asian political identity has become an instrumental expression but one that doesn't entirely transcend what is Chinese American. Shortly after CAUSE changed its name, a Korean American woman joined the board as the first non–Chinese American. Since then, a number of other Asian Americans have joined as board members, and in 2007 CAUSE hired a Japanese American man as its executive director.

The pan-Asian public face is a victory for Woo, who remains a central force behind CAUSE. In the aftermath of the 1996 fund-raising investigation, he has also become involved in a range of political activities, including substantial campaign contributions that have allowed him to become a well-known and often-consulted figure among mainstream political structures.

Woo remains firmly grounded in Southern California and in the political goal of collective action. At the same time, he evinces an outward, transnational focus that capitalizes on his expertise as a broker in local and international business. He has represented Southern California and its transnational trade connections in Asia as chair of the Asia Trade Committee in the Los Angeles mayor's office and has advised the California Assembly Committee on Asia Trade. All of this, including his own business, requires frequent trips to China and Hong Kong. But one of Woo's main vehicles for political participation as a U.S. citizen remains CAUSE and its central mission—how groups like CAUSE can be positioned within the nexus of political empowerment and dialogue with power structures. A pan–Asian American identity is one of his strategies. "We have to move beyond the Chinese community . . . for strength," he says. "But there's no other group to bring everyone together politically, so we should work for CAUSE to do this. We need to form a network to bring all Asian Pacific American groups together, and we need to define how to do this." He is also highly aware of the different political consequences offered by involvement "from below" and "from above."

> You have to develop a reputation among people who have power, that you are their friend, that they can trust you, and that you can bring them support if they need it. And when you're an immigrant, you don't get that connection at the top. You get that connection at the *bottom.*
>
> [You have] to get people to feel that this is an organization that they need to pay attention to; they are convinced that when they talk to you, they talk to the community. [*He starts to laugh.*] The other way to do it is to protest in front of them so they *have* to let you in!

Many new activists had witnessed confrontation on college campuses during the late 1960s, but this has never been the way new Chinese activists envision political participation, no matter how frustrating the situation.

The evolution of CAUSE into a pan–Asian American organization is problematic for the Chinese American membership, even for those who supported the idea. How they see themselves and their individual positionings is not as straightforward or simple as place of birth; it also has to do with the degree to which their everyday American lives are experienced inside and outside the Chinese community. As a realtor in the San Gabriel Valley, Lynn works predominantly with Chinese Americans, half of whom are new immigrants with extensive transnational social and economic connections. She saw the CAUSE name change as a co-optation for larger, questionable goals. "I don't think we've done enough of a job of servicing the Chinese Americans, which is what we started out to do," she says. "We've really strayed from our original intent, which was to focus on getting voting information and bilingual info out to the community. They're going in a different direction."

On the other hand, naturalized activists who have spent more time participating outside the Chinese community agree that CAUSE's embrace of a pan–Asian American identity is needed. Franklin says the group "needs to be encompassing." One of the original founders of CAUSE, Paul Zee, also backs the idea but is pragmatic about what it actually means. Zee left CAUSE and became involved in another project, the A-Team, an Asian American political outreach group.

> I have been promoting this idea that Asians have got to stick together as one unit, one body. Asians need to stick together, period.
>
> The board can be 100 percent Chinese American, but yet perception-wise, you should call it Asian. All in all, in the political dictionary here, Chinese does not exist. It's got to be Asian American.

Winston, a former CAUSE board member, argued early in support of a pan–Asian American identity. In addition to his vocal activism during the 1996 DNC fund-raising controversy, Winston spent part of his law career as one among a few minorities hitting the glass ceiling at a corporate law firm. He went on to become active in the National Asian Pacific American Bar Association.

> I wanted [CAUSE] to be Asian American. I did not want just Chinese American. We had a big argument over that. That was one of the reasons I left after that and never came back to any more meetings. As far as Americans go, we're all the same you know. *Get off it!* Chinese, Japanese, Korean, whatever, *big deal!* Especially for people who don't live in L.A., we're definitely all the same!

Native-born American activists influenced by progressive Asian American sensibilities of the 1960s tend to see the need for expanding identities. Cal is now in his 50s and a native Californian. He is a state employee and part-time city council member in an East San Gabriel Valley community of 100,000. He supported the CAUSE name change as a way of strengthening a Chinese American agenda and a means by which to address his own racializing experiences. He is still trying to persuade constituents that he isn't a foreigner. "I called and left my name with this woman," he says. "Her response was, 'Oh, you don't sound like a Cheng.' I said, 'Oh what does a Cheng sound like?' She says, 'Oh you know, somebody with an accent.' I told her I was *born here* and had lived here my whole life! We are always the perpetual foreigner!"

Brent, the American-born Chinese attorney who talks openly about discriminatory practices in some Southern California law firms, was a CAUSE board member during the name change. He sees the shift in the organization's public face from two perspectives.

> I think there's a lot of sense of loss with the board about going multiethnic. But the sense of loss is overpowered by the benefit, the broadening and sense of empowerment. If it isn't an Asian American organization, if it doesn't represent *more* bodies, what is the concept of turning Asian American?
>
> But we're constantly dealing with so many internal issues. Clearly most foreign-borns don't think about what's come before us, what's been America's history with respect to us.

"With respect to us" foregrounds the importance of larger asymmetrical power relations that must be continually kept in sight. Conceptual foci on "studying up" are as critical in contextualizing social meanings as "studying down." Turning the spotlight on institutions and bureaucracies of power relates directly "to the concept of citizenship in a country that is to be run on a democratic framework and the control that citizens must have to harness managerial manipulation" (Nader 1974, 294). Even if naturalized Chinese activists resist a pan–Asian American categorization, they have a certain degree of powerlessness in changing this mainstream discourse.

CAUSE's annual fund-raising dinner in May 2002 was planned to coincide with Asian Pacific American Heritage Month, which had become a government-sanctioned event in 1977, concurrent with the co-optation of the term *Asian American.* Symbolic enactments are appropriated as a way for power structures to address difference through acceptable events such as parades, proclamations, and food festivals, thus officially "celebrating" diversity in the United States. Virtually all of the usual letters of congratulations that appeared in the CAUSE dinner program booklet conflated *Chinese American* and *Asian Pacific American* or ignored references to Chinese Americans altogether, as shown in a letter from the office of California governor Gray Davis: "I am delighted to extend a warm welcome and to observe Asian Pacific American Heritage Month. It is a pleasure to join you in this celebration of our rich Asian Pacific heritage and traditions" (CAUSE/ Vision 21 2002).

Official recognition of minority discourses simultaneously celebrates the ideals of national belonging and citizenship and instantiates an ascribed subalternity and marginality (Schein 2000). It is an uneasy accommodation within the existing social order (Appiah and Gutmann 1996). But at the same time, the seeds are sown for political mobilization. As Cynthia Enloe (1981) writes, "Over time, state practices may encourage individuals to see themselves as part of not just an artificial state category but as a group which shares important common experiences: oppression, deprivation, and also benefits" (134). New Chinese activists did not know about "America's history with respect to us," but that is largely no longer the case. They now own similar racialized histories and have come to more fully realize the persistence of bounded U.S. racial ideologies that conflate and marginalize regardless of access to economic or social capital or nativity.

The debate surrounding the CAUSE name change thus frames larger identity issues and the way in which new Chinese activists view their membership in the wider community. Charlie Woo realized he was only one of many different colors of small-business owners who wanted the same kind of life he wanted for his own family. They were all inhabitants of "Toy Town," a discursive element that local government attached to the area after businesses got together and approached their city representatives for assistance. This inscribed bounded entity also furthered the politicizing of a common identity and created situational coalition building based on common *economic* experiences as a multiethnic *racial* group.

INCORPORATING PARTISAN IDEOLOGIES

As naturalized Chinese political participation has matured over the past 10 to 15 years, there are already visible differences in political identities supplemented and refined by partisan politics. To the extent that much of established political participation in the United States needs to be labeled, tagged, and otherwise identified, new activists have also adopted Republican and Democratic memberships. This addition to the political terrain of new Chinese activist involvement does not take away from the salience of a politically racialized identity, nor does partisan politics obscure the larger goal of empowerment. However, it is another form of political heterogeneity and tension, in both intragroup difference among naturalized Chinese activists and intergroup difference with American-born progressives. Among naturalized immigrants, it has already taken a toll in terms of mobilization and organization.

From 2000 to 2003, CAUSE became CV21, merging with Vision 21, which had earlier broken away from CAUSE.[12] The remarriage was short-lived. The public perception was that CAUSE was more closely aligned with the Democrats while Vision 21 adherents were Republican. The desire to maintain nonpartisanship is addressed in board meetings quite vehemently, and during this period, the CV21 board did include members from both sides of the aisle. By law, CAUSE is not permitted to make partisan endorsements. Members, of course, are free to individually support whomever or whatever issue they wish. But it is not so surprising that CAUSE came to be identified with the Democrats. Speakers and invited guests at functions like the annual Political Institute have been primarily Democrats. However, it may also be said that the preponderance of Democratic speakers has more to do with the fact that, at least until the recall of Gray Davis in 2003, California had been Democratic since the late 1990s. In addition, CAUSE leaders like Charlie Woo are Democrats, and most members of the board during this period described themselves as Democrats. In previous years, when some of CAUSE's earlier leaders were Republican, organization newsletters gave prominent mention to members' participation in the 1996 Republican National Convention. The CV21 experiment points to the difficulties in finding common ground among what might appear to most outsiders and mainstream political structures as a homogeneous group of activist immigrants. Taken one step farther, this becomes part and parcel of the increasing heterogeneity that exists among Asian Americans generally, the challenges inherent in a commonly accepted group political agenda, and the continuing inability or lack of desire by power structures to see any differences beyond the all-purpose Asian Pacific American rubric.

By the 1990s, new political infrastructures among naturalized immigrants displayed diversity and confidence; new activists did not need just a few organizations within which to enact their political identities. In addition, there were simply more people who were at a point in their life histories to become politically involved. For example, a decade ago a Chinese American name on a municipal ballot was still a rarity. In 2003, more than a dozen Chinese American candidates were on the ballots in 11 San Gabriel cities, often vying against each other.[13] Already, more than two dozen Chinese Americans, most of them post-1965 new activists, have been elected to local-level positions in the San Gabriel Valley. After CV21 broke up, Vision 21 morphed into another political group, also with a pan-Asian outlook—the A-Team, which has intermittent periods of activity. In 2002, it was a Republican organization that included Chinese, Japanese, and Korean Americans who backed California Republican gubernatorial candidate Bill Simon. The original umbrella unfurled by CAUSE is no longer large enough to shelter everyone.

Some scholarship has shown that naturalized Asian citizens generally do not possess deeply held philosophical beliefs about party affiliation, but this is certainly not the case among the new Chinese activists (Ong and Lee 2001). It must be said, however, that the use of *any* political ascription is in itself extremely limiting. The terrain shifts as rapidly as new issues emerge, as will be shown in the following examples. Among new activists, party affiliations run the gamut of so-called conservative to liberal values (Omatsu 1989).

New Chinese activists who are entrepreneurial small-business owners and those who are self-employed are more conservative regarding issues that progressive activists often see as falling within the realm of social justice— affirmative action, welfare rights, and other safety net measures. Republican stances on these subjects appeal to this conservatism. Lynn relates her party affiliation primarily to her own business struggles.

> I'm Republican. I think, being in business, I've had to compete with others in order to be selected as the representative to market their homes or property. I never felt that because I'm Asian or Chinese I am entitled to that market share. I *always* have to fight for it.
>
> There is a difference in thinking of Asian Americans coming of age in the sixties—like affirmative action. I don't think affirmative action really elevates [education]. It brings down the standards.

Unlike new Chinese Democrats, those who call themselves Republicans seem to have had fewer racializing experiences in their American lives or have not internalized them in the same way. It is not uncommon for activists who are conservative on social issues to minimize the role racism and racializing experiences have had in their own life histories. Franklin was just 27 when his company decided to subsidize his master's degree. He says he was one of the youngest managers and the only Chinese American. "I've never really been discriminated against," he says. "At least not blatantly. There were probably situations where . . . I don't know. But in terms of opportunities, if I'm able to perform, I get that opportunity, and when I don't get that opportunity, I didn't do my homework."

Those who have worked in U.S. corporate settings for some years and have fought for promotions and a level playing field are chagrined by these types of comments. Stanton has no doubt about the relationship between his racialization and his lack of promotions, two facts that have been instrumental in inscribing his identity.

> I look at it this way. As an Asian American, as a Chinese American, as a minority in this country, we should be identifying with the Democrats. Republicans are an exclusive group rather than inclusive.
>
> I look at so many Chinese Americans and there are so many Republicans. Their rationale is this—you should be self-reliant. That means you should make enough money to take care of yourself and family and not worry about anybody else. This is their mentality.

Stanton credits his view on equality to both his African American mentor/boss and an earlier supervisor who offered more radical visions of social justice.

> When I got my Ph.D., I met a guy who was a socialist. That was my first job and he influenced me. He used to have a May Day party. In those days, the early seventies, Vietnam was going on. There was a big demonstration throughout the [United States]. Lots of people stopped working for one day, and he let all of us off that day, and we all went marching.
>
> That was my first march on Antiwar Day. I felt very strongly about that. . . . Why were we killing all these people? He had a lot of influence on me. I saw a picture of a very successful businessman, yet he was still very much worried about society and issues.

Lena's years of working at a credit union after she became a citizen were not idyllic. As mentioned in Chapter 4, she was singled out, the butt of racial stereotyping, sexual innuendo, and suspicion. These first American experiences are still with her. She is a staunch Democrat. A few years ago, she and another new Chinese activist and Republican squared off in a debate. The issue was paid family leave, and in 2002 California became the first state to authorize it. The law stipulates that most California workers get half their salary while they take time off to care for ill family members or newborns. It was a bitterly divided ideological contest in which traditional political coalitions of labor squared off against management and big business. Many new activists who are themselves employers did not support the bill because of the worry over additional taxes—about $46 a year per worker—which they said would be added to the cost of their doing business. The Republican who debated Lena runs his own small company of about a dozen workers in South San Gabriel Valley. He adopted the business stance saying: "We cannot have this. We cannot make money." Lena presented the other side, favored by progressive Democrats: "Of course you are in business and you want to make money, but . . . you can't just use business to make money. You've got to help those who need it. We help minorities, the disabled. . . . That's the philosophy the Democrats have. If you think about our cultural traditions, the Democrats are right about this. It's a better fit."

However, for those activists, both foreign-born and native-born, who ideologically align themselves with Democrats, the challenge is forging coalitions with the naturalized community. At least in the Southern California ethnoburbs, the Chinese electorate appears to be turning Republican (Ong and Nakanishi 2003). During the early 1980s, when most post-1965 Chinese immigrants started becoming U.S. citizens and only a few were getting politically involved, registered Democrats in Monterey Park still outnumbered Republicans 43 percent to 31 percent (Ong and Lee 2001). Not only were many of these Chinese American Democrats so-called baby boomers, but their parents were also Democrats. Part-time San Gabriel Valley councilman Cal was born in Southern California, and his politicization began as a youngster listening to stories his father told him about being a young working-class welder and union member in the San Francisco shipyards. "My dad made a conscious effort to become an American citizen so he could vote on a regular basis," he says, his eyes lighting up when he relates a comment his father always made. "'The Democrats represent the working people and the Republicans all the rich people!' Even though he was a respected business owner, he never forgot his labor roots."

However, as Monterey Park's burgeoning population of naturalized citizens began to include more professionals and entrepreneurial business owners, Republican registration grew. By the late 1980s, Republicans had achieved a slight majority, 37 percent to 35 percent (Ong and Lee 2001). Statewide in California, however, partisanship among Asian Americans is a different picture. In 2004, Democrats still outnumbered Republicans among registered voters. Of those elected to the California Assembly in 2004, five of the seven Asian Americans—all native-born—were considered progressive Democrats whose political life histories bore the imprint of the 1960s.[14] In 2008, Asian American voters in California were still leaning Democratic at 33 percent, with Republican registration at 16 percent. However, 17 percent of Asian American voters said they were independent, and 34 percent said they were nonpartisan (National Asian American Survey 2008). Regardless of party affiliation, however, naturalized activists in Southern California, including new Chinese, have yet to breach the borders of local electoral politics. That will no doubt change.[15]

The difficulties of attaining consensus within the growing naturalized Chinese American community speak to a larger problem. At this point, there appears to be broad-based agreement among current activists that the continuing racialization of Chinese Americans by mainstream political structures presents a major hurdle to full political empowerment. Even those new activists who have not had deep racializing experiences recognize the need for equal opportunity. If this is the case, it remains to be seen how closely the growing ideological differences new Chinese activists are exhibiting can be aligned with a pan–Asian American identity that for the most part still embraces a progressive Asian American social stance. There is evidence that both sides are beginning to make adjustments aimed at fashioning other kinds of bases for inclusiveness. Native-born and foreign-born activists alike are very aware that the value and rewards of being categorized racially point to keeping an eye on the larger issue of group integration (Espiritu 1992). The remainder of this chapter explores some of the inherent political tradeoffs being negotiated between the two groups and how this dialectic is currently enacted and accommodated, undergoing transformative redefinition in the process.

Outside the Box

As new-activist political participation begins to mature, the conundrum over collective group identity forms an imperfect circle. Divergent life histories created different paths for new immigrant activists and those who are native-born and resulted in different politicized roots. However, with their immigration to and subsequent citizenship in the United States, naturalized Chinese activists have now experienced three decades of the imposition of new structures of power and categorization. For most of them, this encompasses the entire repertoire of their adult life histories. The same time frame also applies to the personal political histories of native-born progressives. Both groups thus have a common history based on continuing forms of shared marginalization as citizens. It is the embrace of a common *political* history, dynamically fashioned as a response to hegemony. It is new and does not presuppose any primordial origins. Given that mutability is inherent in this process of identity construction, the point where these two paths meet in this imperfect circle is not permanent, nor is it likely to be so.

While new-activist Chinese professionalized themselves through college and graduate educations in the United States during the 1970s and 1980s, native-born activists of the 1960s, including some former radicals, were pursuing similar projects. Social outcomes of the 1960s, including affirmative action programs in both education and employment, offered new opportunities for Asian Americans. The result was that "young professionals altered the political terrain in our communities" (Omatsu 1989, 147). They organized pan–Asian American advocacy groups in law, medicine, journalism, science, and business. Despite the professional credentials of these groups, their core ideologies centered on their members' realization of their marginality. Collective mobilization allowed them to use those credentials and their positions inside established structures to alter discourse regarding Asian Americans. For example, a half dozen of the primarily young Chinese and Japanese American-born journalists, such as myself, who were working for major newspapers and television stations in Southern California founded the Asian American Journalists Association in 1981. Part of the original mission statement was to ensure that the organizations employing us covered Asian Pacific American communities with fairness and accuracy.

As Omatsu (1989) observes, progressives redefined the vocabulary for political contestation. During the 1960s, radical activists embraced the words *consciousness, ideology, revolution,* and *liberation.* Now, more familiar terminology includes *advocacy, empowerment, access,* and *legitimacy,* all of which have also become part of the lexicon for new Chinese activists.

UNCOVERING DIVERGENCE: WHOSE AGENDA?

In Chapter 1, I began with the description of a small event at a CAUSE board meeting, where Ric, an American-born activist, and Larry, a naturalized citizen activist, discussed California's Proposition 54. Actually, Ric didn't see much point in discussion. A progressive stance advocated that the proposition be rejected on its face—it was racially discriminatory. Although Larry was among those CAUSE board members voting no on 54, he wanted a better explanation. Weeks later, Larry was still complaining about being pegged as a go-along: "He [Ric] said, 'Omigod, can you imagine if an outsider looked at us and we *supported* Proposition 54?' It was a lousy piece of legislation. But I thought he was just giving me the standard rhetoric without thinking . . . he was doing that as a liberal minority person who's doing what he's expected to do."

Larry is an example of a new Chinese activist who considers himself progressive—up to a point. As a successful businessman in Southern California, he knows that government doesn't always have his best interests in mind. Racism, however, is a complicated issue for Larry. He talks about the racial experiences he has had in the United States, the least of which were comments from other college students who told him to "go back to your own country." He was another contributor to the Democrats who got lumped in with foreigners who were Asian. He fully realizes that he is still seen as a foreigner, but he has been trying to move beyond that in a way that he says progressive Asian American activists can't.

> I think people from that [1960s] generation are boxed in. I don't think I'm boxed in. I want to be convinced, not just because [progressives] oppose something so how *dare we not*?! I think that in Southern California, ethnic tension is not high on most people's list—not like jobs.
> Bringing up race creates a wedge issue. . . . Whites are picking on us, we're picking on them, and I don't like that. You might defeat them now, but they're going to screw you the next chance they get you in a back alley.

Fundamentally, he endorses collective pan–Asian American political action. The differences have more to do with method; a new-activist approach understands that racialization is a central problem but contestation is more indirect. However, Larry believes a naturalized activist agenda does not differ greatly from one that American-born activists promote. "I just don't want to copy everything they say and everything they do," he says. "I want to incorporate it into what I consider to be very distinct and different characteristics of the Asian American community. I'm not buying a progressive agenda wholesale." He gives an example:

> Sometimes it's even laughable. I remember when the OCA [Organization of Chinese Americans] letter supporting Bill Lann Lee said *all* concerned

Americans who support Bill Lann Lee . . . and then they went one step further to define who all those Americans are.[16] Blacks, Latinos, Asians, gays, and lesbians.

There were no whites in their definition of "concerned Americans"! I mean, with stuff like that, you're never going to accomplish anything. And I think constant complaining isn't going to accomplish anything.

New activists like Marlon say they are more flexible in seeing racism in ways that are not prescriptively confining.

Funny thing about native-born Americans. They've experienced racial discrimination when they were kids. They knew they couldn't do well, not because they weren't trying but because of institutional impediments. But if you grow up in a society where there's more homogeneity, you're less conscious, mostly, of racial discrimination.

So I think in the back of the mind of any minority here, they have a schizophrenic experience. They want to ignore the racial factor, but somehow it always comes back to haunt us. [Naturalized citizens] make use of whatever suits them. Which is okay. I'm seven foot two, I play basketball. I'm five six, I play table tennis.

Sam still hasn't forgotten his first experiences with American-born Asians and their confrontational political style. He was a student at UCLA during the early 1970s and recalls being somewhat nonplussed by Asian Americans who wore Mao jackets and espoused socialism: "In Hong Kong we knew about Communism in China, and that was a bad thing, but here you had the antiwar movement and the hippies, and some people thought Mao was a big deal! That was kind of interesting." The Mao jackets are gone now, but Sam and other new Chinese activists still think those Asians who were born in the United States are not working enough on empowerment from the inside.

ABCs are sometimes not all that aggressive in making connections. FOBs are better at making connections. ABCs are sheltered in their own groups. When I first came here, we were in Echo Park and Silverlake [neighborhoods of Los Angeles]. I just didn't think too much about whether my English was good or not. We came here and we said, well now, we have to speak English, so we just did it. If you think about things too much, you'll really screw yourself up!

Naturalized Chinese activists say that even their own American-born children don't have the same aggressive drive they had as immigrants. Marlon complains that his son doesn't see opportunities as he does:

> One day I went to pick him up and saw him coming out with a bunch of kids. I said, maybe you should introduce me to some of your [friends'] parents. He said, "Why do you want to do that?" I said, "Maybe to get some business from them." He said, "We don't make friends for that." Native-born Americans are not entrepreneurial! They don't see relationships as an opportunity to make contacts!
>
> I'm saying, as an immigrant, I look at America as a land of opportunity. That's taken for granted if you're born here. So in the wider context of politics, you can do the same thing. You can look at networking. I told him he would never survive in Asia!

Winston is like many naturalized activists who see the difference between himself and those born in the United States as a matter of historical frameworks: "Whether you are white or yellow and grew up in this country and went to college in the sixties, . . . you still have the spirit of the sixties. That's why a lot of [ABCs] are very public-interest oriented and a lot of them are liberal Democrats. If you weren't in America or the Western world during those years, you missed out. There's a big difference between the two groups."

One of the major differences is the argument over affirmative action in education. Naturalized activists believe in equal opportunity—not a system they say penalizes their children because they are Chinese American. Says Winston: "[We] do not want to give special preference to blacks or Latinos—no affirmative action. ABCs are more willing to go with affirmative action. But [we] fought very hard to come to this country and value education more than anything. [Immigrants] want their children, *their* ABCs, to get the best education they can, and they're not willing to give up a few places to other [minorities]."

Although Veronica says she is a Democrat, the affiliation has little relevance to her personal beliefs about some social justice issues. Asian activists who are more progressive would call her a conservative.

> I really resent people who say "You owe me." When I got here, I had two suitcases. Everything I have now I worked for. If you do the same, you'd be there, too.
>
> For ten years I worked at the county hospital. A lot of the patients are illegal immigrants who come here to have babies. They get welfare, and you

and I pay for it. Hey listen, I came legally, I worked for it, I never asked for handouts. I never got a dime of welfare!

During the 1960s and 1970s, support for social programs like affirmative action in education and employment became part of the ideological mantra for many progressive and native-born Asians. Many of them had themselves been beneficiaries and were able to see the value of these social efforts. They continue to believe that although much has changed during the past 30 years with regard to Asian American educational attainment, employment, and opportunities for advancement, this is by no means a completed picture and does not apply across the spectrum to all ethnic groups in the Asian Pacific American community. New Chinese activists, on the other hand, were not part of this initial effort to expand opportunities for Americans of color and do not see Chinese Americans, at least not those like themselves, as needing affirmative action. In higher education, they see Chinese Americans now subject to discrimination that *limits* their numbers.

Yet, in many areas of American life, new Chinese activists are aware that their high levels of educational attainment and social and economic success do not translate into full equality. Franklin still embraces Asian American political activities because he believes that "something has to come into play" to ensure that public policy is not discriminatory.

> I was lucky I wasn't in an internment camp. I'm sure that was no fun. I can see the issue of civil rights, but . . . it's got to be a case-by-case basis. I generally do not believe in affirmative action in employment.
>
> Especially for *prior wrongs*—I don't agree with that. I like to see the best person. If I have a medical problem, I want to go to the best person, I don't care what color. And from a selfish standpoint, Asians do better without affirmative action.

Progressive American-born Asians like Ronald don't think that the need for affirmative action has disappeared, and he is open in his displeasure with those who think otherwise.

> Oh *I see* . . . let him or her go to work for a large American company and really want to move up, and let them sit there for maybe 10 or 15 years with their degree from Stanford . . . then they're going to come *crawling*. . . . Let 'em wait, and if they have any fairness at all in their souls, they're going to say, "I guess you guys were right. There are limitations in this country."

Analysis of some of CAUSE's board decisions on controversial statewide propositions over the past decade shows a record that does not completely align with a progressive Asian American agenda. In the case of Proposition 187, the so-called Illegal Aliens Measure, in 1994, CAUSE's discussion and its subsequent board vote more closely resonate with statewide Asian American opinion.[17] CAUSE *did* decide to oppose the proposition, but its position reflected neither the protracted board discussion nor the lack of unanimity.

Four years later, California Proposition 227 outlawing bilingual education passed, 61 percent to 39 percent. CAUSE board members recommended a yes vote in support of English immersion and English-only classes. Many new Chinese activists, of course, did not need bilingual assistance when they arrived as college students, and their American-born children do not need it either. Statewide, 57 percent of Asian Americans voted yes, which perhaps is indicative of an increasingly conservative and majority immigrant electorate. Again, progressive Asian American groups such as APALC opposed the measure.

In 2002, Proposition 52, Election Day Voter Registration, was endorsed by an assemblage of progressive Asian American organizations as well as groups such as the American Civil Liberties Union, Common Cause, and the League of Women Voters. Those supporting the measure saw it as a way to increase normally dismal voter turnout. CAUSE voted to oppose the proposition, and on election day, so did 60 percent of California's electorate. Some members echoed conservative concerns that the measure would increase voter fraud. But more progressive, naturalized activists like Stanton were incensed by CAUSE's opposition: "I thought it would be a natural to support it. I said, 'What the *hell* are we doing?' I thought for us to promote voter registration and promote political participation—that's our mission! I'm disgusted . . . very frustrated."

In contextualizing the political issues of both naturalized and American-born activists, one point needs to be revisited. When they enact their politicized identities, activists involved in groups like APALC or CAUSE represent their own interests, but inherent in their organizational names are also claims to represent *all* Asian Americans. Given that the leaders of these types of community-based organizations can be considered elites, and given the heterogeneity of class and ethnicity that exists in twenty-first-century Asian America, this seems a difficult task.

Criticism of progressive projects, such as those already outlined, has been muted, perhaps because most of the dominant discourses in Asian American communities are controlled by a largely progressive leadership. In historical hindsight, young radicals of the 1960s have been taken to task for trying to organize among poorer immigrant communities. They were not always successful at consciousness-raising among the working poor. Some scholars believe they were ineffective because of language barriers and also because "for the people" did not translate into *with the people* owing to class-based or generational differences between college students and immigrants (Kwong 2001). Now, with Asian American leaders increasingly professionalized, the same might be said of the interface with contemporary flows of poor immigrants. These criticisms aside, it is still important to understand the vitality of place that these revolutionary ideas occupy in notions of community building. As progressive Asian American leaders address social injustices, the creativity they show in contesting racialized identities helped to lay the foundation for later successful social movements on issues such as Japanese American redress.

New Chinese activists who have arrived after 1965 face similar challenges within the changing immigrant communities. New activists are still a small percentage of the immigrant population, but with their social and economic capital, they have been instrumental in transforming the economic and social fabric of the community for themselves and for working-class immigrants.

One early Saturday morning in the summer of 2002, the topic of discussion at a downtown Los Angeles hotel is concerned with more inclusion. A dozen or so new Chinese activists have given up part of their weekends to have coffee and talk about political empowerment. The subject of "new immigrants" comes up, and everyone generally acknowledges that reaching this population is important. One woman says: "We've been a group of well-informed, elite Chinese Americans, but we lack communication. How do we bring immigrants in, and how do we empower these people?" Everyone knows who "these people" are. They are categorized as small-business owners, the working poor, and laborers. Many are already U.S. citizens, part of the new immigrant majority, but their status does not automatically translate into further participation. New activists see them as having neither the time nor the financial resources to be involved politically, although given the 1960s history of some earlier immigrant workers, this view might seem patronizing. CAUSE, however, is targeting this cohort, and the group has expended much of its energy and resources on them. Partisanship aside, voter education followed by voter registration means more Chinese American votes and therefore more political power. For new Chinese activists, empowerment is a matter of their leadership enhanced by post-1980 working-class Chinese citizens.

After many of the naturalized Chinese activists came to the United States, labor requirements in the U.S. economy changed once again, with concomitant changes in U.S. immigration policies. Since the 1980s, the numbers of Chinese admitted as professionals have declined, although professionals have increasingly used the family ties category (Hing 2003). In addition, thousands more from China were allowed entry as political refugees fleeing from Communist countries (this preference was eliminated in 1980). The national impetus for continued Asian immigration still focuses on cheap labor. The majority of Asian immigrants are working class and still come to the United States via kinship ties irrespective of job status. In addition, there is another significant change in the demographics of immigration. Since the mid-1980s, more women than men have been coming from throughout Asia and the Pacific to fill burgeoning numbers of low-paying jobs in expanding U.S. production sites that existed in the 1990s. Claims of representation among new Chinese activists, therefore, have to address not only class differences but, now, shifting gender ratios as well. In other words, "these people" are predominantly working-class women. Gender issues are not yet a focus among most naturalized activists.

Organizationally, integrating class heterogeneity is a problem not only for naturalized Chinese activists but also for progressive Asian American groups. The leaders and governing boards of progressive groups like APALC look very much like the CAUSE board; they are entrepreneurs, lawyers, and corporate department heads. And although progressive organizations may deal programmatically with working-class issues, their leadership is also part of another, different class and elite network. The complex, internal stratification that exists in the Asian American community once again points not only to the difficulties of representation, but to the concomitant complexities of building consensus that will facilitate group action.

Conclusion

The 1990s posed new challenges for both native-born and foreign-born activists as they fashioned politicized identities. Among new activists, political participation became more polished—part of an accumulated history of life

experiences and events. Like radical and progressive Asian American activists of the 1960s, naturalized Chinese formed part of a critical mass, a cohort
of U.S. citizens with common histories and similar goals. This community
maturation process was instrumental in helping groups like CAUSE articulate their message of empowerment publicly.

Broadly speaking, collective action was funneled into the formation of
grassroots associations specifically political in character. This included politically partisan endeavors. These new inroads brought new activists into political arenas dominated not just by progressive Asian American leadership
but by the larger narratives of national politics and ideologies. As with Asian
Americans of past generations, much of the ascription of a politicized racial
identity was beyond group control, as new activists discovered during the
1996 DNC fund-raising controversy. These new narratives were embedded
in the wider frameworks of power and knowledge that publicly determine
the outlines of rational and acceptable discourses.

The desire of naturalized activists to broaden their political involvement
has altered the political landscape. But the transformation has been both
opportunity and curse. The stories of successful, entrepreneurial immigrants
are empirical half-truths that "reflect the historical interplay of power and
politics locally, nationally and internationally" (Crouch 1996, 351). In many
ways, this discourse is the 1990s version of the 1960s Asian American model
minority myth, whose exceptionalism was grounded in primordial essen-
tialisms. The exceptionalism that new Chinese activists face is played out
against a backdrop of cultural immutability whose history can be unearthed
in the foreign Other, now embedding itself in the middle of the American
body politic. Yet, like the "positives" of the minority myth that Mike Woo
uncomfortably acknowledges, the discourse of exceptionalism has also enabled new Chinese activists to perform models of entrepreneurialism, transnational networking, and other forms of economic and social capital for
the purpose of altering power relations. In this, they have had more effect
and success at local-level participation. The insertion of CAUSE interns in
Sacramento, for example, and the attention that mainstream political leadership now pays to CAUSE events in Southern California are evidence of
political recognition.

However, there is by no means a complete or cohesive whole in political
projects exemplified by groups like CAUSE. The accumulation of maturing
life experiences in the United States, including differing political ideologies,

adds complexity to goals of collective action. Issues such as affirmative action and addressing class and gender have split opinion. Underlying these concerns is the attention that must be paid to the ongoing migration and naturalization of large numbers of new working-class Chinese Americans whose roots/routes of politicization are vastly different from those of post-1965 naturalized activists. Particularly the more progressive of these activists worry that newer cohorts of naturalized Chinese Americans are beginning their participation as political and social conservatives.

The lack of intragroup cohesion is further complicated by the wider project of pan–Asian American identity that some Chinese activists began during the 1990s. Embrace of a pan–Asian American political identity is a turning point in a new-activist Chinese life history; it is tacit recognition of these activists' place in U.S. racial projects and assent that, at least in public political arenas, racial alignments are a way to more effectively contest political disparity. In the context of the U.S. political system, they have realized that unity of voice is a way to evade majority constructions of marginality that shunt aside minority perspectives. This reinterpretation can lead to empowerment. In the next chapter, a campaign for public office affords a valuable and visible opportunity for analysis of how new politicized identities and group actions are enacted on the ground.

SIX

Seeking New Allies,
Building New Community

Political Accommodations and the Power of Race

At the end of the day, new Chinese activists who have shaped the heart of this ethnography through their life histories acknowledge the task and the responsibility they share with other active Asian Americans, including the native-born, in negotiating common strategies for inclusion. Lily Chen, whose first political experiences brought pain, believes the success of this task depends largely on building history together. "Getting it together is the key for all of us," she says. "It takes common experience and even real suffering to bring people together. You have to hurt. You have to really suffer before you realize you need political power." She makes a cutting motion, her extended fingers slicing across her wrist. "It's not like every day we all think alike. It's the issues that can bring us all together."

Sam is aware that he is part of a larger Asian American polity that includes both foreign-born and native-born, whose success in the pursuit of social justice and equality will accrue to him and his family. "I can see why ABCs are more conscious of being a minority, yeah," he says. "We're learning from each other. I am Asian American here. That's the future of Los Angeles. We are part of this multicultural community." Kenton also emphasizes partnerships, but eventually, he says, the numbers of new immigrants will mean that the partnership will tilt in his direction: "Yes, you will be seeing immigrants. . . . They have experiences in the political world and they will become leaders. ABCs will still play a very important role—

they are committed and devoted. The only thing, I hope the future leaders will accept *all* Asian Americans, the ABCs, the FOBs, the Japanese, the Chinese—*everybody*."

To this end, one of the major collective goals is political representation at local and state levels under the pan–Asian American banner. Increasingly, there is a trajectory of alignment and accommodation, as can be seen in the electoral campaigns of Mike Eng and Judy Chu in the Monterey Park area. These two American-born progressives fashioned roles for themselves in the new immigrant collectivity and, in the process, pulled new Chinese activists farther inside the pan–Asian American tent. They did so by representing themselves as bridge builders who understood and were active participants in a *shared community history*. With specific election goals in sight, both candidates and their Asian American supporters bonded around a common history of local racial experiences that allowed for a cohesive whole. At least temporarily, the partnership made room for some of the ideological differences described in Chapter 5. This tacking back and forth once again emphasizes "that identities are not things, they are matters of social dispute" (England 1999, 39) and that they are fluid and situated in historical and social circumstances.

THE POLITICAL MENU: SPECIALS OF THE DAY

During the 1970s and 1980s, the time-worn Golden Dragon Restaurant on North Broadway in L.A.'s Chinatown was emblematic of a Chinese American community past, its banquet room a site where Chinese Americans practiced a communal identity. "In December 1980," Mike Woo remembers, "I had my very first fund-raiser in this room." A grandson of Chinatown immigrants, he returned repeatedly to the Golden Dragon during his 20-plus years of running for office to raise money from supporters, to share memories of collective struggle, and to invoke his own family's deep roots in Chinatown. The headquarters of the Woo Family Association, its walls lined with faded portraits and photographs of all the family heads, is within walking distance of the Golden Dragon.

But as post-1965 Chinese immigration shifted away from Chinatown and headed east into the San Gabriel Valley and beyond, so too did emblems and manifestations of Chinese American identity. Now, Ocean Star in Monterey Park fulfills the role that the Golden Dragon did for Asian

Americans of the 1970s and 1980s. It is an acknowledged site of a new Chinese American community identity that pays homage to a newer generation of Chinese immigrants. "Imagine a restaurant so enormous that the hostesses have to communicate with each other via walkie-talkie," the *Los Angeles Times* wrote of the restaurant in 2004. "Imagine seafood so fresh that the walls are lined with fish tanks. . . . You have just visualized any number of restaurants in Hong Kong. . . . This may not be a trip to Hong Kong, but it's as close as you can come without crossing the ocean" (*Los Angeles Times* 2004).

Just before Thanksgiving 2002, Ocean Star was the scene of another political fund-raiser for another candidate named Mike. More than 600 people showed up to support Mike Eng, who announced his candidacy for Monterey Park City Council—his first try at elective office. Eng is an American-born Chinese and a former self-proclaimed radical turned progressive who grew up during the 1970s. Like many other American-born Chinese in Southern California, his family roots are in Chinatown where his grandfather was a restaurant worker. Eng spent his college years at the University of Hawaii contemplating the ministry but decided law was his calling. At UCLA's law school, he was involved in a number of radical and social justice issues on campus and was instrumental in starting the nation's first college class on Asian American legal history. The course continues to be taught. For most of his professional career, Eng has been an immigration attorney and remains active in a number of progressive Asian American organizations. During the mid-1980s, Eng did what a lot of other professional Asian American activists did once they achieved some stability in their careers—he helped form an advocacy group called the West San Gabriel Valley Asian Pacific Democratic Club. The pan-Asian group aimed much of its grassroots work at voter registration among new naturalized citizens, but it also gave progressive and politically active Asian Americans a chance to begin building networks among new immigrants who were becoming involved in supporting candidates and issues.

Eng also joined CAUSE during the late 1990s. On this evening in 2002, most of the current CAUSE board and many members show up to contribute to his campaign. Also in attendance, now a quarter century older, are many of Eng's American-born contemporaries from the 1960s and 1970s. The familiar faces of other longtime community organizers, social service providers, and political activists like Mike Woo give the event a hint of déjà vu. But the evening belongs to the post-1965 naturalized Chinese immigrants who fill most of the tables. A glance at the registration roster reveals an overwhelming professional and entrepreneurial presence. Many of these same people were heavily involved in the election of Eng's equally political spouse, Judy Chu, to the California State Assembly a year earlier. The political lives of these two progressive Asian Americans reveal the common contemporary terrain that naturalized and American-born activists share and the dialectics that derive from this cohabitation.

· · ·

In 1985, Chu was the first Asian American elected to the Garvey School Board, an area that includes Monterey Park, San Gabriel, and Rosemead. Like Eng, Chu comes from a working-class and labor background. Her father was a member of the Machinists Union, her mother was a Teamsters cannery worker. Chu grew up in South Los Angeles and says that her politicization as a woman of color crystallized at UCLA during the Vietnam War. Courses in ethnic and women's studies convinced her to change from being a math major to pursuing a doctorate in clinical psychology. Her research focused on the adjustment processes of Vietnamese refugees. Like other Asian Americans who professed radicalism as students, Chu turned toward a more progressive stance once she married and began teaching at East Los Angeles College. Living in the San Gabriel Valley, she was an eyewitness to the sundering of old-time politics as the demographics of Monterey Park began to change. At the height of nativist backlash in Monterey Park, when the city council urged Congress to adopt English as the official U.S. language, both Chu and Eng were vocal in their opposition. The outlines of their political maturation can be seen in these initial efforts at building alliances 20 years ago. Both have nurtured this goal and return to it repeatedly when they speak at public functions.

Chu's visible presence in local politics came to fruition in 1988 when she was able to capitalize on a coalition of Latinos and a growing base of post-1965 Chinese citizens to win a seat on the Monterey Park City Council. Her upward trajectory toward statewide politics seemed assured until 1994, when she challenged a Latina incumbent for the State Assembly and was defeated decisively. Four years later, Chu lost the seat again to another Latina. Finally, on her third attempt in 2001, she captured nearly 59 percent of the votes with broad crossover voting from Latinos and strong backing from labor leaders.

Chinese Americans, especially the large numbers of naturalized immigrants who make the 49th Assembly District home, saw Chu's campaign as a way to gain political recognition. They were particularly focused on getting her elected after so many defeats. Lily Chen, who can't help but recall her own role as political pathbreaker, says it took the better part of a decade and concerted planning from a coalition of new activists like herself and American-born activists to achieve victory for Chu. "This is a strong signal that local residents are more accepting of us," she says. "They see we can represent them and that we can get votes beyond just our own ethnic group."

New Chinese activists involved in groups like CAUSE also saw Chu's election as a historic moment in terms of political recognition and empowerment. Since nonprofits are not permitted to endorse candidates, CAUSE focused on a nonpartisan call to get out the vote, theorizing that more Chinese American voters would mean more votes for Chu. Brent recalls that the campaign became a bone of contention, not ideologically but methodologically, between American-born and naturalized activists. New Chinese activists on the board won.

> The foreign-born were all adamant about Judy. This is one great shot to get a Chinese American assemblyperson in there. We've got to spend the money! They outnumber the native-borns and they had the votes.
>
> Nobody's really arguing that Judy wouldn't be a good assemblyperson. The difference was basically all the American-born Chinese were much more fiscally conservative on it.

CAUSE waged its get-out-the-vote campaign through a series of public service announcements on Chinese-language television stations and a half dozen of the major Chinese-language newspapers in the San Gabriel Valley. As previously discussed, media can control the discursive terrain by deciding what issues will be given prominence and therefore legitimacy in public arenas. The CAUSE project demonstrates how ethnic media is symbolic of the immigrant experience—one that differs markedly from that of the native-born, who have less proficiency with the Chinese language.

For highly literate immigrant populations like the Chinese who are readers of robust print industries in their homelands, the vernacular press in the United States has historically been an important link. It has been an active participant in creating community presence and forging community identity. For example, at the turn of the twentieth century, when first-generation immigrants from Japan who spoke and read Japanese dominated settlements of immigrants in Southern California, the daily *Rafu Shimpo* newspaper had tens of thousands of readers. Printed in Japanese with some English, it communicated the pulse of a vital, socially engaged community whose activities and opinions were offered for community consumption. The *Rafu* was forced to stop publication during the evacuation and internment of Japanese Americans during World War II, but it was one of the first community organizations to rehabilitate itself after the war. It became a uniting voice for returning internees building a postwar community.

The tens of thousands of Chinese-speaking and Chinese-reading immigrants who continue to settle in suburban enclaves are voracious consumers of foreign-language media, which also provide a community link and a sense of belonging and incorporation into a transnational Chinese American life (J. Fong 1996). As previously stated, the life histories of naturalized Chinese initially show politics to be not only anathema but a real physical risk. Yet their experiences before immigration also point out the informed nature of this "apolitical" population. As Sam mentioned, everybody in Hong Kong "quietly read the newspapers." Reading habits made the move to the new home and, for many new immigrants, have helped ease the transition of immigration and provided a route to political knowledge in the new community. Sam and other activists are keenly aware of this. "The Chinese-language newspapers really helped to connect to the community and to find out we have a forum," Sam says, "and that increased awareness. It's more fun to read about more things in the community that the *L.A. Times* would not even report. ABCs don't read those [Chinese language] newspapers."

With the increase in the Chinese population since 1965, the number of newspapers serving the San Gabriel Valley and beyond has also grown. Like many of the new immigrants, some of these papers can be classified as transnational in their coverage and economic ties. They have both local and global reach, with numerous overseas branches in North America, Europe, Australia, and the Pacific. Two of the largest San Gabriel Valley newspapers, *Sing Tao Daily* and *International Daily News*, have given heavy coverage to local Asian American political candidates and regularly cover CAUSE events. Sam says aspects of transnational coverage that also foster ties across borders are facilitated by communications technology. "On the block" is an ever-widening area for new immigrants. Sam laughs to think that no local politician or any wannabes would ignore this rich source of community identity. "Now Judy Chu knows she better pick up the newspapers every day!" he says. "Before, they wouldn't pick up a Chinese newspaper because they thought, oh it's nothing. Technology has really helped. They just e-mail the whole thing over here from Taiwan or Hong Kong, and we do the same. We've become more economically and politically connected."

Chinese Americans without Chinese language skills may have greater choice in mainstream news sources, but their access to the specificities of a quotidian Chinese American life as reported in the pages of vernacular newspapers is limited because of the absence of such coverage in conventional sources. As Chu and Eng learned, the vernacular media can be a valuable tool in forging community membership and discourse.

Chu's departure for Sacramento after 13 years on the Monterey Park City Council paved the way for Eng to take over her seat on the council. Although he was well known as Chu's spouse, Eng also capitalized on his own record of progressive politics. He built coalitions among Latinos, labor unions, and labor groups. Perhaps most striking, however, was his open inclusion of and reliance on new immigrant activists. His bilingual Chinese-English campaign literature (replete with photographs of himself and Chu) emphasized his progressive roots—supporting senior citizens, funding youth scholarships, touting memberships in Democratic grassroots organizations and Asian American labor alliances—but he also embraced and promoted entrepreneurial and business issues that many new Chinese activists favored.

The evening program at the Ocean Star fund-raiser, which began with Chu introducing her spouse, summoned up the past and the present in Monterey Park. She made subtle allusions to a 1960s activism disdainful of capital elevated over community and referenced common history closer to home.

> In the mid-eighties, there were many new immigrants and there was a backlash against *us*. It was a rough period in this city of ours, but Mike worked hard to stop that backlash. He worked to improve the community and to build bridges between people. From the beginning of his career, he was determined to use the skills he has, not to make money, but to serve the community.

Speaking after dinner, Eng wove a tapestry of progressive political symbols, with broad allusions to Martin Luther King's speeches laced with a strong appeal to the new demographics.

> I have a vision of a city where the workforce and working families are treated with dignity. I see a city where ethnic diversity is seen as an asset not as a weakness, a city where that which unites us is infinitely greater than anything that divides us!
>
> I have a vision of a city that welcomes new immigrants and sees them as an integral part of our cultural workforce. Immigrants can be seen as an asset—they need not be a millstone, isn't that right? We need these immigrants!

Most telling, however, was Eng's embrace of new business and real estate development in Monterey Park. As previously discussed, many Asian American activists during the 1960s and 1970s had been vocal and confrontational about corporate development in enclaves like Chinatown and Little Tokyo. Monterey Park was torn apart during the 1980s by what established residents saw as rampant overdevelopment by new Chinese immigrants. But for many new Chinese activists, business development and other entrepreneurial activities are a litmus test both in their own lives and for those they would support politically. Eng's homage to this shift in constituency was stark.

> My vision is our vision to build and build. I see a Monterey Park Marketplace Mall with over 500,000 square feet, which could be the city's largest shopping center and running with over a million dollars sales tax revenues and business fees creating over a thousand jobs a year! You like that vision? [*Vigorous clapping from the audience.*]
>
> Because that vision could become a reality with a Krispy Kreme, an In-N-Out Burger, a Nordstrom, a Barnes and Noble, an LA Fitness Center, and one of the first drive-through Starbucks in the United States! A Home Depot, a Target, a Bed, Bath, and Beyond—I see that happening now, not 10 years from now! [*Continuous clapping.*]

Eng got more votes than anyone else. He joined Betty Tom Chu and Monterey Park mayor David Lau to form a Chinese American majority on the city council. Things had changed a lot since Lily Chen's defeat.

A week later, on a Sunday afternoon, Eng and Chu hosted a victory party for Eng's campaign volunteers. Nearly 100 people sat down to celebrate with a Chinese buffet lunch at a senior citizens day center. A decade before, during Mike Woo's run for Los Angeles mayor, new Chinese activists who cut their political teeth on that campaign complained about not having an organizational apparatus that could get out the vote and raise money and awareness about candidates and issues relevant to Chinese Americans. According to them, they lacked a political machine, the pejorative definitions of such notwithstanding. Said one naturalized activist of the earlier Woo campaign, "How do we create, if not a machine, a mechanism that works—an institutional approach as it applies to Asian Americans, which is a must in politics—and then take it to the next step?" The view around the room on that Sunday, with the presence of not just the two elected officials but the scores of community volunteers and contributors supporting them, had all the markers of a local political machine with effects reaching far beyond Monterey Park.[1]

The role new Chinese Americans played in this victory was unambiguous. Against the backdrop of a large congratulatory sign with bright red Chinese lettering, Eng gave special thanks and small gifts to the dozens of Chinese-speaking volunteers who canvassed neighborhoods registering voters for Eng, the Chinese speakers who handled phone banks, and even a Chinese-speaking press relations officer who made sure that Eng's name appeared regularly in area newspapers. Eng talked about his campaign as successfully "working those ties for common goals." Even two new activists who label themselves Republicans saw the larger picture in getting this progressive Democrat elected. "You know, ABCs look at this process as community service," one of them said. "Mike is a Democrat and his political agenda is totally different from mine, but I'm supporting him for city council. I've seen him in action. I know he does a lot of things for the good of the whole community." The other new Republican activist added: "I don't want anything from Mike. I know his heart is in the right place. I wanted him to win because he is a good leader and he will do good for Asian Americans and the whole society."

Eng and Chu have a balancing act—as do most politicians—in trying to make good on such disparate campaign promises as a drive-through coffee shop and labor representation. Chu, the new assemblywoman, spoke about it at a CAUSE function in 2002.

> Yes, I feel the pull from these different constituencies. I have a responsibility to carry legislation that's important to Asian American communities, like bilingual laws, hate crimes, the typical type of progressive Asian American issues.

I think there are issues where there is no consensus and other issues where there is a great deal of consensus. I think there are certain fundamental ones that we can all work on. And those issues for which we have some agreement, we have to work on a united voice. Of course I recognize the diversity within our community and the variety of opinions.

In these new power relationships between American-born and naturalized citizens, there will be inevitable fissures in negotiating consensus. Like other new activists, Kenton is cautious about criticizing Chu but is nonetheless frank in talking about some of the current tension.

Of course, that's already happened. In Hong Kong or Taiwan, sometimes you can bend the rules a little bit, especially if you're dealing with a developer. But Judy sees things very black and white. Sometimes if you don't *openly* oppose [a project], then those people can swallow it, they can understand it. But she would vote no, and that really upset some people! They said, "When you ran for office I supported you, but *now* I ask you for these small things and you won't do it, and not only won't you do it, you vote *against it*!"

I'm not saying Judy is wrong because she has her own perspective, but there is a gap, a conflict. If she had been an immigrant, it might have been different. The differences are not only style but focus and understanding the new immigrant community. I'm *not* talking about violating the law! [But] Judy, being an ABC, doesn't have that knowledge or understanding.

Chu still has overwhelming support from naturalized Chinese, but for those like Leonard, there is an underlying, mostly unspoken restiveness. "Right now, I see this as a partnership," he says. "At this point I don't think the new immigrants have any desire or any plans to replace the likes of Judy. Eventually maybe, but right now it's a very supportive system. Right now there's no one comparable to help them." Kenton is also thinking about substitutions among established American-born political leadership. "[They] bring a different focus," he says. "I hate to use the word *replacement*. . . . These new immigrants are willing to work with Judy because she has certain things and connections they don't have yet, and they're more than happy to support her. She will upset certain individuals but she has done a pretty good job."

Recently, the subject of participation is causing concern, ironically not because naturalized Chinese aren't active but because they *are*. This fact, once again, turns on its head the idea that new immigrants are passive and uninterested in participating. A flood of naturalized Chinese American candidates running for local offices in Southern California, some qualified but most less so, means that they are starting to cancel each other out at the polls. Local-level appointive and elective office is where political experience takes root for most politicians, and whereas qualifications, training, and campaign monies are perhaps not as important there, these issues assume a more critical importance in larger, statewide races. In addition, the complexities of redistricting, which often determine who has the best chance of getting elected, require an experiential sophistication and knowledge of backroom politicking that most first-time candidates do not possess. As Lily Chen and others realized a decade before Chu's eventual win, this becomes crucial if getting more Asian Americans elected is a mobilizing goal, especially because other political and special interest groups are lobbying hard for their own versions of gerrymandered maps.

Some CAUSE members, for their part, say they will continue to focus on candidate training, particularly among new Chinese immigrants, and try to winnow out those individuals who have little chance of winning but who can split the vote. Needless to say, this plan is laden with conflict. Naturalized citizens hold dear the tenet that pretty much anyone can run for public office. CAUSE members like Larry must balance the need to get as many people on board politically as possible with the desire to ensure that candidates are qualified and their campaigns winnable. Accusations of king-making also need to be avoided. As Larry says:

> I think it's time for us to get together and talk about, "Okay, whose time is it to run?" I don't want to talk about rigging elections of course, but you know other groups like Jews and Latinos will try to groom the best candidate and try to control these ridiculous egomaniacs who want to run for office to stay out of it.
>
> Can we ever get enough influence that we can do this? If you want to extrapolate and say that should be an Asian American goal and not just a Chinese American goal, so be it!

That American-born Asian political leaders like Chu and Eng have worked to enable a more inclusive pan-Asian political identity speaks to their responsiveness to the challenge of heterogeneity. What is occurring is an *emergent* and *evolving* relationship between foreign-born and native-born activist citizens in which each group seeks to discover areas where commonality can form the basis for collective action and where issues of less agreement are either temporarily tabled or worked on through intergroup negotiation in nonpublic arenas. Heterogeneity will always be one of the biggest challenges facing a unified Asian American political identity. The awareness that different groups possess historically disparate cultural models but also bring special attributes of sociality, including ways of networking, can strengthen the whole.

In campaigns like Eng's, it is possible to discern political negotiation and compromise. Entrepreneurship and development are core issues for many naturalized Chinese. In areas like Monterey Park, which needs to strengthen and expand its civic tax base, Eng can embrace the idea of economic development as long as naturalized activists can cede ground on a core progressive issue such as labor protection and workers' rights. The two issues need not be in opposition. In this politics of recognition, the naming of collective group activity under a pan-Asian identity functions as an external, public marker of unity. Beneath this reside the ever-flowing currents and eddies of internally negotiated group dynamics.

NEW CHINESE ACTIVISTS: A ONE-GENERATION ANOMALY?

Generationally, it goes without saying that naturalized activists are a unique bunch. Any of their children born here are ABCs. How do immigrant parents see their children's futures? How will the positionings of those children be expressed politically and racially? Will they be as politically active? Many of the children whose parents populate this ethnography are still in high school or college, with a few beginning to venture out; they are products of Americanized lives that are categorically different from their parents' experiences. Larry sees definite differences in his children's generation. "It takes a special mentality to be an immigrant," he says. "I don't care whether it's a Mexican immigrant or what. It takes a certain risk-taking attitude that if somebody else can do it, I want to do it. I don't know what drives my kids . . . all they want to do is play video games." Veronica worries that her children don't value being Chinese:

> I noticed that when I picked them up at school, they get really embarrassed when I talk to them in Chinese. They were *embarrassed to be Chinese*! They should be glad they have two cultures that can work together. I gave up. They took German.

Chinese culture is still important. You never question your parents, you never say no, you just do. And parents should *always* take care of the kids' education. When I hear about [white] families—the kids have to borrow money to go to school. I say, "God, you *have* to do that?" It's quite shocking, really!

Marlon watched with disgust the generational conflict between some of his friends and what he saw as their underachieving daughter. "She wants to study moviemaking," he says, laughing in derision, "which drives her parents nuts! They want their children to be engineers, to have a good job. They don't want their daughter going to film school and then becoming permanently unemployed! The parents almost cried—they've *never* seen education leading to unemployment!"

Universal parental worries notwithstanding, post-1965 immigrants are not much different from Asians of earlier generations in their concerns for their offspring's futures (Takahashi 1997). If the American-born children of naturalized Chinese follow paths similar to those of previous American-born children of immigrants, if they begin to internalize and identify not only with their American lives but with previous lives centered around the cultural hearth where family roots and historical experiences are found, then the expectation is that they may also come to see themselves as citizens of color. As Min and Kim (2000) suggest, this is despite educational or economic integration, which "may make them feel comfortable. . . . Yet, other structural factors force them to accept their ethnic or pan-ethnic Asian identity" (742).

Virtually all of the first-generation American-born children have parents who continue to maintain transnational ties to Asia. By high school, the children are themselves at least occasional travelers to Asia. And while they are grounded as citizens in their American communities, they also possess a sense of the familiar in Asia. Asia becomes a recognizable ethnoscape, both identifiable and customary (Appadurai 1991). This quotidian life is facilitated by new Chinese activists who are able to maintain homes in Southern California and in Asia. In Lynn's case, she and her husband often shuttle between Cerritos and Taipei and spend extended periods at their homes in each city. Their two college-age children see these constant border crossings as normal.

Some Asian Americans experience this transnational reality with a cultural fluidity unknown to any previous Asian generation. For people like

Mike Woo, the seeming advantages of this life create concern about the political sensibilities of this latest Asian American cohort.

> If a lot of these kids end up getting good jobs, buying nice cars, nice houses, and disappearing into the suburbs and don't maintain any connection back to the community, I think the potential influence and [political] clout will be lost. We haven't had a Vincent Chin incident in a while. I hate to say that's what it takes, but sometimes that's what needs to happen to galvanize an otherwise apathetic community.

Erik, who is in his 30s, was born in Southern California and is too young to remember how Vincent Chin's 1982 murder spurred Asian Americans to collective political action. But in college, he read enough about it to understand its importance. "It was so horrible and violent," he says; "it doesn't matter if you're Chinese or Japanese—you're a human being! It erupts emotionally!" He is also too young to remember the transformative 1960s or the movement for social justice in the United States: "Yeah, I saw it all on the History Channel." Neither was he old enough to vote for Mike Woo when Woo ran for mayor of Los Angeles during the 1990s, but his parents did. Their support of Woo has since become part of the fabric of his own politicized history.

> I remember as a kid when he ran for mayor. My parents donated a lot of money to Michael. They really believed in him. My dad was very vocal about it [Woo's loss to Riordan]. He thought it was racism.
>   Same with Judy [Chu]. My parents have been huge supporters of Judy, and they don't even live in Monterey Park. They felt like, okay, we've taken care of our family. We've got enough money, we're feeding ourselves . . . we've *all* experienced either subtle or obvious discrimination and that *pisses* them off! I know both my parents have their Chinese immigrant stories.

Erik's parents came to the United States in 1967. Like most post-1965 activist families, Erik's has deep political connections. Both sides of the family supported Chiang Kai-shek and were forced to leave China for Taiwan. His father, whom Erik calls a patriot, was admitted to the United States under the special skills quota. Like other post-1965 immigrants, they settled away from Chinatown, in eastern Los Angeles County where their appearance at the local supermarket—Erik in his baby stroller—elicited long stares. Erik says that his parents "didn't hang out in Chinatown because Chinatown Chinese were Cantonese and we're Mandarin. . . . It's like we were talking to Brazilians!"

Erik could be one of those young Asian Americans who worry Mike Woo except for the fact that he is already talking enthusiastically about political involvement, including an eventual run for public office. He attended a private high school in Los Angeles and is an alumnus of both Stanford and Harvard. Erik has joined the family business after working at a major software company. He has already traveled extensively in Asia and, for a time, worked overseas. Despite this life of privilege and a first-rate education (or perhaps because of it), Erik learned very early about the isolation racial difference can create.

> I grew up around that classic old, white world . . . white shirts and hair above the collar. It was like parties at [this] club and that [other] stupid club. I competed with those kids, I live amongst them. I do business with them now.
>
> But here's the thing that *sticks* with me. My senior year of high school and I'm at this club, and this other kid walks up to me and says, "Oh, are you the one taking the pictures?" Like I said, "Man, I'm actually *here* for the party!" I left. I was shocked. I felt . . . you know . . . I was in shock.

As with first-generation naturalized Chinese activists, shock turned to commitment.

> You know, I will enjoy financial success, but I will use that to do more than just buy toys and vacations in Jackson Hole. I will want to redirect some of that to help out, to get the community to the next level, and to be one of the representatives along the way because *I* experienced things as an Asian American and I believe even my children will 20 years out. That's why we need to protect ourselves.

Erik's life experiences as a native-born Asian American connect him to the wider pan-Asian community, which is unlike the more ethnic-specific focus of his parents.

> My girlfriend is Japanese. I hang out with Koreans. I speak almost as much Korean as I do Chinese. The fact that you're not Chinese is irrelevant to me. When it comes to political empowerment, my generation is more APA [Asian Pacific American] oriented.
>
> We realize if we splinter ourselves and we don't cooperate, *we don't mean anything!* We were all born in America, English is our first language. We have enough common ground. Like the Abercrombie & Fitch controversy.[2] What was more important was that APAs came *together* on this issue. *All* the groups were cooperating.

Erik may embrace a broader pan-Asian collectivity, but his views on political issues cannot be glossed as either liberal or conservative.

> I'm a *California Republican*! I'm socially liberal, fiscally conservative. I'm pro-choice, I'm against the death penalty, but I don't like taxes and I don't like how much I have to pay. I think the glass ceiling is bullshit. I think you allow it to be there. Screw that! I worked for [a major brokerage house] and was a director at 27. It wasn't because I was Chinese but because I worked my ass off and I made money for the company, so they promoted me.
>
> My parents worked their butts off—welfare . . . I don't believe in welfare. But I'd rather have welfare than have people who have nowhere to go except to resort to crime. I'm a privatist, and welfare is a valuable tool to stop people from falling into the cracks. Can it be administered differently? Absolutely!

His opinions about affirmative action echo those of many first-generation post-1965 Chinese activists.

> I never thought about it because it didn't affect me. It was about the black kids. I don't have a good opinion about it. It hurts as many people as it helps. Affirmative action doesn't help us. It's one of those messy, complicated, emotionally driven issues. I don't have a good answer now. Give me 12 years and I'll have a good sound bite.

Presumably, by that time, he's "absolutely" going to run for office. He says he will be an example of a new kind of Asian American candidate, reaching beyond the limits of ethnicity.

> We're going to be more sophisticated, more policy driven. My generation, I don't think they're going to ride a Chinese platform as much. The way we'll have to operate is at a mainstream level. Gotta work the parties, gotta know the right people, gotta know how to raise an inordinate amount of money.
>
> You can't do that with just the Chinese American community. You've got to have that simply as an arrow in your quiver. There's no way a single ethnic group can get there alone. Everyone has got to be thinking multiracial.

Finally, adding more complexity to the ever-burgeoning heterogeneity that is Asian America are the continuing flows of Chinese immigrants who now include a cohort of younger, foreign-born, and recently naturalized citizens. Post-1965 new activists are now in their late 50s and 60s. They have been participating politically long enough to be called "old guard" by these younger naturalized citizens who also want to begin carving out their own space and place and who will necessarily become future leaders. What follows is a brief glimpse of yet another layer in the project that is the (re)construction of a politicized Asian American identity.

MARCH 2004

A U.S. immigration official speaks to the crowd: "We will be passing out voter registration cards for you to fill out—*this is your newly acquired right and you should exercise it!* You can also apply for a U.S. passport. You should have already turned in all your foreign documents." It is 7:30 in the morning, and already, lines of people snake around the outside of the Los Angeles Convention Center. They stream into the cavernous building, rushing to get good seats. More than 5,000 in all, they are a sea of people dressed in red, white, and blue. Half of them are excited new U.S. citizens-to-be. They clutch green cards; other forms of temporary, precitizenship documentation; and their letters from what was formerly the Immigration and Naturalization Service.[3] The other half of the crowd—family and friends—are equally excited, with their arms full of American flags; red, white, and blue bouquets; stuffed animals; and video cameras to record the historic moment.

Among the crowd is a young man from northern China who came here with his family during the late 1980s. His parents are both respected university graduates who paid for their positions as young intellectuals by being "reeducated" during the Cultural Revolution. They worked as laborers on a rural farm where, they told their young son, it was not uncommon to see and hear about others who had been sent down committing suicide. The experience left his mother traumatized; she wants nothing to do with politics. His father, on the other hand, was politically radicalized. He grabbed at the first chance, 20 years later, to take his family away from China.

They settled in Monterey Park. Young Steven started public school speaking not a word of English. Now he is a student at UCLA with few memories of China. He has yet to return and exudes an unconscious sense of self that many American-born Chinese exhibit. He is bilingual, speaking English without accent and subscribing to all forms of Chinese-language media. He has a mix of primarily Asian American friends, both foreign-born and native-born. The Chinese woman he is dating was born in the United States. While growing up, he says, his father told him that "politics is the only way you can change things." He has adopted his father's political stance. Steven has thought about citizenship for some time now but finally decided during college to make it a priority. He eventually wants to run for political office here, so becoming a U.S. citizen is a necessary step toward that goal.

Steven has already volunteered for political activities and met many older Asian American activists—both naturalized and native-born. Several have become part-time mentors. As one new Chinese activist commented about Steven and others like him: "They represent the new leadership arena of young immigrants. They're very comfortable here in America and they also understand immigrant issues." Although Steven's identity and his views on political issues have yet to fully mature, his decision to be involved with both naturalized Chinese Americans and progressive native-born activists indicates his awareness of his racialized status and his desire to work in the Asian American community. Ideologically, his current political philosophy regarding relevant Asian American issues is somewhat similar to Erik's.

Steven, however, does not have Erik's country club background. Although well educated, Steven is a product of public schooling and a middle-class upbringing. Born nearly two decades after the 1960s, he understands and supports the transformative nature of the fight for equal justice and civil rights, especially as it is still espoused among his older mentors. He is highly supportive of naturalized citizen and immigrant rights and issues, such as bilingual ballots. However, surrounded by high numbers of Asian and Asian American students at UCLA, he is less sure about the need for affirmative action in higher education. He thinks entrepreneurial business efforts among immigrants need to be supported, but he reserves some of his strongest criticism for those Chinese Americans who think only about making money and "living and working and associating in areas where there are only Chinese so they don't see the larger community issues." He voted a progressive, Democratic ticket in November 2004. He thinks that some of the current new Chinese activist leadership in Southern California isn't doing enough to foster the next generation—people like himself. Like Erik, he *is* still young and relatively inexperienced and says he feels an age bias from current political leaders. "Sometimes I have a hard time communicating with them," he remarks. He has also worked on a few community projects with progressive American-born activists who are closer in age to his parents, and met with much the same reception. During the next few years, he will begin paying his dues in terms of additional community and political experiences, and his age will no doubt become less of an issue.

As both naturalized and American-born activists begin to yield leadership over the next decade or so, some of the bench strength in the next round of Asian American politics will come from a new naturalized generation. Like Steven, they will be in their early to mid-30s. He will not be alone. Sharing the same bench will be a fusion of another first generation of Chinese Americans, like Erik, and still other American-born activists-to-be who will represent a fourth, fifth, or even sixth generation of native-born American citizen. *All* of their perceptions of racialized marginalities and strategies of political inclusion and empowerment will be vastly different from those of their elders.

. . .

I hereby declare on oath that I absolutely and entirely renounce and abjure all allegiance and fidelity to any foreign prince, potentate, state, or sovereignty of whom or which I have heretofore been a subject or citizen; that I will support and defend the Constitution and laws of the United States of America . . .

Finishing the pledge in unison, the new U.S. citizens, Steven included, clap and cheer. Above the tumult, he yells, "I did it!" He poses for pictures, clutching a small American flag and his voter registration card.

Conclusion

At the beginning of the twenty-first century, Asian American political activists, both native-born and foreign-born, are working to forge alliances that will allow a united group to advance and increase its level of representation in mainstream political structures and gain access to the resources these structures can offer. On the ground, and in the midst of these myriad negotiations, this collective political action seems fraught with conflict and impossibilities.

On one hand, naturalized Chinese are beginning to become advocates and members of a pan–Asian American political accord. They are vocal supporters of and are generous financially in affirming progressive Asian

American leadership, including native-born electoral candidates who still maintain hegemony in this political alliance. Their support will most likely continue as naturalized activists recognize that the native-born possess political experiences and positionings that they have not yet achieved.

On the other hand, there is also an implicit tension based on the realization that unconditional support from the naturalized community cannot always be viewed with certainty. American-born participants in positions of influence and leadership are carefully strategizing and brokering relationships with the new Asian American immigrant majority. They have been attentive to immigrant issues and recognize the inherent numerical strength of the new community.

However, while this project of group redefinition is accommodated, a pan–Asian American political alliance incorporating the current crop of politically participatory native-born and foreign-born is poised to be eclipsed by the coming of age of a new generation. Members of this younger generation experience economic and social privilege rooted in the relatively higher class standing they inherited from their immigrant parents. But even from this more privileged vantage point, some of the children still appear to be fully cognizant of their family's racialized history in the United States and how this reconciles with broader pan–Asian American categorizations. Other first-generation young adults who have come from Asia since the 1980s, with class roots that may not be as privileged, also have a racialized awareness of belonging to an Asian American sensibility. In determining the trajectory of the new generation, class must not be forgotten, as it has also grown in complexity since the arrival of the post-1965 immigrant population and looms as a core challenge to a pan–Asian American unity.

Less well observed at this time is whether future Asian American political activists are equally receptive to a wider and more diversified approach to the racialized experiences of all people of color and how color and class are mutually constitutive (Brodkin 2000). Asian American activists of the 1960s understood the dialectics of race and class in hegemonic nation-state projects that were and continue to be "central to political contestations over control of the materialities of society" (Goldberg 2002, 109). The attention given to these larger schemes of power has guided the ideology and agenda of progressive activists—an ideology predicated on the notion of heterogeneous inclusion and the concomitant right of individuals to participate in and benefit from state belonging.

The degree to which this legacy has been effectively passed on to a new generation of political participants, both native-born and foreign-born, has been a point of concern and self-criticism among progressive leaders (Leong 1999). This would seem an especially critical point of responsibility for education and discussion as new Chinese activists who *have* acquired knowledge of the experiences of other minorities in the United States have clearly had their own perspectives broadened and liberalized in the process.

Chapter 7 summarizes how racial and cultural difference constructs—simultaneously—the rights of citizenship and, in this shifting terrain, lends new potential to ways of belonging.

SEVEN

Still the Problem of the Twenty-first Century

Toward a Theory of Racialized Identity

The newest chapter in the more than 150-year history of Asian America reveals uncompromising evidence that among post-1965 Chinese immigrants who become political activists, ascribed racial categorizations provide a major impetus guiding their political participation in the United States. This racialized status is in opposition to their putative socioeconomic success. Although there have been and will continue to be changes in the script, the original story line remains largely unedited; racial categorizations persist that classify and subjectify all Americans of Asian ancestry, regardless of nativity. In this context, the fundamental contradiction around which U.S. citizenship is framed in the "unrelenting march toward freedom and democracy" is that, of course, the ideal of what a liberal American democracy can offer is not fully descriptive of the experience of citizens who are neither white nor initially English-speaking (Hu-DeHart 1996, 246). And although issues of ethnicity, fairness, cultural relativity, and other neoliberal gestures have complicated the discursive terrain, the essentialist views of so many American citizens remains constructed around race, and therefore defines their lives.

What is also uncovered are the ways of agency; individuals who first envision and then work to achieve incorporation into the body politic are also actively engaged in redefinition and resistance. The larger, structural constraints imposed upon their agency instantiate a dialectical maneuvering in which they also use racial strategies to contest and negotiate position.

Reinscribing these dialectics constitutes the fashioning of a new-activist political identity. Its crafting does not occur in a vacuum but is also co-constituted with aspects of class, gender, and generation among naturalized Chinese activists, the rest of Asian America, and mainstream society.

I repeat the questions posed at the beginning of this book: Who are these new politically active Chinese Americans, and what do they want to accomplish? The answers can now be framed in the following manner:

1. They are naturalized citizens who, in the process of constructing new lives as Americans, have come to acknowledge, through life experiences in this country, their status as racialized citizens. It is a status that economic, educational, and occupational achievement does not negate.

2. This acknowledgment also forces an awareness of the discrepancies between their status and their ideal of full emancipatory citizenship. They seek to contest a marginalized position through political participation that will gain them recognition and access via a more collective pan–Asian American model.

3. There is no wholesale abandonment of ethnic connections and networks. Indeed, the ethnic base provides them with their first organizational political engagement at the local level. Subsequent pan-Asian racial identifications expand group instrumentalities in mainstream arenas.

4. Enhanced access to social and economic capital, including the utilization of transnational social networks, helps them to maximize political and empowerment strategies, although not always positively.

5. Accommodation to a new-activist political agenda is occurring among progressive Asian American political leaders. The continuing dialectics of these everyday negotiations between native-born and foreign-born activists will determine the future of political Asian America for at least this generation and, with continuing immigration from Asia, possibly the next.

6. Naturalized Chinese political work is a portrayal of community activism. The nexus of new social activity, its interactions and relationships constitute a transformative process that has created and enabled dynamic community change both in Asian America and in the larger mainstream society.

Acknowledging Racialized Status

The dynamics of a new Chinese activist identity center on these activists' growing understanding of the *commonalities* of American experience that they share with other Asian Americans, both foreign-born like themselves and native-born. The work this entails is embedded in the social construction of identity making. The building of common ground has not always been an achievable goal for Asian Americans and still presents great challenges. The history of Asian immigration to the United States illustrates how social ties among different ethnic immigrants that might have fostered early pan-Asian convergences were blocked. For Asian immigrants, there was no pan-Asian identity largely because U.S. immigration policy and, more importantly, economic and labor requirements partitioned Asian immigration by ethnic group. Partition was followed by exclusion. Citizenship for most Asian immigrants was denied until the 1950s. Despite this, in analyzing recovered Asian American history, "the conventional wisdom concerning the Chinese and their supposed political backwardness needs to be stood on its head. . . . [L]ack of political consciousness was not [a] distinguishing characteristic" (McClain 1994, 3).

In further understanding the political economy of the United States within which Asian immigration has always been framed, immigrants of this post-1965 Chinese "knowledge class" are simply another, more contemporary form of recruited labor. Seen from this perspective, their racial assignments are part of a broader national project of the labor force creation of racialized subjects (Brodkin 2000).

Young, post-1965 Chinese immigrants who would later become politically active also immigrated as highly politically conscious individuals. Politics, however, translated not into participation but into fear, and most focused only on availing themselves of the educational and economic opportunities American safety offered. Although a number were college students during the turbulent 1960s and witnessed the contestation—ideological and physical—commonplace on many U.S. college campuses, they often viewed it with a sense of bemusement or disdain. They defined themselves as foreign students and noncitizens who had positive imaginings and attitudes toward the United States. This is in contrast to American-born Asian radicals who were politically active as college students.

However, new Chinese are similar to other progressive Asian American activists who finished school, began working, and then established advocacy and professional groups.

Although some early immigrants were heavily involved as student activists on U.S. campuses, political recognition and the agency requisite for reclaiming an Asian American community history were the purviews of the American-born, not the immigrant. With longevity in the United States, however, came an increasing exposure to racial subjectifications. As first-generation immigrant Chinese who display urbanized Asian roots and acquire Western educations, professional careers, and other socioeconomic benefits, new Chinese activists see themselves as especially qualified for the role of modern U.S. citizen. What better, more capable, competent, and skilled profile could a new citizen possess? Or so they believed. The oft-repeated word *shock* is descriptively concise as they become more immersed in their American lives.

Discrepant Citizenships

The social and psychological investment inherent in deciding to become a U.S. citizen upped the ante for what new Chinese activists assumed full citizenship guaranteed—the promise of participation as citizens within parameters of democratic equality and freedom. The sense of anticipation attached to becoming new citizens is profound. Most have never experienced full citizenship but have known only a twilight of being fractionally so identified. And although others may have been citizens of another nation, this, too, has been fraught with discomfort and political upheaval. All new Chinese activists have family histories deeply tied to other political processes. All were raised to view political participation with, at the very least, suspicion. More commonly, prevailing attitudes include apprehension and fear. They have juxtaposed this intense life experience with an equally powerful vision of liberal democracy. There is no doubt that they are ardent subscribers to American freedoms. The realization that their citizenship in fact hinges on larger narratives involving racial positionings and definitions about who qualifies for full membership leads to their politicization. The desire to organize and act upon their marginality is constructed within the parameters of sanctioned, existing structural pluralities.

Salience of the Ethnic Connection

Expectations of what an American life and democracy offer juxtaposed with the reality of events and life experiences galvanized co-ethnic Chinese Americans into action. Early civic engagements among new activists were local and ethnically organized but outside traditional enclaves like Chinatown. In addition, unfamiliarity with the U.S. political system as well as extant Asian American political and community coalitions promoted ethnicity among new activists. Ethnically based political projects were an outcome of the phenomenal growth of post-1965 immigrants and their massed settlement in the reconfigured spaces and places of the ethnoburbs. These communities perform as new outposts of economic activity, much of it transnational and governed by restructured global economies in which both highly skilled professionals and low-wage laborers find economic niches (Li 1998).

In constructing American lives, many new activists had the economic wherewithal during the 1980s to select suburbs outside the Los Angeles core. Existing multicultural areas were white or Latino with far fewer Asian Americans. A smaller portion of first-generation immigrants and their families have also moved into even more affluent, predominantly white neighborhoods. They selected suburban living in anticipation of a better lifestyle, including superior educational opportunities for their American-born children.

The diversity of multicultural influences, class differences, and the continuing migration of Chinese make ethnoburbs particularly vital and dynamic spaces for social interaction and for the dawning of political mobilization and action. Chinese parents-cum-activists organized by using their ethnic base as an efficacious means for gaining representation in the wider community. The result was a transformation of power relations and recognition of these new players who had challenged established local structures. Organizing along ethnic lines is certainly not new, nor is the skill with which political structures co-opt ethnicity, as the example of U.S. political parties mining European immigrant communities for votes illustrates (Roediger 1991). Moreover, the fact that new activists have begun to construct group cohesion through empowerment tactics privileging race does not mean that ethnic strategies can be considered epiphenomenal. Particularly in urban areas where ethnic populations reached critical mass, ethnicity as a means to political participation ought to be regarded as co-constitutive and, like racial ascriptions, be analyzed through specific historical frameworks governing the political economy of the United States (Fujita and O'Brien 1991).

Local-ities of the Transnational Field

Transnational social practices and a multifocal outlook are normative aspects of a naturalized-activist political identity. Multiple and situational identities and the use of transnational strategies are ways of performing new citizenships that are also socially transformative (Itzigsohn 2000a; Vertovec 1999).

Many new activists do see themselves as brokers and links between the United States and China. Indeed, this has always been the case for Asian Americans. Being Chinese and American has always carried with it a political dimension in global frameworks of unequal power, the development of identity concurrent with the dialectics of transnational dialogue between the two countries (Y. Chen 2006). New activists are conscious of and promote the leverage they gain from using transnational social practices to benefit strategies of inclusion. But simultaneously, two points need to be emphasized regarding transnational social fields. Those who practice the transnational in local communities should not be regarded as presenting "severe risks of compromised political loyalties," as was assumed in the 1996 DNC fund-raising controversy and the 1999 case of Wen Ho Lee (Wu and Lim Youngberg 2001, 338). Neither should a transnational life be considered part of the "exemplary communities of the transnational moment" (Tololyan 1996, 4). A focus on either model, of ideal or of pathology, elides discussion about the ways in which institutions of power co-opt and reconstruct transnationality for their own convenience or in order to reinforce a status of outsider noncitizen and foreigner.

The degree to which new activists view ethnic connections and networks that afford the advantages of transnational proficiency as simply *normative* has created tension over the political boundaries of citizenship. Reconstructions of place/space, avenues of capital, modes of cultural reproduction, and consciousness of being there *and* here—the morphological aspects of a transnational life—have all contributed to a new-activist politicized identity. But these transnational enactments are not always capable of evading local or national borders. There are concrete limits to the skills and capital that new activists have acquired in American society. Racialization speaks directly to those limits and challenges theories of transnational evasions practiced by free-floating, deterritorialized subjects.

The work of new activists redefines the ways in which transnational practices benefit the local in a manner that also continues to build a community-based identity encompassing all Asian Americans. To speak to this indigenous foundation is to rearticulate what has been privileged from the beginning—"the notion that racial factors influence the participation [of] and receptivity toward certain groups in American society" and, furthermore, that although "many formal impediments have been steadily chipped away, formidable resistance remains" (Watanabe 2001, 369).

Naturalized activists have been both condemned and lauded for their ability to perform transnationally. However, whether such performance is accepted or not, the routinization of transnational life within local matrices is now part of quotidian Asian America.

Dialectical Negotiations between Naturalized and Native-Born Activists

Moving beyond ethnic models of grassroots political participation has brought new Chinese activists into the sphere of progressive Asian Americans, where contestations and compromises over a representational political identity often exist. On this interactive field stand new-activist leaders, like Charlie Woo, who already have a history of politicized involvement with ethnic-based organizations and also with progressive Asian Americans and mainstream political structures. Woo is adding his voice to and purposefully engaging some aspects of a progressive agenda. He is seeking a wider and more influential role for immigrant citizens. Also taking the field are American-born leaders like Mike Eng, who has a community history among naturalized activists. He is part of a progressive, American-born group whose trajectory includes building new social relationships among naturalized activists and, at the same time, adding to an Asian American power base by strategizing new ways of achieving political inclusion in power structures. The field has space for allowing and negotiating intragroup difference, a constant shifting and balancing of agenda that need not detract from the larger project of a pan-Asian empowerment in structures of U.S. political power.

After nearly two decades of localized political participation, the next stage of new Chinese political involvement is unfolding. In the aftermath of the DNC fund-raising controversy and the case of Wen Ho Lee, new activists have not been reluctant to seek recognition beyond suburban city halls, at state and national levels. Seen from the vantage point of Asian American history and within the context of time, the evolution of a new Chinese activist identity refocuses theories of Asian American immigration and integration. Post-1965 new activists, of course, are not immigrants in the same mold as the grandparents and great-grandparents of most Asian Americans. Freed from some of the structural constraints that impeded earlier generations of Asian immigrants, such as the nullification and denial of citizenship, new Chinese American activism highlights the agency and speed with which first-generation immigrants can, and already have, translated their politicization into collective action.

There should be little surprise, then, when new activists, having reached a stage in their lives that political participation became necessary—for example, to contest negative stereotyping of their presence or to protect and promote business interests or their children's educations—involved themselves initially in ethnic-specific pursuits during the 1980s. But Asian American scholars and observers of participatory politics, including this author, may have been premature in believing political mobilization would be *permanently* fractured along ethnic fault lines. There will always be ethnic divisions in the ever-changing project of a collective Asian American political identity, but these boundaries need not render the whole ineffectual. Ethnicity still matters, but at the same time it is less salient in confronting the larger inequalities and conflations of the racial state (Bonilla-Silva 1996; Omi and Winant 1994). This becomes especially relevant as naturalized immigrants begin to assess the wider meanings of racialized citizenship. At present, the name change of CAUSE to include *Asian American* may be largely cosmetic, as some members have pointed out, but it still reflects serious, reasoned thought among leaders about their willingness to incorporate other instrumentalities of political action.

To speak of a pan-Asian America is first to recognize the dynamic transformation that this collective identity continues to undergo. As important is whether the progressive roots of a pan–Asian American politics will continue or will be hybridized. Already there is evidence of its transformation, particularly as these changes and differences in agenda are mirrored in electoral politics. No Asian American candidate from Los Angeles or any of the surrounding ethnoburbs—native-born or foreign-born—would attempt to win an election without courting naturalized voters and paying attention to issues that are important to them. The transformation is not without conflict, but neither was the construction of pan–Asian American-ness during the early 1970s. The radical roots of the Asian American move-ment were shed, and the grafting of progressive issues gave weight to the shifting social service and professional leadership that constituted Asian America during the 1980s. If history is a guide, it may be likely that the more conservative elements of a naturalized activist agenda that attends to only business or immigrant issues will also be shed for more progressive or centrist positions. For example, numerous racializing experiences have made many new activists highly attentive to broader social justice issues in-volving not just Asian Pacific Americans but other citizens of color as well. In addition, the CAUSE name change may be interpreted as the result of a nascent accommodation.

The modification, including a change in agenda focus, took some time to accomplish simply because a number of active CAUSE members did not support it. Some of them finally acceded to the majority, but others did not. Lynn had been speaking for some time about leaving the organization, but the name change was the final straw and she dropped out. She felt strongly that much work still needed to be done among Chinese immigrants on the issue of voter education and registration and was unhappy with what she saw as a "dilution" of purpose. Other members of CAUSE who have been displeased with some of the organization's public stances on various election issues have also left. Jettisoning elements of division is a normal process for any group. Aside from the obvious effect of promoting internal group cohesion, it also creates a unified front that makes a bigger impression on power structures. The negative side of coalitional politics, however, is that not everybody gets equal time, and on those issues where there is real dis-agreement, spirited and meaningful discussion can be lost.

CAUSE is still paying attention to its Chinese American immigrant membership in place-based activities such as voter registration in the San Gabriel Valley, but in 2004, the group began publishing a political newslet-ter, *CAUSE & Effects: An Asian American Political Journal.* The lead article in the inaugural edition is "The Absence of Asian Americans" (CAUSE 2004, 1). Other articles highlight the untapped voter potential of the wider

Asian American community, partisan party affiliations, and the conversion of population growth into political power. In short, these are crossover subjects that equally concern many progressive activists.

Community Transformations

Clearly, Asian immigrants *do* desire integration into American society. By the 1990s, they were becoming naturalized citizens much earlier and at rates significantly higher than other immigrant groups (Lien et al. 2001). Yet voter registration and voting remain low among naturalized and native-born Asian Americans. Those active in CAUSE are clearly cognizant of the challenges involved in educating new Asian citizens so they understand that they have a stake in exercising their citizenship politically. As CAUSE has matured over the past decade, its primary goal continues: to educate new Chinese Americans about participatory democracy and get them to vote. Activist members are aware of the socioeconomic diversity among new immigrant citizens, and they feel strongly about their responsibility in literally translating the exigencies of the participatory process and each citizen's role. It is a big job.

Voting is a primary way of exercising one's citizenship, but CAUSE has also worked to educate beyond the ballot box and to effect change through internships, public forums, and petitions. This is again one of the reasons why CAUSE spends its time and resources on ethnic media outlets as a way to build and foster community discourses among a primarily Chinese-speaking audience. For their part, American-born progressives like Judy Chu, who forged a multiracial, multiethnic, and naturalized coalition to finally win office, have become adroit at servicing new immigrant citizen constituencies. New activists want to be full partners in assuring that this happens. There does appear to be at least some dissatisfaction with American-born leadership on some issues that new Chinese activists deem important, but the degree of disaffection remains at a simmer.

What is *not said*, however, is perhaps as important to recognize. While new accommodations are enacted in the everyday of any political negotiation, immigrants are already the majority not just in Asian America but among Asian American voters, with Chinese the largest subgroup. It thus follows that if there is an Asian American collectivity, immigrants like new

Chinese activists will soon be key producers of the agenda. In many ways, they already are. Having altered the local landscape with their financial capital, they are considered indispensable for their contributions in electoral politics, the 1996 DNC fund-raising controversy notwithstanding. Their financial support of various community causes has made up for dwindling government funding to social service organizations.[1] In this regard, they are creating social linkages that are transforming community.

Out of sight of most mainstream institutions and organizations, however, new activists are working from below in shaping their own and other new Asian immigrants' awareness of their adopted communities. Power structures still have not allowed most of these actors to share the stage. Nevertheless, new activists have constructed their own roles, individually and through group mobilization. They have creatively produced their own organizations as well as an institutional dynamic that is responsible for much of the incorporation of immigrants into the politics of participation. And the emphasis is on incorporation. Quite clearly, the dominant, classical theory of assimilation predictive of a single outcome of homogenization and the requirement that newcomers erase their memories and sentiments in order to be accepted does not fully apply here (Alba and Nee 1997). The absorption of minority differences in relation to the majority has been thoroughly critiqued as being overly static and tied to a specific set of historical circumstances related to the "whitening" of various groups of European immigrants at the turn of the twentieth century. This particular theoretical synthesis has shown that the perceptions of even the most racially disparaged European groups shifted over time as Europeans became incorporated into the U.S. body politic (Brodkin 1998). This is not the assimilative example of the Asian American experience, and scholars and others who point to the color of the majority of post-1965 immigrants are less sanguine about the same possibilities of whiteness applying to racially categorized immigrants. Key ingredients for successful individual assimilation include education, exposure to U.S. society, English-language proficiency, economic positioning, and even place of residence (Zhou 2004). Yet even though it has been shown that new activists qualify on every count, their continuing racialization by mainstream narratives defines their subjectification and subsequent politicization.

The uncovering of new activists' political work privileges their agency, but also exposed are the concealed structural impediments that still exist for them—and native-born Asians as well. Political incorporation is still uneven, contested ground, and the terrain is ever-shifting. Not only are there different patterns and rates of adaptation, including different levels of political participation among new Chinese activists, but there is not always a unified core of American society into which immigrants are "expected" to fit. That core is itself a moving target—a fluid and heterogeneous collection of cultures and social practices, albeit still foundational as Christian and Anglo-Saxon (Appiah and Gutmann 1996). Thus, the foregrounding of race in this book presents challenges to more traditional scholarship on assimilation. Whitening has not occurred for Asian Americans.

New activists perform a cultural synthesis, a repertoire of the ties of ethnicity inclusive of a broader racial outlook and a transnational amalgam of social practices that also continue to be grounded in and defined by territory. A politicized new-activist identity shows the lack of a need to throw away one's ethnicity in order to embrace citizenship. It is the ethnic base upon which *future* participation in politics begins (Lien 2001).

Conclusion

In interrogating the routinizations of race in their everyday lives, new activists are devising their own counternarratives. Acknowledgement of a racialized citizenship is a key strength in their empowerment strategies, and recognizing the intractability of racial categorization in American society lies at the core of their alignment with a pan–Asian American political identity. For the present, those new activists who have made CAUSE their principal means of political participation seem to be further implementing parts of a progressive agenda. Although a number of CAUSE members do not embrace affirmative action and see it as a hindrance for more highly educated Chinese Americans, there appears to be a new awareness that this is not so for all Asian Americans. A recent issue of *CAUSE & Effects*, for example, was devoted entirely to this divisive issue, looking at both sides of the subject from an Asian American perspective "in order to better understand the issues and opportunities" (CAUSE 2004, 2). Reprinted at length was an article by a progressive Asian American legal group refuting the model minority myth and calling for Asian Americans "living in a diverse, multiracial, multi-ethnic, and multilingual society [to be] concerned about issues of social justice" (CAUSE 2004, 6).

Even though a pan–Asian American partnership will continue to have numerous divisions, it is still a "community of interest" that can coalesce and mobilize (Hum 2004). In a community of shared interests, racial identity can continue to provide a powerful incentive for centering political attitudes and influencing group political mobilization. In pursuing U.S. citizenship and testing and acting upon politicized identities, naturalized Chinese activists are breaking new ground in community grassroots political projects and redefining what Asian American politics will look like. In addition to the sweeping transformations new Asian immigrants have already wrought in suburban Southern California, their potential to redefine the parameters of community politics in Asian America and beyond is without precedent. Thus far in their politicized lives, they have had the majority of their success—success as defined by depth and degree of participation and organization, and the ability to transform power relations—at the local level. The reconfigured ethnoburbs provided the place and space for the emergence of a new activist ethnic politics. The local as a site of contestation is held in common with progressive Asian Americans as well. Local community and grassroots political participation is an area in which a pan–Asian American presence was first realized and is still most visible.

Incorporation and integration are occurring among new activists, but their citizenship and participation in a broader pan-Asian alliance are still discrepant within a nationalist project that continues to insist upon cultural homogeneity no matter what national discourses might otherwise advertise in the name of diversity (Williams 1989). As has been shown in theories of the racial state, even as the state seeks to subsume and minimize divergence, it is active both in promoting and in intensifying racial and cultural differences (Enloe 1981). So in many ways, the belief in diversity that both naturalized and native-born participants see as essential to democratic tradition remains in conflict with other metanarratives and ideologies that discourage such diversity—the latter having a much longer history than the former. The reality is that in the United States, diversity is often perceived as a *destabilizing* force in a body politic intent on consensus.

Despite this, the work of naturalized Chinese activists defies narrow definitions of assimilation and homogenization. The dynamism with which these new citizens display their desire to be integrated into American democratic life is an expression of how they view their new allegiance—but that vision is not blind. By immigrating and then choosing to become naturalized, they have given their consent to be governed, but they also want their citizenship to be fully sanctioned. They do not see themselves as probationary citizens, nor do they want others to view them as such. In their aggressive struggle against marginalization, naturalized activists have wholeheartedly embraced the virtues of public engagement, participation, and community centeredness in a fashion that Alexis de Tocqueville saw as uniquely American.

> No sooner do you set foot upon American ground, than you are stunned by a kind of tumult; a confused clamor is heard on every side; and a thousand simultaneous voices demand the satisfaction of their social wants. . . . I am not sure that, upon the whole, this is not the greatest advantage of democracy; and I am less inclined to applaud it for what it does, than for what it causes to be done. (Tocqueville 1984, 108–109)

New Chinese American activists believe that in the doing, they can make a difference in bringing about positive social change. Inherent in this explicit political agenda is faith in collective struggle with other Americans of Asian ancestry and the power of social movements to rearticulate entitlement and belonging.

Reference Matter

Selected Survey Results from the 2000 Democratic National Convention

From August 14 to 17, 2000, the Democratic National Convention took place at the Wilshire Grand Hotel in downtown Los Angeles. During the four days and three evenings of the convention, I attended events sponsored by the Asian Pacific Islander American Caucus of the Democratic National Committee. The events included daily caucus briefings, private meetings, luncheons, and dinners. Asian Pacific Islander (API) Democrats were randomly sampled as they entered or left these gatherings or were prevailed upon during mealtimes and between scheduled events. The four-page survey was intended for descriptive purposes only and included 26 questions relating to Asian Pacific Americans and the political process. It was formulated with assistance from Mitch Chang, James Lai, Don Nakanishi, and Paul Ong as part of a graduate research project I conducted in cooperation with the UCLA Asian American Studies Center. There were 306 individuals who answered the structured survey, although not everyone answered every question, so total numbers differ.

Ethnic Breakdown of Those Surveyed

Korean	26.2%
Chinese	22.3%
Japanese	17.9%
Filipino	16.3%
Multiple ethnicities	5.3%

Pacific Islander	1.7%
Cambodian	1.0%
Vietnamese	0.3%
Other	9.0%

Birthplace

United States	50.1%
Korea	20.1%
Philippines	11.0%
India	6.7%
China	3.7%
Hong Kong	2.3%
Japan	1.7%
Taiwan	1.3%
Cambodia	0.7%
Pacific Islands	0.3%
Vietnam	0.3%
Other	1.8%

TABLE I

Question: What is your opinion of the following statement?

APIs don't get their money's worth when they give money to political candidates, parties, or issues.

Agree	*Disagree*
244	55
(81.6%)	(18.4%)

Total Asian Pacific American respondents = 299.

TABLE 2

Question: What is your opinion of the following statement?

Democratic investigators discriminated against APIs by tracking campaign contributors based solely on the fact that they had Asian surnames.

Agree	*Disagree*
272	27
(91%)	(9%)

Total Asian Pacific American respondents = 299.

TABLE 3

Question: What is your opinion of the following statement?

Mainstream news media reports on the fund-raising investigation made few distinctions between Asians and APIs and thus often racially categorized an entire community.

Agree	*Disagree*
290	11
(96.3%)	(3.7%)

Total Asian Pacific American respondents = 301.

TABLE 4

Question: What is your opinion of the following statement?

The fund-raising investigation reflected negatively on APIs and limited their ability to participate fully in the political process, such as being considered for federal or cabinet-level appointments.

	Agree	*Disagree*
Foreign-born	21	2
(n = 23)	(91.3%)	(8.7%)
Native-born	39	5
(n = 44)	(88.6%)	(11.4%)

Total Chinese American respondents = 67. At the time of this survey, President Bill Clinton had just named Norm Mineta secretary of commerce, the first Asian Pacific American cabinet member. Rumors were rife, as was the backroom politicking, that a second Asian American—former University of California, Berkeley, chancellor Chang-Lin Tien—might be appointed secretary of energy, if Al Gore were elected president.

TABLE 5

Question: What is your opinion of the following statement?

The fund-raising investigation made me think about getting involved in the political process, and I felt it compromised or lessened opportunities for me to be an equal partner.

	Agree	Disagree
Foreign-born	17	5
(n = 22)	(77.3%)	(22.7%)
Native-born	31	10
(n = 41)	(75.6%)	(24.4%)

Total Chinese American respondents = 63.

TABLE 6

Question: What is your opinion of the following statement?

Because of what happened to API contributors, I am more cautious now if I am asked to give money or help on a political issue.

	Agree	Disagree
Foreign-born	11	12
(n = 23)	(48%)	(52%)
Native-born	21	23
(n = 44)	47.7%	(52.3%)

Total Chinese American respondents = 67.

Los Angeles County Communities with Chinese Populations (including Taiwanese) of More Than 20 Percent

Community	%
Alhambra	32.46
Arcadia	33.51
East San Gabriel	28.41
Hacienda Heights	22.59
Monterey Park	39.67
Rosemead	28.10
Rowland Heights	23.63
San Gabriel	31.75
San Marino	41.94
Temple City	28.36
Walnut	27.46

Percentages are from Garoogian (2005). According to the 2000 U.S. census, the total Chinese population (including Taiwanese) in Los Angeles County was 3.43 percent.

Statistics are necessarily limiting and tell only part of the story of the rapid growth of the post-1965 Chinese community, not only in Los Angeles County, but in Southern California. Other areas that have also shown increases are Cerritos, Diamond Bar, El Monte, Palos Verdes Estates, Rancho Cucamonga, Rancho Palos Verdes, South Pasadena, and West Covina.

Socioeconomic Differences

The following table compares selected occupational categories of foreign-born Chinese, native-born Chinese, and whites as well as a similar comparison of poverty rates among the three groups.

	White (%)	Native-born (%)	Foreign-born (%)
Professional	22	39	33
Managerial/ business	16	22	17
Self-employed	11	10	11
Service	3	2	10
Poverty family	5	3	10

All data are from Wong (2006).

Notes

INTRODUCTION

1. In the 1970s, Asian American community activists lobbied government agencies such as the Census Bureau for the more encompassing name, Asian Pacific American. It was not until 2000 that Pacific Islander Americans, lobbying for their own category, were given separate recognition in the census.

2. The study using focus groups and telephone interviews was commissioned by the Committee of 100 in conjunction with the Anti-Defamation League in 2001. Excerpts are available on the Committee of 100 website. It analyzed numerous attitudes and perceptions about Asian and Chinese Americans and was conducted in the aftermath of the 1996 fund-raising scandal and the 1999 spying case of Wen Ho Lee (see Chapter 5).

CHAPTER I

1. In 2003, the organization changed its name to Center for Asian Americans United for Self Empowerment.

2. This mission statement appeared in the organization's first newsletter in spring 1994 (*OUR CAUSE*, 1994a). A key phrase addressed the group's constituency: "dedicated to the empowerment of Chinese-Americans in the U.S.A." By 2004, the wording had changed to "dedicated to advancing the political empowerment of the Asian Pacific Islander American community."

3. Enactment of an Asian American political identity is largely a public performance; however, many of the activists in this ethnography have also worked behind the scenes—and continue to do so—on highly sensitive issues, campaigns, and other concerns for which they have requested anonymity. I have respected

their privacy either by not identifying them or by using a first-name pseudonym. When both first and last names appear in the text, the subject is considered a public figure, has run or is running for or has been appointed to public office, or already is an elected official.

4. FOB refers to new immigrants, those who are "fresh off the boat." Among Asian Americans, the term has been considered a derogatory description, but many new post-1965 politically active Chinese have appropriated it as an empowering self-ascription. American-born Chinese are often called ABCs by both native-born and foreign-born; the term is usually descriptive, with no valuation.

CHAPTER 2

1. American-born activists like Mary Uyematsu Kao, who now works in the Asian American Studies Center at UCLA, remember the Tiao-yu Tai demonstrators in Los Angeles as especially informed and radicalized anti-imperialists.

2. The sojourner myth has been ubiquitous in scholarly writings about Asian "unassimilability" since its initial appearance in a 1953 doctoral dissertation. The definition of an immigrant who clings to his or her own group and is unwilling to organize as a permanent resident produces deviance; its modern incarnation is that Asian Americans are perpetual foreigners with suspect loyalties. Post-1960s discussion opened competing views of this thesis and not only posited new ways of recovering community history by analyzing the power structures denying inclusion but also privileged a large body of evidence of agency and resistance (P. Yang 2000).

3. An underresearched subject is the direct role that anthropologists and other social scientists played in reifying the institutionalized racial aspects of camp experience. The funding of a six-year-long ethnographic study of the camps (referred to as "laboratories") was described as lavish by 1940 standards. Monies came from the University of California and the Giannini, Columbia, and Rockefeller foundations. Its primary aim appeared to be to document the "positive" effects of internment as well as methods by which inmate behavior might be managed more effectively. Rioting, work stoppages, and food strikes in the camps were catalogued as deviant behavior. See Suzuki (1986).

4. For further discussion of the influence on radical Asian Americans of black nationalist ideologies such as internal colonialism, communal self-determination, nonintegration, and the Nation of Islam as promoted by Malcolm X, see Diane Fujino, *The Revolutionary Life of Yuri Kochiyama* (Minneapolis: University of Minnesota Press, 2005), and Yuri Kochiyama, *Passing It On* (Los Angeles: UCLA Asian American Studies Center Press, 2004).

5. Debates over U.S. census designations also point to agency and collective political pressure from Asian American communities in the formation of public policy, which in turn shapes racial discourse. Classifications exist as a direct result

of dynamic and complex negotiations between state interests and pan-ethnic demands including ethnic-specific challenges. See Espiritu, Le, and Omi (2000).

6. As a young television reporter, I was invited to speak at a conference sponsored by Chinese American engineers and scientists in the fall of 1975. I was astounded when more than 250 employees showed up, among them Ronald. The audience quickly expanded the topic of television news to job promotion and the glass ceiling (one of the first times I had heard this term used).

7. The Chinese Consolidated Benevolent Association formed as an amalgam of different family associations during the 1930s in an attempt to stop internecine conflict and competition. Although the political power of the organization and the family associations waned during the late 1970s and early 1980s as a younger, American-born generation of leadership with more broad-based networking and organizational skills reached maturity, familial ties remain undiluted. The organization could still provide significant amounts of monetary support. Its presence as an "official sponsor" during events like the Chinatown Parade or political fundraisers like Woo's was still seen as a critical part of ritualized public performance.

8. During the mid-1970s, Takei was the first Asian American to run for Los Angeles City Council. He is another son of the Crenshaw area and ran what was called an Asian American campaign. In fact, it was primarily Japanese American. Many of his campaign workers were Japanese American college students and recent graduates who had been active in campus political issues and whose parents still lived in Crenshaw. Takei lost to an African American who capitalized on both the endorsement of Los Angeles' first black mayor, Tom Bradley, and the changing demographics of the Crenshaw area.

9. In March 1991, just 13 days before the beating of Rodney King, Soon Ja Du shot and killed 15-year-old Latasha Harlins, after the two argued over a carton of orange juice. The shooting was recorded on the store's security camera and aired repeatedly on television news. Du was given a fine and probation, angering many people. On the first night of the rioting, Empire Liquor was torched four times. Each time and without assistance from firefighters, who were deployed on countless other blazes, the mostly African American neighbors put out the fires, saving the store.

10. The story of the *Golden Venture* was a particularly graphic episode of human smuggling. In June 1993, more than 200 undocumented Chinese had paid for illegal entry into the United States aboard an unsafe ship with the only toilet reserved for the crew. In the dead of night off the New Jersey shore, the crew grounded the ship. Nearly a dozen people drowned in the ensuing terror, others were arrested, and many were subsequently deported to China. The images of "yellow hordes" and Asian crime syndicates in global finance's backyard stuck in media reports and helped to create further immigrant backlash.

CHAPTER 3

1. For a better understanding of this complex issue from the perspective of both the Hong Kong Chinese and the British, see Chan (1997) and Hook (1997).

2. The transformation of community by Chinese immigrants, initially Taiwanese, in areas of the San Gabriel Valley is well documented, but there are now significant numbers of Chinese immigrants with social and economic capital who are rapidly moving beyond these traditional post-1965 points of entry. For example, the city of Palos Verdes Estates is an hour south of downtown Los Angeles and overlooks the Pacific Ocean. It is an enclave with a small school system consistently ranked among the best in California and where the median family income is more than $130,000 per year and homes routinely sell in excess of $4 million (*Los Angeles Times* 2007). During the 1980s and 1990s, Palos Verdes Estates was overwhelmingly white. By 2000, nearly 13 percent of the city's population of 2,500 was new Chinese immigrants, many from either Mainland China or Hong Kong (Garoogian 2005, 10).

CHAPTER 4

1. Two authors who have captured the story of the resistance to new Chinese immigrants in Monterey Park are John Horton (1995) and Leland Saito (1998).

2. The change in demographics is quite dramatic. Some communities, such as Arcadia, Rowland Heights, Baldwin Park, and El Monte, registered growth in Chinese populations that exceeded 1,000 percent. In 1980, Los Angeles County was about 1 percent Chinese, but by 2000 it had grown to more than 3 percent. See Appendix 2 for more details.

3. During this period, local news media in Los Angeles aired stories about new Chinese immigrants buying tony homes in the San Marino area, not with statements of credit and qualification from financial institutions but with suitcases of cash.

4. I interviewed Chen for KNBC News in Los Angeles shortly after her election. It was her first mainstream television news interview. Following the newscast, a number of viewers wrote to say that they couldn't believe a foreigner had been elected. Others found fault with Chen's accented English.

5. In an August 1984 television interview I conducted with Gene Mornell, chair of the Los Angeles County Human Relations Commission, Mornell spoke of his office's investigation into racist graffiti, billboards, and tracts directed at Chinese Americans in Monterey Park.

6. In April 2001, a U.S. Navy spy plane collided in midair with a Chinese fighter jet in the South China Sea. The Chinese pilot was killed, and the 24-member navy crew was forced to make an emergency landing on Hainan Island, China's southernmost province. Initially expressing "regret," the Bush

administration demanded the plane's release and sent navy destroyers to Hainan. The crew was released after 11 days and after U.S. officials said they were "very sorry" for the incident. News stories compared the U.S. spying in China to a Chinese plane flying surveillance off the Florida coast and wondered how the U.S. might react to that situation.

7. The Noguchi case began in 1969 and became a cause célèbre in Los Angeles, with widespread media coverage. The original charges against Noguchi were a bizarre list of incidents of mismanagement and incompetence. Noguchi's attorney blamed racism, the abysmal lack of understanding of the Japanese culture, and the fact that Noguchi was born in Japan. Activist Japanese Americans raised nearly $50,000 in 1969 to challenge the county and win reinstatement for Noguchi. In 1982, he was demoted and transferred out of the coroner's office. Despite community pressure from a coalition of Asian Americans, he was not reinstated.

8. A handful of new-activist women are beginning to get elected in suburban communities. In March 2003, Taiwan-born Laura Lee was elected to the city council in the City of Cerritos. Lee fits the personal, educational, and occupational profile of many other new activist women. She is married with two grown daughters, has a master's degree in biology from the State College of Virginia, and was a medical researcher before becoming a real estate broker in Cerritos in 1979. With regard to wider elective office such as the California State Legislature, foreign-born Chinese women have yet to make their mark, but American-born Chinese women are already making history, with four elected since the late 1990s.

CHAPTER 5

1. PACS are independent political action committees that contribute to candidates or issues. They are not the official committees of particular candidates or political parties but can be affiliated. Common Cause describes PACs as special-interest groups with specific legislative and issue agendas.

2. Aside from David Lang and Paul Zee, a third naturalized activist, Eugene Chang, was also at the El Monte coffee shop. Chang eventually moved to Taiwan and began working in a stock brokerage.

3. The OCA was founded in 1973 as a general advocacy group addressing issues related to social justice, equal opportunity, and the cultural heritage of Chinese Americans specifically and Asian Americans generally. OCA is similar to older organizations such as the Japanese American Citizens League and the National Association for the Advancement of Colored People. OCA is nonprofit and seeks a broader agenda aimed at legislative and policy initiatives.

4. At the Ninth Annual Dinner in 2002, major sponsors listed in the program included the Burger King Corporation, Kaiser Permanente, KSCI-TV, the City of Los Angeles Department of Water and Power, the Panda Restaurant Group, State

Farm Mutual Automobile Company, the Wallis Foundation, and the Weingart Foundation. CAUSE board members purchased individual tables, as did a number of Chinese American professional associations and banks. Other Asian American groups bought tables as well, including the Asian Business League and the Japanese American Citizens League. The program had full-page ads from both Democratic and Republican candidates with the disclaimer that CAUSE endorses no one and that "all candidates have been given the opportunity to advertise on an equal basis."

5. APALC was formed in 1983 and is considered a leading voice of progressive Asian America. It holds numerous news conferences, and mainstream media tap staff members to comment on issues such as welfare rights, immigrant and worker rights, voting rights, and domestic violence. Its primary mission is to address civil rights issues and to provide legal services to the Asian Pacific American community. In 2008 it became affiliated with the Asian American Justice Center in Washington, D.C.

6. In 1996, soft money was seen as especially desirable in that it fell outside legal limits on direct contributions to federal candidates. It also was given with virtually no strings attached and could be used in other areas of a campaign.

7. With global restructuring, the patrolling of national boundaries to ferret out exactly *where* campaign monies originate has gotten quite complex. U.S. law bars foreign nationals, governments, and corporations from contributing to U.S. elections. Political parties receiving money from a foreign source are obligated to return the money. Noncitizens who have legal permanent residence may contribute money. U.S. subsidiaries of foreign corporations may also contribute, providing that the transnational subsidiary earns profits in this country (U.S. Commission on Civil Rights 1998). The questionable contributions came from Asian sources—individuals and transnational corporations doing business outside the United States or Asians living here but not citizens (for example, the Buddhist nuns in Hacienda Heights who contributed to Vice President Al Gore's campaign). Other monies could not be traced properly to anyone—citizen or not.

8. Against legal advice, a few naturalized Chinese activists continue to be outspoken about being targeted by federal and DNC investigators. They speak at community functions and in university classrooms about their experience and the toll it has taken on their families, both economically, in lawyers' fees, and psychologically, in what they see as continuing government harassment. None has curtailed campaign contributions or stopped participating in community politics. Some believe that federal authorities continue to monitor their political activities.

9. By 2000, federal investigators had spent more than $30 million on the investigation. Twenty-two people were charged with mostly minor violations of election law; 17 were convicted. Huang reached a deal to plead guilty only to

making two small contributions to Democratic campaigns in California in 1993 and 1994. There was no admission of wrongdoing for any fund-raising during the 1996 reelection campaign, and the Justice Department agreed that no further charges would be brought against him. Hsia was convicted on five charges of filing false reports with federal election officials on donations to Vice President Al Gore. Of the $7 million raised by Huang and other Asian Americans, the DNC eventually returned about $3 million to donors in 1996. Common Cause estimates that during the 1996 campaign both the Democratic and Republican parties raised record amounts of soft money—more than a quarter of a billion dollars. No high-level official in the DNC, the White House, or the presidential or vice presidential reelection campaigns was ever charged.

10. Republican congressman Christopher Cox chaired the bipartisan House Select Committee on U.S. National Security and Military/Commercial Concerns with the People's Republic of China, which issued the three-volume report— hence the abbreviated name Cox Report. A redacted version of the report was made public in May 1999, but a third of it remains classified.

11. Mineta got his start in local politics and eventually was elected mayor of San Jose. He was also a U.S. congressman and served as U.S. secretary of transportation. He was interned at Heart Mountain, Wyoming, during World War II. I covered a news story involving Mineta during his mayoral tenure during the late 1970s. He came home one day to find racial graffiti and the word "JAP" spray painted on his garage door. Instead of removing it, he called a press conference in his driveway to denounce racism.

12. According to group founders, much of the seed money for Vision 21 came from Cyrus Tang, a China-born entrepreneur who moved to the United States in the 1950s. Tang was educated at the Illinois Institute of Technology and founded a multibillion-dollar business in industrial steel and pharmaceuticals. With political and personality disagreements leading to a rift in CAUSE during the late 1990s, Vision 21 founders sought out their own funding and made contacts with Tang, who reportedly donated several million dollars. Vision 21 is now defunct.

13. CAUSE conducted a mass e-mailing to its members and others interested in the March 2003 local elections in Southern California. Cerritos, El Monte, Gardena, Monterey Park, Rosemead, San Gabriel, San Marino, South El Monte, South Pasadena, and Temple City all had at least one Chinese American candidate on the ballot. It was not uncommon to find two, and Monterey Park fielded six candidates for three positions. A few months before, San Marino elected its first Chinese American city councilman, orthopedic surgeon Matthew Lin, who later became mayor.

14. The seven members of the 2004 Asian Pacific American Caucus in the California State Legislature constitute the largest cohort of Asian Americans

ever elected statewide. Of the 2004 caucus, only Leland Yee of San Francisco is foreign-born. He came to the United States with his parents when he was just three years old. In 1962, Hawaii-born Korean American attorney Alfred Song was elected to the assembly as a Democrat—the first Asian American in the state body.

15. One exception is former Republican congressman Jay Kim. Kim was born in South Korea and came to the United States in 1961 on a student visa to finish his graduate degree at the University of Southern California. A business entrepreneur, Kim owned a civil engineering firm when he was elected to represent the conservative Diamond Bar area. In 1997, Kim and his wife pleaded guilty to federal charges of illegal campaign contributions. He was sentenced to house arrest and lost his seat in Congress. The five Korean multinational corporations convicted of channeling illegal funds to Kim were fined a total of $1.6 million, the largest fine at the time in U.S. history.

16. In August 2000, President Clinton named former NAACP lawyer Bill Lann Lee as assistant U.S. attorney general for civil rights—the nation's top civil rights law enforcer and the first Asian American in that position. Clinton had nominated him as acting attorney general three years earlier, but Republicans led by Utah senator Orrin Hatch objected, saying Lee did not support equality for *all* Americans. Clinton finally circumvented the Republicans by making his appointment during a congressional recess. Lee served fewer than five months before the Republicans gained the White House.

17. The Illegal Aliens Measure (the official moniker on the state ballot summary) to deny health care, social services, and education to the undocumented passed overwhelmingly, 59 percent to 41 percent. Asian Pacific American civil rights and political advocacy groups joined a coalition of other progressive and liberal organizations to advocate a no vote on the proposition. Early state polling before the vote showed that Asian Americans were heavily *in favor* of it (Associated Press 1994). As election day neared, opinion gradually shifted and narrowed. Asian Americans voted in support of denying social services to undocumented workers, 52 percent to 48 percent (Morris 2000; Field Poll 1995).

CHAPTER 6

1. Chu represented the San Gabriel Valley area in the California Assembly until she was forced out by term limits in 2006. That year, Eng ran for and was elected to the same seat, where he continues as a state assemblyman. In 2007, Chu was elected to the California State Board of Equalization. In 2009, she announced her candidacy for U.S. Congress to fill the vacated seat of the Obama administration's newly appointed secretary of labor, Hilda Solis.

2. In April 2002, clothing retailer Abercrombie & Fitch found itself at the center of controversy when it sold a line of T-shirts imprinted with what detractors la-

beled a racist depiction of Asians. Asian American students at Stanford University called for a national boycott, which was endorsed by more established community groups such as the Organization of Chinese Americans. The national boycott and resulting media coverage occurred with extraordinary speed; students used mass e-mailings and websites to emphasize that they would not tolerate racial jabs. In doing so, they invoked a progressive message of shared history: "The racist shirts are remnants of the racial oppression faced by Asian Americans and bring back that intolerant ideology to today" (Boycott-af.com 2002). Abercrombie & Fitch pulled the products from store shelves and issued an apology.

3. After the terrorist attacks of September 11, 2001, the Immigration and Naturalization Service became known as the Citizenship and Immigration Services of the U.S. Department of Homeland Security.

CHAPTER 7

1. In July 2004, a full-page advertisement in the *Los Angeles Times* listed the year's top contributors to the United Way. Of the five individuals leading the list, two were post-1965 Chinese immigrants. Hong Kong–born Dominic Ng, the president of East-West Bancorp, is a major civic contributor. His own personal contributions and fund-raising for United Way set a $66 million record. Ng was surpassed only by a subsequent chair, Andrew Cherng, founder and owner of Panda Restaurant Group. Cherng, who was born outside Nanjing, and his wife, Peggy, have donated heavily to community and educational organizations.

References

Alba, Richard, and Victor Nee. 1997. "Rethinking Assimilation Theory for a New Era of Immigration." *International Migration Review* 31 (2): 826–874.

Anagnost, Ann. 1997. *National Past-times: Narrative, Representation, and Power in Modern China.* Durham, N.C.: Duke University Press.

Anderson, Benedict. 1991. *Imagined Communities: Reflections on the Origin and Spread of Nationalism.* London: Verso.

Anthias, Floya. 1999. "Beyond Unities of Identity in High Modernity." *Identities* 6 (1): 121–144.

Aoki, Andrew L., and Don T. Nakanishi. 2001. "Asian Pacific Americans and the New Minority Politics." *PS: Political Science and Politics* 34 (3): 605–610.

Appadurai, Arjun. 1991. "Global Ethnoscapes: Note and Queries for a Transnational Anthropology." In *Recapturing Anthropology,* edited by R. G. Fox, 191–210. Santa Fe, N.M.: School of American Research Press.

————. 1997. *Modernity at Large: Cultural Dimensions of Globalization.* Minneapolis: University of Minnesota Press.

Appiah, K. Anthony, and Amy Gutmann. 1996. *Color Conscious: The Political Morality of Race.* Princeton, N.J.: Princeton University Press.

Asad, Talal. 1991. "From the History of Colonial Anthropology to the Anthropology of Western Hegemony." In *Colonial Situations: Essays on the Contextualization of Knowledge,* edited by G. Stocking Jr., 314–324. Madison: University of Wisconsin Press.

Asian Pacific American Institute for Congressional Studies. 1996. *A Call to Action: Briefing Package on Asian Pacific Americans and the Campaign Finance Controversy.* Washington, D.C.: APAICS.

Associated Press. 1994. "Campaign Briefs: Hispanic Voters Split on California Immigrants." *New York Times*, October 13.

———. 1999. "Asian American Scientists File a Bias Complaint." *New York Times*, December 24.

———. 2000. "Asian American Activism on Rise in Wake of Wen Ho Lee Indictment." *Pacific Citizen*, February 27.

Bai, Shouyi, ed. 1982. *An Outline History of China*. Beijing: Foreign Language Press.

Barth, Frederick. 1969. *Ethnic Groups and Boundaries*. Boston: Little, Brown.

Basch, Linda, Nina Glick Schiller, and Cristina Blanc. 1994. *Nations Unbound: Transnational Projects, Postcolonial Predicaments, and Deterritorialized Nation-States*. Amsterdam: Gordon and Breach.

Billings, Deborah L. 2000. "Organizing in Exile: The Reconstruction of Community." In *The Maya Diaspora: Guatemalan Roots, New American Lives*, edited by J. Loucky and Marilyn Moors, 74–92. Philadelphia: Temple University Press.

Bonacich, Edna, Lucie Cheng, Norma Chinchilla, Nora Hamilton, and Paul Ong, eds. 1994. *Global Production: The Apparel Industry in the Pacific Rim*. Philadelphia: Temple University Press.

Bonilla-Silva, Eduardo. 1996. "Rethinking Racism: Toward a Structural Interpretation." *American Sociological Review* 62 (June): 465–480.

Bookman, Ann, and Sandra Morgen. 1988. *Women and the Politics of Empowerment*. Philadelphia: Temple University Press.

Bourdieu, Pierre. 1977. *Outline of a Theory of Practice*. Cambridge: Cambridge University Press.

Boycott-af.com. 2002. "Don't Support Racism, Don't Shop Abercrombie and Fitch!" http://www.boycott-af.com.

Brenner, Robert. 2002. *The Boom and the Bubble*. New York: Verso.

Brodkin, Karen. 1998. *How Jews Became White Folks and What That Says about Race in America*. New Brunswick, N.J.: Rutgers University Press.

———. 2000. "Global Capitalism: What's Race Got to Do with It?" *American Ethnologist* 27 (2): 237–256.

———. 2003. "On the Politics of Being Jewish in a Multiracial State." *Anthropologica* 45: 57–65.

Cannon, Lou. 1997. "Scars Remain Five Years after Los Angeles Riots." *Washington Post*, April 4.

Castles, Stephen, and Alastair Davidson. 2000. *Citizenship and Migration: Globalization and the Politics of Belonging*. London: MacMillan Press.

CAUSE. 2004. *CAUSE & Effects: An Asian American Political Journal*. Vol. 1. Pasadena, Calif.: CAUSE.

CAUSE/Vision 21. 2002. Ninth Annual Dinner Program. Pasadena, Calif.

Chan, Ming K. 1997. "The Legacy of British Administration of Hong Kong: A View from Hong Kong." *China Quarterly* 151: 567–582.

Chang, Gordon. 2001. "Asian Americans and Politics: Some Perspectives from History." In *Asian Americans and Politics: Perspectives, Experiences, Prospects*, edited by G. Chang, 13–38. Washington, D.C.: Woodrow Wilson Center Press.

Chen, May Ying. 1978. "Teaching a Course on Asian American Women." In *Counterpoint: Perspectives on Asian America*, edited by E. Gee, 234–239. Los Angeles: University of California, Los Angeles, Asian American Studies Center.

Chen, Yong. 2006. "Understanding Chinese American Transnationalism during the Early Twentieth Century: An Economic Perspective." In *Chinese American Transnationalism: The Flow of People, Resources, and Ideas between China and America during the Exclusion Era*, edited by S. Chan, 156–173. Philadelphia: Temple University Press.

Ching, Leo T. S. 2001. *Becoming "Japanese": Colonial Taiwan and the Politics of Identity Formation*. Berkeley: University of California Press.

Chong, Key Ray. 1984. *Americans and the Chinese Reform and Revolution, 1898–1922*. New York: University Press of America.

Clifford, Frank. 1993. "Riordan Wins Mayor's Race." *Los Angeles Times*, June 9.

Clifford, James. 1994. "Diasporas." *Cultural Anthropology* 9 (3): 302–338.

Committee of 100. 1999. Press release. "C100 Pleads for Integrity and Honor in Wen Ho Lee Case." http://www.committee100.org/media/media_eng/081099.html (accessed July 1, 2006).

———. 2001. *American Attitudes toward Chinese Americans and Asian Americans*. New York: Committee of 100.

Constable, Nicole. 1997. *Maid to Order in Hong Kong: Stories of Filipina Workers*. Ithaca, N.Y.: Cornell University Press.

Cose, Ellis. 1993. *The Rage of a Privileged Class*. New York: HarperCollins.

Crenshaw, Kimberle, and Neil Gotanda, eds. 1995. *Critical Race Theory: The Key Writings That Formed the Movement*. New York: The New Press.

Crouch, Sheila L. 1996. "The Success of the Cuban Success Story: Ethnicity, Power, and Politics." *Identities* 2 (4): 351–384.

Davis, Mike. 1992. *City of Quartz: Excavating the Future in Los Angeles*. New York: Vintage.

Der, Henry. 2001. "Roots of a Civil Rights Activist." In *Asian Americans: The Movement and the Moment*, edited by S. Louie and Glenn Omatsu, 156–169. Los Angeles: University of California, Los Angeles, Asian American Studies Center.

Dikotter, Frank. 1990. "Group Definition and the Idea of 'Race' in Modern China (1793–1949)." *Ethnic and Racial Studies* 13 (3): 420–432.

Dirlik, Arif. 1997. "Critical Reflections on 'Chinese Capitalism' as Paradigm." *Identities* 3 (3): 303–330.

———. 1996. "The Global in the Local." In *Global/Local: Cultural Production and the Transnational Imaginary*, edited by R. Wilson and W. Dissanayake, 21–45. Durham, N.C.: Duke University Press.

Duara, Prasenjit. 1991. "Knowledge and Power in the Discourse of Modernity: The Campaigns against Popular Religion in Early Twentieth-Century China." *Journal of Asian Studies* 50 (1): 53–66.

England, Sarah. 1999. "Negotiating Race and Place in the Garifuna Diaspora: Identity Formation and Transnational Grassroots Politics in New York City and Honduras." *Identities* 6 (1): 5–53.

Enloe, Cynthia. 1981. "The Growth of the State and Ethnic Mobilization: The American Experience." *Ethnic and Racial Studies* 4 (2): 123–136.

Espiritu, Yen Le. 1992. *Asian American Panethnicity: Bridging Institutions and Identities*. Philadelphia: Temple University Press.

Espiritu, Yen Le, and Michael Omi. 2000. "Who Are You Calling Asian? Shifting Identity Claims, Racial Classification and the Census." In *The State of Asian Pacific America: Transforming Race Relations*, edited by L.E.A.P. Los Angeles: Leadership Education for Asian Pacific Public Policy Institute and University of California, Los Angeles, Asian American Studies Center.

Ferriss, Susan, and Ricardo Sandoval. 1997. *The Fight in the Fields: Cesar Chavez and the Farmworkers Movement*. New York: Harcourt Brace.

Field Poll. 1995. "California Opinion Index: A Summary Analysis of Voting in the 1994 General Election." In *Field Poll (The California Poll)*, p. 5. San Francisco: Field Institute.

———. 2003. "As Awareness of Prop. 54 Has Increased, Disposition to Vote Yes Has Declined." In *Field Poll*. Release No. 2091, September 11. San Francisco: Field Institute.

Fink, Leon, and Alvis Dunn. 2000. "The Maya of Morganton: Exploring Worker Identity within the Global Marketplace." In *The Maya Diaspora: Guatemalan Roots, New American Lives*, edited by J. Loucky and Marilyn Moors, 175–196. Philadelphia: Temple University Press.

Fletcher, Michael. 1996. "Asian Americans Resent Stereotyping in Gift Flap." *Washington Post*, October 23.

Foner, Nancy. 1997. "What's New about Transnationalism? New York Immigrants Today and at the Turn of the Century." *Diaspora* 6 (3): 355–372.

Fong, Daniel. 1994. "Our CAUSE, a Chinese Americans United for Self Empowerment Publication." In *Editor's Corner*, Vol. 1, Spring.

Fong, Joe Chung. 1996. "Transnational Newspapers: The Making of the Post-1965

Globalized/Localized San Gabriel Valley Chinese Community." *Amerasia Journal* 22 (3): 65–77.

Fujita, Steven, and David O'Brien. 1991. *Japanese American Ethnicity: The Persistence of Community.* Seattle: University of Washington Press.

Garoogian, David. 2005. *The Asian Databook.* Millerton, N.Y.: Grey House Publishing.

Gee, Emma, ed. 1976. *Counterpoint: Perspectives on Asian America.* Los Angeles: Asian American Studies Center.

Geertz, Clifford. 1973. *The Interpretation of Cultures: Selected Essays.* New York: Basic Books.

Giddens, Anthony. 1991. *Modernity and Self-Identity: Self and Society in the Late Modern Age.* Stanford, Calif.: Stanford University Press.

Gladney, Dru C. 1998. *Ethnic Identity in China: The Making of a Muslim Minority.* New York: Harcourt Brace.

Glenn, Evelyn. 2000. "Citizenship and Inequality: Historical and Global Perspectives." *Social Problems* 47 (1): 1–20.

Glick Schiller, Nina, and Georges E. Fouron. 1999. "Transnational Lives and National Identities: The Identity Politics of Haitian Immigrants." In *Transnationalism from Below*, edited by M. Smith and Luis Guarnizo, 130–161. New Brunswick, N.J.: Transaction Publishers.

Goldberg, David Theo. 2002. *The Racial State.* Oxford: Blackwell.

Gotanda, Neil. 1995. "Critical Legal Studies, Critical Race Theory and Asian American Studies." *Amerasia Journal* 21 (1 and 2): 127–135.

———. 2001. "Citizenship Nullification: The Impossibility of Asian American Politics." In *Asian Americans and Politics: Perspectives, Experiences, Prospects*, edited by G. Chang, 79–101. Washington, D.C.: Woodrow Wilson Center Press.

Gowan, Peter. 1999. *The Global Gamble: Washington's Faustian Bid for World Dominance.* New York: Verso.

Gregory, Steven. 1998. *Black Corona: Race and the Politics of Place in an Urban Community.* Princeton, N.J.: Princeton University Press.

Guarnizo, Luis E., and Michael Peter Smith. 1999. "The Locations of Transnationalism." In *Transnationalism from Below*, edited by M. P. Smith and L. Guarnizo, 3–34. New Brunswick, N.J.: Transaction Publishers.

Gupta, Akhil, and James Ferguson. 1999. "Beyond 'Culture': Space, Identity, and the Politics of Difference." In *Culture, Power, Place Explorations in Critical Anthropology*, edited by A. Gupta and James Ferguson, 33–51. Durham, N.C.: Duke University Press.

Ha, Julie. 1997. "Mike Woo Reflects on L.A. Five Years after the Riots." *Rafu Shimpo* (Los Angeles), April 7.

Hall, Stuart. 1990. "Cultural Identity and Diaspora." In *Identity: Community, Culture, Difference*, edited by J. Rutherford, 222–237. London: Lawrence & Wishart.

Hannerz, Ulf. 1993. "The Withering Away of the Nation?" *Ethnos* 58 (3–4): 377–391.

———. 1996. *Transnational Connections: Culture, People, Places*. New York: Routledge.

Harrell, Stevan. 2001. "The Anthropology of Reform and the Reform of Anthropology: Anthropological Narratives of Recovery and Progress in China." *Annual Review of Anthropology* 30: 139–161.

Harrison, Faye V. 1995. "The Persistent Power of 'Race' in the Cultural and Political Economy of Racism." *Annual Review of Anthropology* 24: 47–74.

Hayano, David M. 1981. "Ethnic Identification and Disidentification: Japanese American Views of Chinese Americans." *Ethnic Groups* 3 (2): 157–171.

Hing, Bill Ong. 2003. "Making and Remaking Asian Pacific America: Immigration Policy." In *Asian American Politics: Law, Participation and Policy*, edited by D. Nakanishi and J. Lai, 81–88. Oxford: Rowman and Littlefield.

Ho, Fred. 2000a. "Fists for Revolution: The Revolutionary History of I Wor Kuen / League of Revolutionary Struggle." In *Legacy to Liberation: Politics and Culture of Revolutionary Asian Pacific America*, 3–13. San Francisco: Big Red Media.

———, ed. 2000b. *Legacy to Liberation: Politics and Culture of Revolutionary Asian Pacific America*. San Francisco: Big Red Media.

Hook, Brian. 1997. "British Views of the Legacy of Colonial Administration in Hong Kong." *China Quarterly* 151 (September): 553–566.

Horton, John. 1995. *The Politics of Diversity: Immigration, Resistance, and Change in Monterey Park, California*. Philadelphia: Temple University Press.

Hu-DeHart, Evelyn. 1996. "P.C. and the Politics of Multiculturalism in Higher Education." In *Race*, edited by Roger Sanjek and Steven Gregory, 243–256. New Brunswick, N.J.: Rutgers University Press.

———. 1999. *Across the Pacific: Asian Americans and Globalization*. Philadelphia: Temple University Press.

Hum, Tarry. 2004. "Asian Immigrant Settlements in New York City: Defining 'Communities of Interest.'" *AAPI Nexus* 2 (2): 20–48.

Iijima, Chris. 2001. "Pontifications on the Distinction between Grains of Sand and Yellow Pearls." In *Asian Americans: The Movement and the Moment*, edited by S. Louie and Glenn Omatsu, 3–15. Los Angeles: University of California, Los Angeles, Asian American Studies Center.

Itzigsohn, Jose. 2000a. "Immigration and the Boundaries of Citizenship: The Institutions of Immigrants' Political Transnationalism." *International Migration Review* 34 (4): 1126–1154.

———. 2000b. "Living Transnational Lives." *Diaspora* 10 (2): 281–296.

Jalal al-'Azm, Sadik. 2000. "Orientalism and Orientalism in Reverse." In *Orientalism: A Reader*, edited by A. L. Macfie, 217–238. New York: New York University Press.

Jiobu, Robert M. 1996. "Recent Asian Pacific Immigrants: The Demographics Background." In *The State of Asian Pacific America: Reframing the Immigration Debate*, edited by Bill Ong Hing and Ronald Lee, 35–58. Los Angeles: LEAP Asian Pacific American Public Policy Institute and University of California, Los Angeles, Asian American Studies Center.

Jo, Yung-Hwan, ed. 1980. *Political Participation of Asian Americans: Problems and Strategies*. Los Angeles: Pacific/Asian American Mental Health Research Center.

Kang, Connie K. 1999. "Final $1.2 Million Added to Thai Workers' Settlement." *Los Angeles Times*, July 29.

———. 2000. "Southland's Voice to Be Heard in Taiwan Election." *Los Angeles Times*, March 14.

Kim, Claire Jean. 2001. "The Racial Triangulation of Asian Americans." In *Asian Americans and Politics: Perspectives, Experiences, Prospects*, edited by G. Chang, 39–78. Washington, D.C.: Woodrow Wilson Center.

Kondo, Dorinne K. 1990. *Crafting Selves: Power, Gender, and Discourse of Identity in a Japanese Workplace*. Chicago: University of Chicago Press.

Kroskrity, Paul V. 1993. *Language, History, and Identity: Ethnolinguistic Studies of the Arizona Tewa*. Tucson: University of Arizona Press.

Kwong, Peter. 2001. *Chinatown, N.Y.: Labor and Politics, 1930–1950*. New York: The New Press.

Lardner, George, Jr. 1998. "Gore Friend Charged with Violating Law on Contributions." *Washington Post*, July 10.

Lee, Lauren, and J. Harper Liu. 1994. "The Fury: Asian Americans Stand Up to Aggression." *Transpacific* 9: 28.

Lee, Robert G. 1999. *Orientals: Asian Americans in Popular Culture*. Philadelphia: Temple University Press.

Lee, Wen Ho. 2001. *My Country versus Me: The First-Hand Account by the Los Alamos Scientist Who Was Falsely Accused of Being a Spy*. New York: Hyperion.

Leong, Russell. 1999. "Amerasia Dialogue: Glenn Omatsu." *Amerasia Journal* 25 (2): vii–xiv.

Li, Wei. 1998. "Anatomy of a New Ethnic Settlement: The Chinese *Ethnoburb* in Los Angeles." *Urban Studies* 35 (3): 479–501.

Lien, Pei-te. 2001. *The Making of Asian America through Political Participation*. Philadelphia: Temple University Press.

Lien, Pei-te, Christian Collet, Janelle Wong, and S. Karthik Ramakrishnan. 2001. "Asian Pacific American Public Opinion and Political Participation." *PS: Political Science and Politics* 24 (3): 625–630.

Los Angeles Times. 2004. Special Restaurant Issue: "The List, June 20."

———. 2007. "Home Sale Prices." http://www.latimes.com/classified/realestate/transactions (accessed May 21, 2007).

Louie, Steve, and Glenn Omatsu, eds. 2001. *Asian Americans: The Movement and the Moment*. Los Angeles: University of California, Los Angeles, Asian American Studies Center.

Louie, Winnie, and Paul Ong. 1995. *Asian Immigrant Investors and the Immigration Act of 1990: A Policy Research Program Report*. Los Angeles: University of California, Los Angeles, School of Public Policy and Social Research.

Lowry, Rich. 1997. "The Manchurian Candidates." *National Review*, March 24.

Lum, Sadie. 2006. "Asian American Women and Revolution: A Personal View (1983)." In *Chinese American Voices: From the Gold Rush to the Present*, edited by J. Yung, Gordon Chang, and Him Mark Lai, 327–335. Berkeley: University of California Press.

Ma, Huan. 1997. *The Overall Survey of the Ocean's Shores: 1433*. Translated by J. V. G. Mills. Bangkok: White Lotus Press.

Ma, Laurence J. C., and Carolyn Cartier. 2003. *The Chinese Diaspora: Space, Place, Mobility, and Identity*. Oxford: Rowman and Littlefield.

Mahler, Sarah. 1999. "Theoretical and Empirical Contributions toward a Research Agenda for Transnationalism." In *Transnationalism from Below*, edited by M. Smith and L. Guarnizo, 64–100. New Brunswick, N.J.: Transaction Publishers.

Malkki, Liisa H. 1999. "National Geographic: The Rooting of Peoples and the Territorialization of National Identity among Scholars and Refugees." In *Culture, Power and Place: Explorations in Critical Anthropology*, edited by A. Gupta and James Ferguson, 52–74. Durham, N.C.: Duke University Press.

Massey, Douglas S. 1981. "Dimensions of the New Immigration to the United States and Prospects for Assimilation." *Annual Review of Sociology* 7: 57–85.

Matsuda, Mari. 1995. "Looking to the Bottom: Critical Legal Studies and Reparations." In *Critical Race Theory*, edited by K. Crenshaw and N. Gotanda, 63–79. New York: The New Press.

McClain, Charles. 1994. *In Search of Equality: The Chinese Struggle against Discrimination in Nineteenth-Century America*. Berkeley: University of California Press.

McGeary, Johanna. 1999. "The Next Cold War?" *Time*, June 7.

Michaelson, Judith. 1981. "Stevenson Ignores Foe but He's Hardly in a Corner." *Los Angeles Times*, April 5.

Miller, Daniel. 1992. "The Young and the Restless in Trinidad: A Case of the Local and the Global in Mass Consumption." In *Consuming Technologies: Media and Information in Domestic Spaces*, edited by Roger Silverstone and Eric Hirsch, 48–66. London: Routledge.

Min, Pyong Gap, and Mehdi Bozorgmehr. 2000. "Immigrant Entrepreneurship and Business Patterns: A Comparison of Koreans and Iranians in Los Angeles." *International Migration Review* 34 (3): 707–738.

Min, Pyong Gap, and Rose Kim. 2000. "Formation of Ethnic and Racial Identities: Narratives by Young Asian American Professionals." *Ethnic and Racial Studies* 23 (4): 735–760.

Mintz, Sidney. 1986. *Sweetness and Power: The Place of Sugar in Modern History*. New York: Penguin Books.

———. 1998. "The Localization of Anthropological Practice: From Area Studies to Transnationalism." *Critique of Anthropology* 18 (2): 117–133.

Mitchell, Katharyne. 1996. "In Whose Interest? Transnational Capital and the Production of Multiculturalism in Canada." In *Global/Local: Cultural Production and the Transnational Imaginary*, edited by R. Wilson and W. Dissanayake, 219–251. Durham, N.C.: Duke University Press.

Monterey Park, City of. 2004. *The History of Monterey Park*. Monterey Park, Calif.: City of Monterey Park.

Morris, Irwin L. 2000. "African American Voting on Proposition 187: Rethinking the Prevalence of Interminority Conflict." *Political Research Quarterly* 53 (1): 77–98.

Nader, Laura. 1974. "Up the Anthropologist: Perspectives Gained from Studying Up." In *Reinventing Anthropology*, edited by D. Hymes, 284–311. New York: Vintage Books.

Nakanishi, Don. 1991. "The Next Swing Vote? Asian Pacific Americans and California Politics." In *Racial and Ethnic Politics in California*, edited by B. Jackson and M. Preston, 25–49. Berkeley, Calif.: IGS Press.

———. 2001. "Beyond Electoral Politics: Renewing a Search for a Paradigm of Asian Pacific American Politics." In *Asian Americans and Politics: Perspectives, Experiences, Prospects*, edited by G. Chang, 102–129. Washington, D.C.: Woodrow Wilson Center Press.

National Asian American Survey. 2008. http://www.naasurvey.com.

National Diao-yu Islands Action Committee. 1971. "Reaction of Chinese Students in America." Tiao-yu Tai Special of the National Diao-yu Islands Action Committee, Berkeley.

Nee, Victor G., and Brett De Bary Nee. 1974. *Longtime Californ': A Documentary Study of an American Chinatown*. Boston: Houghton Mifflin Sentry.

Ng, Wing Chung. 1999. *The Chinese in Vancouver, 1945–80: The Pursuit of Identity and Power*. Vancouver: University of British Columbia Press.

Nishio, Alan. 1982. "Personal Reflections on the Asian National Movements." *East Wind*, Spring/Summer: 36–38.

Omatsu, Glenn. 1989. "The 'Four Prisons' and the Movements of Liberation: Asian American Activism from the 1960s to the 1990s." *Amerasia Journal* 15 (1): xv–xxx.

———. 1990. "Movement and Process: Building Campaigns for Mass Empowerment." *Amerasia Journal* 16 (1): 63–80.

Omi, Michael, and Howard Winant. 1994. *Racial Formation in the United States: From the 1960s to the 1990s.* New York: Routledge.

Ong, Aihwa. 1997. "'A Momentary Glow of Fraternity': Narratives of Chinese Nationalism and Capitalism." *Identities* 3 (3): 331–366.

———. 1999. *Flexible Citizenship: The Cultural Logics of Transnationality.* Durham, N.C.: Duke University Press.

Ong, Paul, Edna Bonacich, and Lucie Cheng. 1994. *The New Asian Immigration in Los Angeles and Global Restructuring.* Philadelphia: Temple University Press.

Ong, Paul, and Suzanne Hee. 1993a. "The Growth of the Asian Pacific American Population." In *The State of Asian America: Police Issues to the Year 2020,* 11–24. Los Angeles: LEAP Asian Pacific American Public Policy Institute and University of California, Los Angeles, Asian American Studies Center.

———. 1993b. *Losses in the Los Angeles Civil Unrest: April 29–May 1, 1992.* Los Angeles: University of California Center for Pacific Rim Studies.

Ong, Paul, and David Lee. 2001. "Changing of the Guard? The Emerging Immigrant Majority in Asian American Politics." In *Asian Americans and Politics: Perspectives, Experiences, Prospects,* edited by G. Chang, 153–172. Washington, D.C.: Woodrow Wilson Center Press.

Ong, Paul, and Don Nakanishi. 2003. "Becoming Citizens, Becoming Voters: The Naturalization and Political Participation of Asian Pacific Immigrants." In *Asian American Politics: Law, Participation and Policy,* edited by D. Nakanishi and J. Lai, 113–133. Oxford: Rowman and Littlefield.

OUR CAUSE. 1994a. "Mission Statement." Vol. 1, Spring.

———. 1994b. "Citizen of the Year Award Dinner." Vol. 1, Fall.

———. 1995. "CAUSE Legislative Trip to Sacramento." Vol. 2: 2.

———. 1996. "Repairing Potholes in the New Silk Road." Vol. 3: 1.

———. 1997. "CAUSE Registers 353 Voters." Vol. 4: 1.

———. 2001. "CASIC Internship Program Celebrates Its Tenth Year." Vol. 7: 1.

Palumbo-Liu, David. 1999. *Asian/American: Historical Crossings of a Racial Frontier.* Palo Alto, Calif.: Stanford University Press.

Pardo, Mary S. 1998. *Mexican American Women Activists: Identity, Resistance in Two Los Angeles Communities.* Philadelphia: Temple University Press.

Park, Kyeyoung. 1997. *The Korean American Dream: Immigrants and Small Business in New York City.* Ithaca, N.Y.: Cornell University Press.

Parrillo, Vincent. 1982. "Asian Americans in American Politics." In *America's*

Ethnic Politics, edited by J. Roucek and B. Eisenberg, 89–112. Westport, Conn.: Greenwood Press.

Pedraza, Silvia. 1996. "Origins and Destinies: Immigration, Race and Ethnicity in American History." In *Origins and Destinies: Immigration, Race and Ethnicity in American History*, edited by S. Pedraza and R. Rumbaut. Belmont, Calif.: Wadsworth.

Pierson, David. 2004. "Demonstration Decries Taiwan's Recent Election." *Los Angeles Times*, March 28.

Portes, Alejandro. 1995. "Economic Sociology and the Sociology of Immigration: A Conceptual Overview." In *The Economic Sociology of Immigration: Essays on Networks, Ethnicity and Entrepreneurship*, edited by A. Portes, 1–41. New York: Russell Sage Foundation.

———. 1997. "Immigration Theory for a New Century: Some Problems and Opportunities." *International Migration Review* 31 (4): 799–825.

Portes, Alejandro, and Patricia Landolt. 2000. "Social Capital: Promise and Pitfalls of Its Role in Development." *Journal of Latin American Studies* 32: 529–547.

Portes, Alejandro, and Rubén G. Rumbaut, 1990. *Immigrant America: A Portrait*. Berkeley: University of California Press.

Rabin, Jeffrey. 2000. "Chinese Americans Raise Funds for Accused Physicist." *Los Angeles Times*, January 24.

Rafu Shimpo. 1981. "Nikkei Cross Party Lines to Support Candidate." February 5.

Reuben, Julie A. 1998. "Reforming the University: Student Protests and the Demand for a 'Relevant' Curriculum." In *Student Protest: The Sixties and After*, edited by J. G. Degroot, 153–168. New York: Longman.

Risen, James, and Jeff Gerth. 1999. "Breach at Los Alamos: A Special Report: China Stole Nuclear Secrets for Bombs, U.S. Aides Say." *New York Times*, March 6.

Robinson, Cedric J. 1983. *Black Marxism: The Making of a Black Radical Tradition*. London: Zed Biblio Distribution Center.

Roediger, David R. 1991. *The Wages of Whiteness: Race and the Making of the American Working Class*. London: Verso.

Rouse, Roger. 1991. "Mexican Migration and the Social Space of Postmodernism." *Diaspora* 1: 8–23.

Sacks, Karen Brodkin. 1988. *Caring by the Hour: Women, Work, and Organizing at Duke Medical Center*. Urbana: University of Illinois Press.

Safire, William. 1996. "The Asian Connection." *New York Times*, October 7.

Said, Edward. 1979. *Orientalism*. New York: Vintage.

———. 2000. "Arabs, Islam and the Dogmas of the West." In *Orientalism: A Reader*, edited by A. L. Macfie, 104–106. New York: New York University Press.

Saito, Leland. 1998. *Race and Politics: Asian Americans, Latinos, and Whites in a Los Angeles Suburb.* Urbana: University of Illinois Press.

San Juan, E. 1992. *Racial Formations/Critical Transformations.* Atlantic Highlands, N.J.: Humanities Press.

Sanjek, Roger. 1998. *The Future of Us All: Race and Neighborhood Politics in New York City.* Ithaca, N.Y.: Cornell University Press.

Sassen, Saskia. 2000. *Cities in a World Economy.* Thousand Oaks, Calif.: Pine Forge Press.

Schein, Louisa. 2000. *Minority Rules: The Miao and the Feminine in China's Cultural Politics.* Durham, N.C.: Duke University Press.

Schmidt, Robert. 1999. "Crash Landing." *Brill's Content.* November, 67–73.

Schwada, John. 1993. "Wachs Assails Record of Bank Tied to Woo." *Los Angeles Times,* March 11.

Sederberg, Peter C. 1984. *The Politics of Meaning: Power and Explanation in the Construction of Social Reality.* Tucson: University of Arizona Press.

Shanklin, Eugenia. 1999. "The Profession of the Color Blind: Sociocultural Anthropology and Racism in the 21st Century." *American Anthropologist* 100 (3): 669–679.

Shaplen, Jason T., and James Laney. 2004. "China Trades Its Way to Power." *New York Times,* July 12.

Shelby, Tommie. 2005. *We Who Are Dark: The Philosophical Foundations of Black Solidarity.* Cambridge, Mass.: Harvard University Press.

Shiao, Peter. 1994. "CAUSE Fights Voter Intimidation in Monterey Park." *OUR CAUSE.* Vol. 1: 1.

Simon, Richard. 1993. "Exit Poll Finds Voters Sought Lesser of 2 Evils." *Los Angeles Times,* June 9.

Smith, Michael Peter. 1994. "Can You Imagine? Transnational Migration and the Globalization of Grassroots Politics." *Social Text* 39: 15–33.

Smith, Robert C. 2000. "How Durable and New Is Transnational Life? Historical Retrieval through Local Comparison." *Diaspora* 9 (2): 203–233.

Sowell, Thomas. 1981. *Ethnic America.* New York: Basic Books.

Spivak, Gayatri Chakravorty. 1988. "Can the Subaltern Speak?" In *Marxism and the Interpretation of Culture,* edited by C. Nelson and L. Grossberg, 271–313. Urbana: University of Illinois Press.

Steinberg, Stephen. 2001. *The Ethnic Myth: Race, Ethnicity and Class in America.* Boston: Atheneum.

Sterngold, James. 2000. "Nuclear Scientist Set Free after Plea in Secrets Case: Judge Attacks U.S. Conduct." *New York Times,* September 14.

Stout, David. 1999. "Lee's Defenders Say the Scientist Is a Victim of a Witch Hunt against China." *New York Times,* December 12.

Suzuki, Peter T. 1986. "The University of California Japanese Evacuation and Resettlement Study: A Prolegomenon." *Dialectical Anthropology* 10: 189–213.

Takagi, Dana Y. 1996. "Post Civil Rights Politics and Asian American Identity: Admissions and Higher Education." In *Race*, edited by S. Gregory and R. Sanjek, 229–242. New Brunswick, N.J.: Rutgers University Press.

Takahashi, Jere. 1997. *Nisei/Sansei: Shifting Japanese American Identities and Politics.* Philadelphia: Temple University Press.

Takaki, Ronald. 1989. *Strangers from a Different Shore.* Boston: Little, Brown.

Tasaki, Ray. 2001. "Wherever There Is Oppression." In *Asian Americans: The Movement and the Moment*, edited by S. Louie and G. Omatsu, 81–87. Los Angeles: University of California, Los Angeles, Asian American Studies Center.

Tocqueville, Alexis de. 1984. *Democracy in America.* Edited by Richard D. Heffner. New York: Mentor.

Tololyan, Khachig. 1996. "Rethinking Diaspora(s): Stateless Power in the Transnational Moment." *Diaspora* 5 (1): 3–36.

Tseng, Yen-Fen. 1994. "Chinese Ethnic Economy: San Gabriel Valley, Los Angeles County." *Journal of Urban Affairs* 16 (2): 169–189.

Tu, Wei-ming. 1994. *China in Transformation.* Cambridge, Mass.: Harvard University Press.

Turnbull, Spencer K. 2003. "Wen Ho Lee and the Consequences of Enduring Asian American Stereotypes." In *Asian American Politics: Law, Participation, and Policy*, edited by Don Nakanishi and James Lai, 303–316. Oxford: Rowman and Littlefield.

Uhlaner, Carole. 1991. "Political Participation and Discrimination: A Comparative Analysis of Asians, Blacks and Latinos." In *Political Participation and American Democracy*, edited by W. Crotty. Westport, Conn.: Greenwood Press.

U.S. Bureau of the Census. 2000a. *The Asian Population: 2000 Census Brief.* Washington, D.C.: U.S. Department of Commerce.

———. 2000b. "Census 2000 Population, Demographic and Housing Information." California QuickLinks. http://quickfacts.census.gov/qfd/states/06000lk .html (accessed May 19, 2009).

U.S. Census Information Center. 2007. *2007 Statistical Portrait of the Nation's Asian and Native Hawaiian and Pacific Islander Populations.* Washington, D.C.: U.S. Census Bureau.

U.S. Commission on Civil Rights. 1998. *Briefing on Civil Rights Implications in the Treatment of Asian Pacific Americans during the Campaign Finance Controversy.* Washington, D.C.: U.S. Government Printing Office.

U.S. Congress. 1999. *U.S. National Security and Military/Commercial Concerns with the People's Republic of China.* 3 vols. Washington, D.C.: U.S. Government Printing Office.

Uyematsu, Amy. 1971. "The Emergence of Yellow Power in America." In *Roots: An Asian American Reader*, edited by Amy Tachiki, Eddie Wong, and Franklin Odo, 9–13. Los Angeles: University of California, Los Angeles, Asian American Studies Center.

Vertovec, Steven. 1999. "Conceiving and Researching Transnationalism." *Ethnic and Racial Studies* 22 (2): 447–462.

Walsh, Edward, and Guy Gugliotta. 1997. "Chinese Plan to Buy U.S. Influence Alleged." *Washington Post*, July 9.

Wang, L. Ling-chi. 1991. "The Politics of Ethnic Identity and Empowerment: The Asian American Community since the 1960s." *Asian American Policy Review* (Spring): 43–56.

———. 1995. "The Structure of Dual Domination: Toward a Paradigm for the Study of the Chinese Diaspora in the United States." *Amerasia Journal* 21 (1 and 2): 149–169.

———. 1998. "Race, Class, Citizenship and Extraterritoriality: Asian Americans and the 1996 Campaign Finance Scandal." *Amerasia Journal* 24 (1): 1–21.

Watanabe, Paul. 2001. "Building on the Indigenous Base: The Fund-Raising Controversy and the Future of Asian American Political Participation." In *Asian Americans and Politics: Perspectives, Experiences, Prospects*, edited by G. Chang, 367–382. Washington, D.C.: Woodrow Wilson Center Press.

Watson, James L. 1993. "Rites or Beliefs? The Construction of a Unified Culture in Late Imperial China." In *China's Quest for National Identity*, edited by L. Dittmer and S. S. Kim, 80–103. Ithaca, N.Y.: Cornell University Press.

Wayne, Leslie. 1997. "F.E.C. Fines German Citizen for U.S. Campaign Donations." *New York Times*, July 19.

Wilbur, Clarence Martin. 1976. *Sun Yat-sen, Frustrated Patriot*. New York: Columbia University Press.

Williams, Brackette. 1989. "A Class Act: Anthropology and the Race to Nation across Ethnic Terrain." *Annual Review of Anthropology* 18: 401–444.

Wolf, Eric. 1983. *Europe and the People without History*. Berkeley: University of California Press.

Wong, Morrison G. 2006. "Chinese Americans." In *Asian Americans: Contemporary Trends and Issues*, ed. Pyon Gap Min, 110–145. Newbury Park, Calif.: Pine Forge Press.

Wu, Frank, and May Nicholson. 1997. "Have You No Decency? An Analysis of the Racial Aspects of Media Coverage on the John Huang Matter." *Asian American Policy Review* 7: 1–37.

Wu, Frank, and Francey Lim Youngberg. 2001. "People from China Crossing the River: Asian American Political Empowerment and Foreign Influence."

In *Asian Americans and Politics: Perspectives, Experiences, Prospects*, edited by G. Chang, 311–353. Washington, D.C.: Woodrow Wilson Center Press.

Yan, Yunxiang. 1996. *The Flow of Gifts: Reciprocity and Social Networks in a Chinese Village*. Stanford, Calif.: Stanford University Press.

Yang, David C. 2005. "Globalization and the Transnational Asian 'Knowledge Class.'" *Asian Law Journal* 12 (April): 137–160.

Yang, Philip Q. 2000. "The 'Sojourner Hypothesis' Revisited." *Diaspora* 9 (2): 235–258.

Zhou, Min. 1992. *Chinatown: The Socioeconomic Potential of an Urban Enclave*. Philadelphia: Temple University Press.

———. 2004. "Assimilation, the Asian Way." In *Reinventing the Melting Pot: The New Immigrants and What It Means to Be American*, edited by T. Jacoby, 139–153. New York: Basic Books.

Zia, Helen. 2000. *Asian American Dreams: The Emergence of an American People*. New York: Farrar, Straus and Giroux.

Index

ABCs (American-born Chinese), 204*n*4 (chap. 1). *See also* native-born activists

Abercrombie & Fitch boycott, 210*n*2

affirmative action: benefits to Asian Americans, 150; Chinese American opinions on, 146, 175, 177, 192; new vs. native-born activists' views on, 153–54

African Americans. *See* civil rights movement

agency: and decision to migrate, 76; DNC fundraising scandal and, 132; grassroots activism and, 113; and identity construction, 17; in negotiation of inclusion, 120; new Chinese activists' contesting of constraints imposed on, 181, 191–92; and response to Wen Ho Lee case, 139

American identity, impact of new Chinese activists on, 5–6

American imaginaries of immigrants: case studies, 60–71; and identity construction in new Chinese activists, 77–78; as motive for migration, 76

anthropology, need to address race issues in, 5

APALC. *See* Asian Pacific American Legal Center

Asian American, as term: bureaucratization of, 36; introduction of, 31–32

Asian American community, conflict over representativeness in, 16, 25, 119–20

Asian American identity. *See* identity, Asian American; identity, pan-Asian; identity construction in Asian Americans

Asian American issues, mainstream's lack of recognition of, 3

Asian American Journalists Association, 150

Asian American pedagogies, and expansion of U.S. racial discourse, 5

Asian Americans: political donations per capita, 120; political involvement of, 12

Asian American scholars, on nature of political involvement, 12–13

Asian American studies, and building of Asian American identity, 6

Asian Pacific American Legal Center (APALC), 122, 155, 157, 208*n*5

Asian Pacific Americans (APAs): political unification of, 141, 143; as term, 36

Asian Pacific Islander (API): population growth, Chinese Americans and, 24; as term, 36

assimilation: inapplicability of concept to Chinese Americans, 191, 193; key requirements for, 191; and model minority myth, 32–33; new Chinese activists' reinvention of routes to, 82–83, 86; rejection of, 38

asymmetries of power: Asian American challenging of, 8, 12; and concept of citizenship, 143–44; need to address, 8. *See also* hegemonic structures
A-Team, 142, 146

baby-boom generation, and student activism of 1960s, 31
Bamboos, as term, 89
Bradley, Tom, 48
Brent (native-born Chinese American): on CAUSE name change, 143; on Chu campaign, 164; and racialization of identity, 95–96; on U.S.-Chinese relations, 126–27
business cards of new Chinese activists, 134–35
business credentials of new Chinese activists, as advantage, 119

Cal (San Gabriel Valley councilman), 142–143, 148
California Asian-American Student Internship Coalition, 140
California Assembly Committee on Asia Trade, 141
California legislature, Asian Americans in, 148–49, 209n14
campaign finance laws, and foreign contributions, 208n7, 210n15. *See also* DNC fundraising scandal
Canada, Chinese immigrants' strategizing of identities in, 107
capitalism: and Macao, 38; and systematized racism, 29
CASIC. *See* Chinese American Student Internship Coalition
CAUSE (Chinese Americans United for Self-Empowerment): board meeting (summer, 2003), 11, 14–15; Chu (Judy) campaign and, 164; corporate sponsors, 207n4; debate on Proposition 54, 14–15, 16, 17, 150–51; efforts to coordinate Asian American political activism, 170; efforts to subsume membership differences, 118; Eng (Mike) campaign and, 162; founding of, 116–17; fundraising

dinner (2002), 143; Huang (John) and, 129; leadership, 88, 101, 140, 155–57; local focus of, 118–19; media use by, 121; membership, 11–12, 37, 41, 118, 136–37; merger with Vision 21, 145; name change by, 139–44, 188, 203n1 (chap. 1); political diversity in, 145–46, 158–59; political involvement of members, 12; political recognition achieved by, 158; political stance of, 145, 155–56, 192; as representative Chinese American organization, 21–22, 23; representativeness of leadership, 155–57; targeting of working-class immigrants, 156–57; Wen Ho Lee case and, 138; women members, 59
CAUSE agenda, 14, 117, 118, 119, 203n (chap. 1); general advocacy, 121–22; leadership training, 123–24; pan-Asian identity and, 2–3, 139–44; voter registration, 122–23, 156–57, 164, 189, 190
CAUSE & Effects: An Asian American Political Journal, 189–90, 192
Census, U.S., and politicized state racial definitions, 36, 204n5
Center for Asian Americans United for Self Empowerment, 140, 203n1 (chap. 1). *See also* CAUSE
Chang, Eugene, 207n2
charitable contributions by new Chinese activists, 191, 211n1
Chen, Lily: background, 80–81, 85; as catalyst for future activism, 113; election loss of 1985, as racialized exclusion, 86; first foray into politics, 102–3; leadership training, 110, 112; nativist backlash against, 83–84, 86; on pan-Asian unity, 160; on redistricting, 170
Chiang Kai-shek, 60, 173
children of new Chinese activists: and pan-Asian identity, 172; parents' views on, 171–72; political participation in, 176–78; politicization of, 173–74; and transnational identity, 172
Chin, Vincent, 48, 173
China: ethnic diversity in, 74; political conditions in, as cause of migration, 55, 63–64, 71, 85; presentation of

alternative modernities by, 72; U.S. recognition of, 56

China, ascendance of: activists' support of, 39; immigrants' pride in, 75; and mainstream views on new Chinese activists, 7

Chinatowns: as community focal point, 34–35, 45; intrusion of transnational corporations into, 53, 75i; political activism of 1960s and, 34–35

China-United States relations: and DNC fundraising scandal, 130–31; impact on perception of Chinese Americans, 74–75, 125–27; mediation of transnational Chinese in, 125, 140–41; U.S. recognition of China, 56; and Wen Ho Lee case, 135–36

Chinese American community: Chinatowns as focal point of, 34–35, 45; class concerns in, 16; conflict over representativeness in, 16; diversity within, 4; fragmentation of, 101; growing ideological differences within, 149–57; heterogeneity in, 16; impact of female new Chinese activists on, 58–59; impact of new Chinese leadership on, 25; party affiliation in, 144–49

Chinese American Engineers Association, 80–81; activism of, 40

Chinese American groups: community events, described, 23–24; in Southern California, 21–22. *See also* CAUSE

Chinese American identity. *See* identity, Chinese American; identity construction in Chinese Americans

Chinese Americans: migration into Los Angeles suburbs, 42; whitening of, as unlikely event, 191, 192

Chinese American Student Internship Coalition (CASIC), 123–24, 140

Chinese Americans United for Self-Empowerment. *See* CAUSE

Chinese Consolidated Benevolent Association, 45, 205n7

Chinese imaginary, cultural exclusivity in, 73–74

Chinese nationalism: of 1920s and 1930s,

immigrants' support of, 39; contemporary nationalizing discourse, 73–74

Chinese Nationalists, immigrants' support of, 44–45

Chineseness: Hanification of, 73–74; and identity construction in new Chinese activists, 72–77; immigrants' pride in, 72, 74–75; valorization of, and altering of hegemonic terrain, 107

Chinese Students of America, 28

Chu, Betty Tom, 167

Chu, Judy: background, 163; campaigns, 161, 163, 164; Chinese-language media and, 166; Eng campaign and, 166–67; new Chinese activists and, 190; political career, 163–64, 210n1; supporters of, 173; and tensions between native-born and new immigrant activists, 168–69, 170

citizenship: Asian Americans' desire for full rights of, 193–94; Asian immigrants' desire for, 190; asymmetries of power and, 143–44; denial to Asian immigrants, before 1950s, 183; DNC fundraising scandal investigation and, 131; and race, in U.S., 95, 99, 181, 184, 193

citizenship of new Chinese activists: achievement of, as mark of status, 76; activists' expectations for, 184; activists' qualifications for, 184; combined with transnational identity, 82, 83, 89, 103, 106; commitment to stay in U.S., 54, 55, 68; compared to marriage, 73; and negotiating of inclusion, 120–21; and Orientalizing of Chinese American identities, 18; pride in, 70; and risks, 74

Civil Rights Commission hearings, on DNC scandal investigation, 129, 132

civil rights movement: influence on Asian American activism of 1960s, 33, 204n4 (chap. 2); influence on native-born Asian Americans, 95–96; new Chinese activists' views on, 96

class concerns, in Chinese American community, 16

class heterogeneity: in new Chinese immigrants, 59, 83; and political activism, 156–57

population, U.S. Asian, immigration law
changes and, 37–38
proactive response: need for, in Asian
American activism, 136; in Wen Ho Lee
case, 137–38
professional associations, equal employment activism, 39–40
professional credentials of new Chinese
activists, as advantage, 119
progressive politics: morphing of radical
1960s agenda into, 35–36; new Chinese
activists' critique of, 150–51; political
agenda of, 36; redefining of political
vocabulary by, 150
Proposition 52 (Election Day Voter
Registration) 155
Proposition 54 (Anti Race, Ethnicity, Color
or National Origin Classification),
14–15, 150–51
Proposition 187 (Illegal Aliens Measure),
155, 210n17
Proposition 209 (Anti Affirmative Action),
14, 122
Proposition 227 (Anti Bilingual
Education), 155

race, and citizenship, in U.S., 95, 99, 181,
184, 193
race issues: anthropology's need to address,
5; need to historicize, 8
racial consciousness, awakening of, in
1960s, 27. *See also* racialization of
identity
racial data, prohibition on gathering of. *See*
Proposition 54
racial discourse in U.S., Asian American's
expansion of, 5
racial discrimination: in Hong Kong, 56;
new Chinese activists' views on, 96; and
U.S. immigration policy, 57. *See also* job
discrimination; racialized exclusion
racial heterogeneity, empowering narratives
of, 94
racialization of identity, 57, 97–99; acknowledgment of, as empowerment
strategy, 192; and adoption of pan-
Asian identity, 88, 95, 125, 142–43, 159;

in children of new Chinese activists,
172; DNC fundraising scandal and,
132–34; as impetus to political activism, 109, 173, 181, 182, 184, 188–89,
191; new Chinese activists' experience
of, 144, 151–52; as obstacle to political
empowerment, 149; and party affiliation, 146–47; persistence of, 181; and
politicization, 37–40, 173, 174, 181–82;
transnational identity and, 187
racialized exclusion: Chen (Lily) election
loss as, 86; and Chinese American
group identity, 20; community activism
as response to, 37–40; grassroots efforts
against, 103, 104–8; history of, 28–31;
persistence of, 20; racial projects, 32–33;
resistance to, in 19th century, 29, 30–31;
Woo's election losses as, 46–48, 49–50.
See also nativist backlash against influx
of Chinese immigrants
racial politics, and identity of Chinese
Americans, 17
racial projects, and exclusion of Asian
Americans, 32–33
racial targeting, in DNC fundraising scandal investigation, 129–30
racial typologies, 19th century Chinese immigrants and, 29–31
racist characterizations of Chinese
Americans, in Wen Ho Lee case, 138
radical socialist activism, Chinese immigrants' dislike of, 35
Rafu Shimpo newspaper, 165
Reagan administration, 43, 48
Rebuild L.A., 49
reciprocity: in construction of Chinese personhood, 134; and relationship building
in new Chinese activists, 135
redistricting, political savvy needed to influence, 170
refugees, new Chinese activists as, 55, 77
relationship building activities, by new
Chinese activists, 134–35
Reno, Janet, 138
representativeness in Asian American
community: CAUSE leadership and,
155–57; conflict over, 16, 25, 119–20

Republican Chinese Americans: organiza-
tions, 145, 146; support for Eng (Mike),
168; views of, 146–47, 148, 175. *See also*
conservatism
Republican Party, gains in Chinese
American community, 148–49
Republic of China (ROC). *See* Taiwan
restrictive housing covenants, 42
Ric (CAUSE board member), 15, 16, 17–18,
150–51
Richardson, Bill, 139
Riordan, Richard, 50, 115, 116
ROC (Republic of China). *See* Taiwan
Ronald (native-born Asian American),
205n6; on affirmative action, 154; on
American-born identity, 26–27; background, 37; politicization of, 37–39, 40;
transnationalism of, 87
rule of law in Hong Kong, race discrimina-
tion and, 56
rule of law in U.S., attractiveness of, 30

Sacks, Karen Brodkin, 112
Said, Edward, 29
Sam (immigrant from Hong Kong): background, 67–68; on Chinese-language
media, 165–66; on life in Hong Kong,
70, 71; on native-born activists, 152;
on pan-Asian unity, 160; on political activism of 1960s, 96; on political
participation, 102; and racialization of
identity, 97
San Gabriel Valley: CAUSE and, 117, 122;
Chinese American political participation in, 145–46; Chinese-language
media in, 121, 165–66; influx of Chinese
immigrants into, 81, 87, 92, 206n2
(chap. 3)
San Marino: immigrants living in, 95; influx of Chinese immigrants into, 81
second generation. *See* children of new
Chinese activists
Seinan neighborhood, 42
Shuwa corporation, 48
Simon, Bill, 146
Sing Tao Daily newspaper, 165
Sino-Japanese War of 1937, 39, 44

social capital: and challenging of hegemonic structures, 139; immigrants'
accumulation of, 59–60, 78, 91, 134–35,
182; of new Chinese activists, as advantage, 119
social construction of Asian Americans,
global issues and, 47–48
social justice movement, and development
of pan-Asian identity, 124
social networks: and accumulation of social capital, 59–60, 78, 182; native-born
activists' lack of interest in, 152–53
social scientists, and Japanese American
internment, 204n3
sojourner, as term, 55
sojourner myth, 18, 30, 95, 142–43, 204n2
Southern California: housing discrimination in, 42; political affiliation in,
148–49
South Pasadena: grassroots networks used
to challenge dominant discourse, 104–
8; history of, 103–4; influx of Chinese
Americans into, 104
South Pasadena Chinese American Club
(SPCAC), 104–8; get-out-the-vote campaigns, 109–10; leadership, 108
South Pasadena Educational Foundation,
107
SPCAC. *See* South Pasadena Chinese
American Club
spouses of new Chinese activists: male,
views on wives' careers, 91, 93; lack of
spousal activism, 67–68
Stanton (immigrant from Taiwan): background, 72; DNC fundraising scandal
and, 129; on importance of maintaining personal ties to China, 137; on
party affiliation, 147; and political
participation, 75, 94; on Proposition
52, 155; and racialization of identity,
98; radicalization of, 147; transnational
identity of, 72–73, 75; on U.S.-Chinese
relations, 125–26; and Wen Ho Lee
case, 137, 138
state racial definitions, 36, 204n5
stereotypes of Asian Americans: business
acumen, 90; CAUSE advocacy against,

WITHDRAWN

CPSIA information can be obtained
at www.ICGtesting.com
Printed in the USA
LVHW030942110421
684148LV00002B/238

9 780804 762427